CAMBRIDGE LATIN AMERICAN STUDIES

EDITORS

MALCOLM DEAS   CLIFFORD T. SMITH
JOHN STREET

24

THE CRISTERO REBELLION

THE SERIES

THE CRISTERO REBELLION:

THE MEXICAN PEOPLE
BETWEEN CHURCH AND STATE
1926–1929

JEAN A. MEYER

L'Université de Perpignan, France

Translated by Richard Southern

CAMBRIDGE UNIVERSITY PRESS

CAMBRIDGE

LONDON · NEW YORK · MELBOURNE

Published by the Syndics of the Cambridge University Press
The Pitt Building, Trumpington Street, Cambridge CB2 1RP
Bentley House, 200 Euston Road, London NW1 2DB
32 East 57th Street, New York, NY 10022, USA
296 Beaconsfield Parade, Middle Park, Melbourne 3206, Australia

First published 1976

Photoset and printed in Malta by Interprint (Malta) Ltd

Library of Congress Cataloguing in Publication Data
Meyer, Jean A 1942–
The Cristero Rebellion.
(Cambridge Latin American studies; 24)
Translation and revision of the French ed. published
in 1975 under title: La Christiade.
Bibliography: p.
Includes index.
1. Mexico – History – 1910–1946. 2. Church and state
in Mexico. 3. Catholic Church in Mexico. I. Title.
II. Series.
F1234.M683213 1976   322'.1'0972   75-35455
ISBN 0 521 21031 3

CONTENTS

Contents

Contents

ILLUSTRATIONS

PLATES

FIGURES

MAPS

PREFACE

The English version of *La Cristiada* is the last of several versions to appear, which is paradoxical, since it has played a decisive role in the publication of my work in various forms. The work originated as a thesis of 2,500 mimeographed pages, at the end of seven years' research – a manuscript unpublishable as it stood, from which publishers recoiled!

It is the Cambridge University Press who deserve the credit for having restored the author's hope and awakened the interest of other publishers; the encouragement of its academic readers and the invitation to sign a contract to transform this enormous manuscript into a different book led me to rewrite entirely (and not simply to summarise) my thesis. Reassured by the scholarly guarantee that this commitment on the part of the Cambridge University Press represented, the other publishers made up their minds. Siglo XXI published the reconstructed thesis in Mexico (1973–4), recast (but not rewritten) in three almost self-contained volumes (*La Guerra de los Cristeros; El Conflicto entre la Iglesia y el Estado; Los Cristeros: sociedad e ideologia*), under the general title *La Cristiada*. Gallimard published in 1974, in Paris, *Apocalypse et Révolution au Mexique: la guerre des Cristeros* (a collection of documents with commentary), and Payot, also in Paris, brought out in 1975 *La Christiade: l'Eglise, l'Etat et le Peuple dans la Révolution Mexicaine*, a book that corresponds to, without entirely duplicating, the present English edition.

Practical problems and the time needed for translation have caused this book to come out well after the others, but one should bear in mind that it is properly the first, and that what one has here is an original text and not the translation of a French book.

To the Cambridge University Press I express my gratitude; my thanks to its academic readers and its officers who have made this book possible.

August 1975   J.A.M.
Perpignan and Mexico, DF.

CHRONOLOGY OF EVENTS

1921

February. Bomb explosion in doorway of Archbishop's Palace, Mexico City.

May. Red flag hoisted on the Cathedral at Morelia. Violent clashes between Catholics, Socialists, and police. Similar incidents in Jacona (Michoacán).

June. Bomb explosion in Archbishop's Palace, Guadalajara.

July. Profanation of the Church of Gómez Palacio (Durango). Public festivities at Tacambaro to welcome the Bishop.

October. Eucharistic Congress at Puebla.

November. Bomb explosion in the sanctuary of Our Lady of Guadalupe. Demonstration of protest in the streets of Mexico City.

1922

January. Services of expiation.

April. Catholic Workers' Congress at Guadalajara. Violent clashes with State trade unionists.

May–June. Coronation of the Virgins of Morelia and Irapuato. Consecration of several Bishops.

1923

January. Laying of the first stone of the monument to Christ the King; expulsion of the Apostolic Delegate.

March. Looting of the Church of Actopán (Hidalgo).

April. Services of expiation for the insults to the Sacred Heart.

May. The State of Durango limits to 25 the number of priests permitted in the State.

July. Outbreaks of violence in Chihuahua, where the number of priests had been fixed at 75.

August. The State refuses permission to build a new church in El Cubilete (Monument to Christ the King).

December. Rebellion of De la Huerta.

Throughout the year: coronations of the Virgin (Talpa, Mexico City); consecration of six bishops.

1924

4–12 October. Eucharistic Congress in Mexico City, accompanied by ceremonies of unprecedented magnificence, provoking a reaction on the part of the Government. Some Ministries dismiss employees who have taken part directly or indirectly in this demonstration.

ABBREVIATIONS

AAA	Archives of Aurelio Acevedo
AGN	Archivo General de la Nación, Mexico City, 'Presidente' section
DAAC	Departamento de Asuntos Agrarios y Colonización, Mexico City
DSR	Department of State Records, Washington, DC
MID	Military Intelligence Division, Washington, DC
SJ	Archives of the Society of Jesus, Mexican Province
UNAM	Universidad Nacional Autónoma de México, Department of History, Archives of the League and of Palomar and Vizcarra

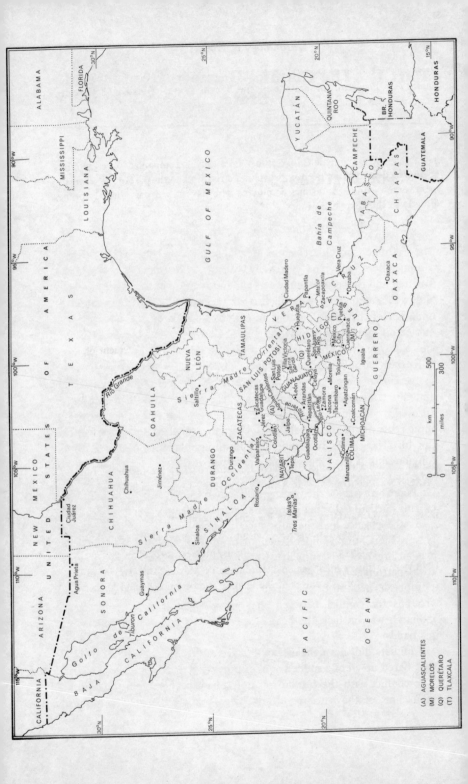

(A) AGUASCALIENTES
(M) MORELOS
(Q) QUERÉTARO
(T) TLAXCALA

Part I   The Conflict Between Church and State

CHAPTER I

The Metamorphoses of the Conflict

From the Conquest to Independence

The Catholic Church arrived in Mexico at the same time as the Spanish conquistadors, and it is extremely difficult to distinguish between the spiritual and the secular in the acts and motivations of the former and the latter; this ambiguity was still further increased by the staunch determination of the Most Catholic monarchs to 'protect' the Church; this 'protection' was the underlying cause of all the conflicts between Church and state in the various regions which made up the Spanish Empire.

Iberian Catholicism, as reformed by Cisneros, was, of course, bound to exercise an overwhelming influence on the society of the New World, and this tendency was reinforced by the ancient chiliastic expectations aroused by the spectacle of a young and newly-discovered universe; the three centuries of the history of New Spain cannot be understood unless the historian bears in mind the ubiquitous presence of the Catholic religion and of the Church that enshrined it. It was, perhaps, the last time that Western medieval Christendom attempted to build the City of God here on earth, at the very moment when Europe was turning its back on this particular Utopia in order to pursue others.

As the essence and the substance of social life, and as an economic power, the Church, under the tight control of the Castilian monarchs, was an organ of government without parallel in history. The system of royal patronage (*Real Patronato*) was the fulfilment of the dreams of Philippe le Bel and of the jurists; in theory, there were no longer any grounds for conflict between the two swords, because the temporal monarch was, in fact, the head of the Church, and held both swords in his hands.

Conflicts did, nevertheless, take place, either in the form of quarrels that flared up all of a sudden or of disputes that dragged on for centuries. The conflict with the Jesuits was only one aspect, though the most obvious one, of the constant efforts being made by Madrid to keep the

1

clergy under its tutelage. (The Palafox incident was one manifestation of this and, even if the Company did not appear in a favourable light on this occasion, and one is inclined to sympathise with the bishop, there is no doubt that the fathers discerned the problem more clearly; the root of it was Caesaro-papism and Regalism.) The dispute with the Jesuits was a manifestation of the state's desire to embrace all things, to intervene in all aspects of the problem, including the economic role of the Church (which was a real source of conflict) and the Indians, who were the apple of discord between the Church and the vested interests. One of the reasons for the expulsion of the Jesuits was, precisely, to be found in the antagonism between them and the colonists of the North at a time when the Jesuits appeared to be trying to convert the whole of that region into one vast 'reservation' for the protection of the Indians.

The best way to evaluate the influence of the Church in New Spain is, to this day, to employ the method of proof *a contrario*: the antagonistic policy of the Bourbons was one of the factors which explain the uprising of 1810. By forfeiting the support of the lower clergy and consequently of the people, and by identifying the cause of ecclesiastical immunity with that of independence, the royal power was destroying its own foundations.

The Independence Movement as a Clerical Reaction

M. N. Farris[1] has observed that the abolition of ecclesiastical immunity was part and parcel of the 'enlightened' policy of the Bourbons and of their programme of Church reform. The temporary decree promulgated by the Viceroy was an immediate response to the requirements of the struggle against the insurgents, who were only too often led by the priests. This was merely the logical conclusion of the Regalist policy initiated in the reign of Charles III.

After centuries in which the Habsburg monarchs, both firmly established in tradition and enjoying popular support and veneration, had rendered as many services to the Church as the latter had to them, the policy of the Bourbons came into direct conflict with a Church that until then had been accustomed to a situation of co-operation and interdependence. The reaction did not, of course, come from the bishops, who were progressive reformers and representatives of the Enlightenment; it came from the sector always considered to be lacking in political consciousness, the very sector that would be found deeply involved in religious conflicts in Mexico as late as the twentieth century – the lower clergy and the popular masses. The history of that era, therefore, evolved within the context of the rupture between the social elite and the Church on the one hand, and between the elite and the masses, on the other; this was true both in Europe and in the Latin American extensions of European conflicts. Those historians who have emphasised the military insignificance of the disturbances of 1767 (expulsion of the Jesuits) and of 1799 (cancellation of the judicial immunity of the clergy) have concentrated too exclusively on the governmental aspect of these problems, when the important thing is that what took place was a rupture between the government and the governed; this left the masses 'disposable', and ready to support a movement of subversion (1810), which was, in fact, to be mobilised by the priests.

This makes it easier to understand the Mexican belief that it was the Francophile ministers in Madrid who were conspiring to liberate America from the Antichrist Napoleon, the offspring of the French Revolution, the Beast of the Apocalypse: 'The Cadiz *Cortes* is composed of heretics, infidels and freethinkers, whom the men of Geneva would be ashamed to have as associates';[2]

likewise, you must understand that we are so far from being heretics that the sole object of our struggle is to defend and protect all the prerogatives of our Holy Religion, which is the main object of our regard, and to encourage the veneration of Our Blessed Lady the Virgin Mary as the visible protector and defender of our enterprise.[3]

This was the reason why the Constitution of Apatzingán (1814) proclaimed Catholicism as the only recognised religion and restored the religious orders suppressed by the Bourbons. When the Spanish Liberals came to power in 1820, the higher clergy of Mexico ceased to be Loyalist and rallied to the cause of Independence; the very bishops who had denounced the diabolical insurrection of Hidalgo and Morelos led the new secessionist movement when their interests were threatened because the king was no longer sufficiently monarchical. For the first time in the history of Mexico the Church was accused of 'taking advantage of the piety and submissiveness of the people' in order to involve the latter in conflicts in which religion would constitute a mere pretext. In 1820 those who made this accusation were the Spanish officials. Thereafter, and as late as 1938, the same accusation was to be repeated by those who governed Mexico. As against this trend, there appeared the pamphlets denouncing the 'Atheistic and Jacobin' government which was conspiring, in diabolical fashion, to destroy the Faith.

The Conflict Between Church and State

The Reform as an Anticlerical Reaction

In March 1822 the Archbishop of Mexico proclaimed that the *Patronato* was dead and that the Church had recovered its liberty. For the moment the objective of the Bourbons, that of subjecting the Church to the modern state, had failed, and the Church thereby recovered an independence which coincided with that of the nation; this marked the beginning of a conflict which was to last for 120 years, in the course of which the state attempted to recover, for its own benefit, the judicial prerogatives of the king. Because of the imperial structure of the Church of Rome, the religious problem was characterised by all the obstacles inherent in any conflict between a state and the Holy See. This first defeat to be suffered by the modern state was to lend an added ferocity to the conflict, and helps to explain the outbreak of a hitherto unknown degree of violence. The wars of the Reform (1857, 1867, and 1876), and the anticlericalism of the Constituents of 1917, the persecution that took place between 1926 and 1938, and the Cristero risings of the same period – all these events were consequences of the Bourbons' Regalist policy and its defeat.

The problem of the recognition of the American states by Rome, complicated as it was by the pressure exerted by Madrid on a succession of Popes who had excessively brief reigns (there were four Pontiffs in the space of nine years), had a profound influence on the history of Mexico. In 1824, Madrid persuaded the Papacy to publish the encyclical *Etsi jamdiu*, which condemned the Independence movement and which incurred for the Church the opprobrious accusation of treason and of collaboration with the Spanish oppressors. The unanimous protest of the Mexican clergy, who declared *ex cathedra* that the Pope had been misled, was of no avail: henceforth, the Liberals were able to assert that the Church was the 'shadow of Spain' under the guise of religion, and that it was necessary to establish a national Church in order to safeguard national independence. The long vacancies in certain sees, which occurred while the authorities awaited the tardy recognition by Rome, did nothing to ease this situation, and meanwhile the influence of Liberalism was growing.

Liberal anticlericalism, which is a term too narrow in scope but hallowed by long usage, was one aspect of the trend towards the secularisation of life and the tendency, in philosophy, to reject the past. To the Liberal, the child of the Enlightenment, it was necessary to *écraser l'infâme*, which was an obstacle to reason and virtue, the incarnation of the past, and a dangerous rival.

4

After a first, and fruitless, attempt (1833–4), the Liberal party realised that it would have to operate less overtly; moreover, there were very few people who, before 1860, would have been bold enough to proclaim openly that they were not good Catholics. In a country where an all-pervading social conformism enjoined religious observance, the protestations of devotion made by the Constituents of 1857 are of purely sociological significance, and it was a pointless gesture to publish a book entitled *Benito Juárez, Católico, Apostólico, Romano*.

Before their victory the Liberals declared that they intended to reform the Church for the common good of all, and even criticised the moral laxity of the clergy; after the victory they recognised frankly that the problem was that of the two swords, and that the state, which was still unstable, was obliged to challenge that eternal institution, the prosperity of which stood out in scandalous contrast to the universal poverty surrounding it.

In this situation of political instability and of the misery of the popular classes whose members lived at the mercy of bandits, there was a Church that had preserved its unity, institutions, practices, and principles. The root cause of the conflict was the contrast between an unstable state and a stable Church, the latter firmly grounded in a continuous tradition: both materially and symbolically, the state gradually placed its servants in the bishops' palaces, which were now those of the Governors, in the seminaries and in the churches. There was a great temptation for the Conservatives, and for their political cousins the Liberals, to try to control the Church. The most obvious conflict was that between the Reform (this term, adopted by the Liberals, embodied an entire political programme) and the Church; but there was a conflict no less real between the Church and the Conservatives. Protection was at times as burdensome as persecution, and during the Imperial era (1863–7) Maximilian, that romantic and confused reincarnation of Joseph II, became embroiled with the Papacy and the Church.

After the sale of the ecclesiastical properties, the 'enlightened' clergy, who were more numerous than is usually supposed, withdrew its support of the Reform, and the 'bourgeois' were condemned by the Church for taking part in what they considered to be a fair method of serving the nation by enriching themselves. The condemnation did, in fact, take place after the application of other religious reforms which regulated the life of a Church that, in law, did not even exist. Thereafter, it was possible to speak of an ecclesiastical party, in opposition to the Reform, which was identified with the purchasers of Church properties. As the

5

ruling class became anticlerical, the common people adopted a clerical outlook. The Reform made charitable activities the responsibility of the public administration – in other words, it abolished them; it secularised all aspects of daily life, and threatened the power of the parish priests.

The people, uninvolved in the political movement that shook the country, unaffected by the international wars, and indifferent to the American invasion, a people thoroughly evangelised and practising a monolithic form of Christianity, reacted violently against the Reform as soon as it affected the sphere of religion; they reacted, in effect, against the Reform as an instrument of persecution, long before they rebelled against its 'liberal' character in the economic sense, in that their basic problem was that of the rural communities and their despoliation.

The Policy of Conciliation (1876–1910)

After his victory in 1867, Juárez was fully occupied with consolidating his power, so he temporarily suspended the anticlerical laws, which had been passed during the period of overt conflict, during a war when it seemed that all was lost; his successor, Sebastián Lerdo de Tejada, the brother of Miguel (the real inspirer of the legal measures promulgated in 1859), exacerbated the religious conflict once more by incorporating those laws into the Constitution. The offensive undertaken by Lerdo must be considered within the context of the construction of the modern state; it coincided with the liquidation of all the centrifugal forces, for the benefit of the central authority. It is in this light that one should regard the Mexican *Kulturkampf.*

This policy provoked the insurrection of the *Religioneros,* a movement which resembled the Vendée and Spanish Carlism. During the course of 1874–5, peasant guerrilla warfare gradually spread throughout the western part of Central Mexico, and forced the President to request extraordinary powers to combat the insurrection which 'has had, and still has, the rare distinction of never having proclaimed any political programme, nor of being commanded by a leader who inspired any respect'.[4]

War under such conditions – that is to say, a war of the people – was bound to take the form of guerrilla warfare, lacking in any overall plan of operations or specific programme of action; bands would be organised, or would fall apart, in accordance with the vicissitudes of the military operations undertaken and the military and economic opportunities that presented themselves. They would be disbanded for the purpose of engaging in labour, sowing, and harvesting. They would then be formed once again in order to capture some town, only to disperse when the Federal troops advanced against them; they buried their arms, unsaddled their horses, and waited for more favourable times.

The Liberal historians, despite all their prejudices against those whom they labelled the 'Cristeros', have been unable to avoid the conclusion that these men deserved a better fate, especially in such cases as that of Socorro Reyes, who in a patriotic war would almost certainly have been a worthy successor of Juan Martín, *El Empecinado*. Socorro Reyes, the leader of a guerrilla band, who with serene fortitude faced his death before a firing squad, fortified by the last rites of the Church, was a fine example of the better type of *Religionero*. Socorro Reyes

was a straightforward and honourable man. In all his public declarations he was frank and truthful, and when he was asked who had encouraged him to take part in the revolution, he said 'my conscience commanded me'. On being taken to the place of execution, he asked permission to say a few words, but this request was denied. However, he asked forgiveness for any offences that his soldiers might have committed during their advance into the outskirts of the town. Socorro Reyes was not a thief or a murderer, and he died in poverty; his presence had been the most solid guarantee for anyone travelling between Morelia and Puruandiro. He forbade his soldiers to loot. The man whom they called 'general' wore only a pair of white breeches and a rough woollen shirt, plain shoes, a felt hat and a borrowed *sarape*. His capital totalled nine and a half *reals*, and out of that sum he provided for a pound's weight of candles to be lit in honour of Our Lord of Salvation from the moment of his death, and he gave one and a half *reals* to an uncle who had come to help him, to enable him to return to his hut. His family were unable to be with him at the last hour, on account of the poverty in which they lived. Socorro Reyes had been born in the San Isidro ravine, in the district of Huaniqueo. He was forty-five years of age, well-built, with a full and long beard. His calm demeanour was evidence of the inward tranquillity of a man whose actions were inspired by sincerity and deeply held convictions.[5]

Such, then, was the character of the popular religious movement that the excellent Federal army proved unable to defeat, even though that army had had fifteen years' combat experience and had overcome Manuel Lozada and all the ambitious generals. The most ambitious of them all, Porfirio Díaz, discerned in this movement his opportunity of attaining his goal after ten years of abortive *coups d'état*, and of representing himself as the First Consul who was capable of establishing peace. Lerdo de Tejada had reawakened the spirit of 1810, and the guerrilla warfare which broke out spontaneously as a result of his policy was evidence of a change sufficiently important to merit some attention.

Porfirio Díaz has been quoted as saying

There are no ... uprisings of the people except when attempts are made to undermine their most deeply held traditions and to diminish their legitimate liberty of conscience. Persecution of the Church, whether or not the clergy enter into the matter, means war, and such a war that the Government can only win it against its own people, through the humiliating, despotic, costly and dangerous support of the United States. Without its religion, Mexico is irretrievably lost.[6]

Díaz, in his striving for unity, obsessed as he was by the expansionist threat of the United States, wanted to establish a government above the warring factions, whereas his predecessors had maintained themselves in power by identifying themselves with specific sectors. The Church, at first ignored and then heaped with favours, though at no time had the law been changed, was still in jeopardy and was yet able to contribute to the unity of the nation by supporting the government. Díaz, a great statesman, was the first to achieve a synthesis between the more intransigent of the Jacobins and the ultra-Papists. The Pax Porfiriana was based on this remarkable stroke of opportunism. The definition of the policy of conciliation, therefore, varied according to the point of view of the interested parties. To the Catholics, it was a *modus vivendi* based on what was in effect tolerance, subject to certain limitations; to the advocates of the separation of Church and state, it was liberalism at its best: in France, in 1905, Ribot was to quote the example of Mexico, and contrast it with that of the United States.

This peace proved advantageous to the institutional Church, which during this period achieved a real reconquest: internal reform, administrative reorganisation, improved training of the clergy and an increase in their number, the mobilisation of the laity, the expansion of the Catholic press and of Catholic education, and the renewal of the strength of the Church in rural areas that had been abandoned since the decline and secularisation of the Regular Orders. This process was so evident that a Liberal spokesman was able to declare that if the parish priests had been eligible to sit in Congress, they would fill it; the government took advantage of this situation and used the parish clergy to keep the provinces peaceful. Don Porfirio, a Freemason like Juárez and Lerdo before him, set an example in this sphere by maintaining continuously cordial relations with the bishops. Cárdenas, the most anticlerical President of all, was to fall back on this policy in order to govern efficiently.

At the same time, the Church was addressing itself vigorously to social problems, after the publication of *Rerum Novarum* and under the influence of German Catholic social thought. The appearance of a new generation of priests and laymen explains this trend: after the Reform the clergy, deprived of its privileged legal status, was thrown back on the masses for support, without forfeiting its spiritual influence among the elite, and it rediscovered the spiritual resources of a dynamic Church. The Liberal victory was a Pyrrhic one, because it aroused the conscience of the clergy and was a reproach to the priests of a population whose emotions were moved by persecution. This process of crystallisation, which was due to the traumatic atmosphere that prevailed, also resulted in the perpetuation of the antagonism between political liberalism and Mexican Catholicism. Apart from a few brilliant exceptions, there were no more Catholic Liberals, nor Liberal Catholics.

The Catholic Congresses (held in 1903, 1904, 1906, and 1909 in Puebla, Morelia, Guadalajara, and Oaxaca), which have received comparatively little attention from historians, provided evidence of the social preoccupations of the Church on the eve of the Revolution – the clergy played a vital role – which contrasted with the indifference displayed by the ruling classes towards the workers. It can be asserted that the Church, at that time, was leading the movement for social reform, a movement which, though timid, nevertheless existed and was a precursor of lateral developments. Who else was criticising the big landowners in these terms?

The worker, in return for this terribly exhausting labour, receives between 18 and 25 centavos a day, which is paid partly in seeds and partly in cash, and even with these low wages, there are some landowners who find ingenious ways of reducing them further ... We understand Socialism ... You rich men, there is no other way open: either you must open your hearts to charity and reduce the hours of work and increase wages, or you are accumulating hatred and resentment ... and your riches and you yourselves will be buried [Banegas y Galván, Bishop of Querétaro].[7]

And the Congress of Oaxaca denounced, on the basis of a detailed study of working-class conditions, 'the unseemly, harsh, despotic and arrogant manner in which the workers in the factories are treated, with grievous damage to their dignity'.[8]

Whether it were the agrarian problem, the Indian problem, the problem of the workers, or work among women and children, the Church was everywhere. The result of this activity, which marked the change of emphasis by the Church from the field of traditional good works to that of social action, was the development of a trade-union movement and the genesis of a new political party. Just as German influence was evident in the Congresses and in the adoption of the Raiffeissen system, it also made itself felt in the organisation of the 'Catholic Workers' Circles', and later in the foundation of a party modelled on the *Zentrum*, the National Catholic party (PCN), which was founded immediately after the fall of Díaz. The Archbishop of Mexico City appears to have taken an active part in its foundation, which was, perhaps, conceived as a move to counter Díaz's efforts to mobilise the Catholics in support of his regime.

The Mexican Revolution (1910–20)

The Catholics did not have a united attitude to the fall of the Díaz regime; the people rejoiced without a second thought, and the lower clergy were ardent supporters of Madero, but some prelates expressed misgivings about this leap into the unknown: 'The strict enforcement of the laws of the Reform is obviously quite consistent with the Revolutionary programme, and we will no longer be able to depend on the tolerance and the spirit of conciliatory supervision of the illustrious General Díaz, who has been, until now, our only defence under God.'[9]

Madero and the Catholics

The Catholics, after Madero's triumphal entry into Mexico City, found themselves with an opportunity of playing a part in politics, and even of founding a party. 'They upbraided us for our imprudence and said that we were preparing, with our audacity, days of mourning and desolation for the Mexican Church.'[10] These words were prophetic. Despite the opposition of the more prudent, the National Catholic party (PCN) was founded, with the encouragement of Madero and the bishops. The Archbishop of Mexico City reassured the Archbishop of Guadalajara, who was a supporter of Díaz: 'Don Francisco Madero Sr. has called to see me, and has made it clear that the intentions of his son are to give full liberty to the Church, not only *de facto*, but also *de jure*.'[11]

The free elections of 1912 resulted in the overwhelming victory of the Catholics in Jalisco and Zacatecas, and a large share of the vote in the Centre and West; this caused alarm among numerous Jacobins, and they persuaded the Government to annul the elections: of the hundred seats won, the Catholics were allowed to keep only twenty-three. Thenceforth the National Catholic party, which controlled numerous municipalities, including Puebla and Toluca, which were state capitals, engaged in a ferocious onslaught on Madero. Trinidad Sánchez Santos, its most prominent journalist, called for the President's assassination and joined the chorus of the right-wing press, which was attacking Madero with unprecedented violence. Less than a year after the elections, Madero was overthrown by a military coup. A few weeks earlier, the bishops had reminded the leaders of the National Catholic party of 'the obedience which is due to duly constituted authority, and the absolutely illicit character of rebellion against those same authorities'.[12] There were rumours at the time of a plot against Madero, and the bishops called upon the two PCN leaders suspected of being involved in it to withdraw their support of it or resign from the party. Ruiz y Flores published an immediate condemnation of the *coup d'état* organised by General Huerta, and both the Church and the PCN expressed their disapproval of the man whom history was to regard as a usurper.

If this was the case, why is it that the faction which was to drive him from power – that is to say, the supporters of Carranza – accused the Church of supporting Huerta? Why did it justify its anticlerical stance on the grounds of this original sin on the part of the Church, and why, even today, is this interpretation universally accepted? Everybody, or almost everybody, supported Huerta, and the Catholics probably did so less enthusiastically than the others, while the bishops took good care not to become involved. It is true that eminent members of the PCN (Tamariz, Elguero, Lozano, Moheno, and García Naranjo) participated in Huerta's government, but who was not a Huerta supporter? As for the PCN, it was dissolved, and its president was arrested. There are three important facts to bear in mind. First, the PCN had engaged in violent attacks on Madero after the 1912 elections and right up to the end, practising party politics of the worst kind. Second, in January 1914 the Church consecrated Mexico to Christ the King, and the Government (that is to say, Huerta's government), gave permission for a large-scale celebration in Mexico City, despite the laws of the Reform which forbade all public religious ceremonies. To Carranza's faction, this was a glaring proof of the alliance between the sword and the holy-water sprinkler, of collusion between the Church and the usurper. Third, the Catholics and the Church took sides against Carranza's faction as soon as the latter achieved prominence; they did not conceal their sympathy for the followers of Villa and Zapata.

The Conflict Between Church and State

Villa, Zapata, and the Catholics

The followers of Zapata were Catholics, and the American Bishop Kelley was able to assert:

Zapata has succeeded in enclosing two States in a ring of steel, his revolution is thoroughly popular, and his soldiers are the only ones who show any inclination for work ... the Church has not been disturbed in the areas controlled by Zapata, the churches are still open, and the Bishop of that region is now [1915] making his annual tour of the diocese to administer the sacrament of Confirmation.[13]

The followers of Zapata did, indeed, respect the churches, and also arranged to have chaplains with their troops. Later, when the entire hierarchy was in exile, one bishop was to remain on the soil of Mexico, Mgr Fulcheri, Bishop of Zamora, and previously Bishop of Cuernavaca, who had come to take refuge in the area controlled by Zapata; it was said that he was also Zapata's confessor. The parish priest of Huautla had copied out the Plan of Ayala on his typewriter; Fr Basurto of Tepoztlán, the parish priest of Tlaltizapán, the priest of Axochiapán who offered Zapata a magnificent horse, the priest of Milpa Alta who was tortured and executed by Carranza's followers, and the priest of Cuautla – all these men were reputed to be adherents of Zapata.

When Zapata entered Mexico City, he carried the standard of the Virgin of Guadalupe and reopened the churches, and the church bells rang out to welcome him. The quarrel between his followers and those of Carranza was symbolised by the practice of devotion to the Virgin of Guadalupe.

The followers of Villa displayed similar attitudes, and Villa and Carranza accused each other of anticlericalism. In fact, the 'antireligious fanaticism' with which Carranza reproached Villa was by no means evident: John Reed, in his *Insurgent Mexico*, attributed many fictitious characteristics to his hero. The anticlerical acts committed by Villa were few in number, and confined to the first few months of his campaign; moreover, they were usually the work of his subordinates, especially Fierro and Urbina. Villa never shared the outlook of the Jacobins, and, when he reached the centre of the country, he realised the danger of cutting himself off from his popular base. Villa's soldiers set the priests free and opened the churches when they captured Morelia and Guadalajara from Carranza; and Villa wrote to Carranza: 'I accuse you of destroying freedom of conscience by persecuting the Church, and of having permitted governments to prohibit religious worship and even to impose fines for activities which are definitely allowed by law, and of having grossly outraged the religious sentiments of the people.'[14]

In Villa's territory there was never any religious persecution, and when, in 1915, Daniel Vanegas, the leader of a band, murdered Fr Refugio Gallardo at Jérez (Zacatecas), he was sentenced to death by his peers, the Villista generals Justo Ávila, Santos Bañuelos, and Isidoro Ávila. Consequently, when forced to choose between Villa and Carranza, the Catholics chose the former, and fought in his army in the Altos de Jalisco, Colima, and western Michoacán.

Carranza and the Constitutionalists

The strong opposition found by the Constitutionalists in some cities under the form of social armed defences was not a sign of sympathy toward Huerta, but it was occasioned by a kind of horror toward the revolutionary soldiers, whom the Catholic clergy made appear bandits who intended to take possession of towns and villages in order to rob, loot, violate and murder.[15]

Because this was what happened and because, when the revolutionaries were followers of Carranza, the process was accompanied by sacrilege and persecution, the behaviour of the peasants is not at all surprising. The Carrancistas concluded that the priests had turned the people against them by their propaganda, and that all their enemies were in the pay of the bishops. It was said that Zapata had received one and a half million gold pesos.

This new anticlericalism stemmed from the same basic motivations as that of the eighteenth and nineteenth centuries; in 1914, the Constitutionalists republished a pamphlet dating from the time of Maximilian,[16] thus establishing continuity with the former age. Although the philosophical presuppositions on which this new anticlericalism was based were identical, the tendency now acquired an unprecedented violence and sectarian fervour in the northern region, which was so strongly influenced by the United States and from which Carranza's movement drew its principal support.

After their victory, Carranza and his followers drew up a new Constitution, and the articles relating to the Church aroused far more passion among the deputies than the legislation favouring the workers or the declaration of the state's ownership of the riches of the subsoil. Article 130 had the effect of denying the Church any legal personality, and gave the Government power to intervene in accordance with the law in matters relating to worship and external discipline; monastic vows and religious Orders were prohibited, and the Church and the clergy were deprived of the right to own property, teach, or vote. Article 130 also gave the states of the Federation the power to decide the number of priests and the spiritual requirements of each locality (this provision was to be of crucial importance in the 1926 crisis). The same Article outlawed any political party having a religious affiliation.

Some of these provisions were merely the confirmation or the logical development of earlier legislation, but the Constitution of 1917 also gave the state the right to administer the 'clerical profession'. The Catholics were identified with the Church, and as a result became second-class citizens, without any place in civic life.

The Church again found itself in the same legal predicament as in 1821; after the passing of a century, the state had acquired, for its own benefit, the *Patronato* exercised by the kings of Spain. This new-found power was to be exercised by an aggressively anti-Catholic state, from whose decisions there was no appeal, because it had no juridical relationship with Rome. A moderate minority had expressed its misgivings at the Constituent Congress: 'The provisions of this new law may lead to peace or to war, and any serious error on the part of the Constituent Congress may perhaps provoke a new conflagration in the country, when the flames of the last conflict have not yet been extinguished.'[17] Dreading this war, they were predicting it with great accuracy when they mocked at the Jacobin proposals in these terms:

The Committee has asserted that we must prevent the distorted interpretations which are the result of religious instruction . . . but this does not go far enough; it should follow the logic of its Jacobin premises; it should not be content . . . with smashing the images of the Saints, pulling the rosaries to pieces, tearing down the Crucifixes, getting rid of Novenas and suchlike frivolities, shutting the door against the priests, and abolishing freedom of association so that nobody can go to Church to make contact with the clergy; it should destroy religious freedom altogether, and after that, in an orgy of sated intolerance, the committee will be able to promulgate this one article: in the Mexican Republic there will only be guarantees for those who think as we do.[18]

In 1918 and 1919 the enforcement of this law provoked a serious conflict in the state of Jalisco when the Governor attempted to limit the number of priests and oblige the clergy to register with the Ministry of the Interior. After the expulsion of Archbishop Orozco, the Catholics embarked on a year-long battle that ended in their victory: the suspension of religious worship, an economic boycott and a strike, accompanied by agitation in the rural areas, obliged the Governor and the local legislature to repeal the offending decree.

President Carranza, even before Diéguez, the Governor of Jalisco, had decided to seek a compromise, had sought a *rapprochement* with the Church for reasons of national and international politics (Mexico had been excluded from the Peace Conference because of the anticlerical legislation of 1917). The *Diario Oficial* published a proposal for the amendment of Article 130, preceded by a denunciation of the 'colossal and inopportune fanaticism' which 'had portrayed the unjustly punished clergy as victims'.[19] Carranza fell from power before there was time to put this constitutional amendment into effect, but the Catholics now had proof that the Constitution could be modified.

The Church responded to Carranza's gestures with goodwill: in 1919 the United States Government found itself under great pressure to undertake military intervention in Mexico. The Catholics who had been members of the interventionist faction withdrew from it in 1919 at the express bidding of the Mexican bishops, as was stated publicly by Bishop Kelley, the President of the Catholic Extension Society and author of the virulent pamphlet *The Book of Red and Yellow*, who was an ardent champion of interventionism. The Mexican bishops had good reason to be hopeful, and the public demonstration of 17 October 1919 proved that their convictions were well founded: on that day the Government authorised a big procession in the streets of Mexico City to celebrate the coronation of the Virgin of Guadalupe. October 1919 erased the memory of January 1914. Carranza was now bestowing the same favour as that granted by Huerta.

Obregón and Opportunism (1920–4)

The offensive against Carranza had provoked the hurried reconciliation (according to the terms of the Plan of Agua Prieta) of all the factions. Why was this not able to embrace the Church, now that the nation was entering a period of reconstruction? This, it would seem, is what Obregón desired. However, it was still necessary to proceed with caution, dealing tactfully with the Jacobins, and avoiding the resurgence of a dangerous Catholic party. Nevertheless, the hostile attitude of the United States, which refused to recognise Obregón's Government, imposed the need for a conciliatory approach. The Federal executive power, following the example of Díaz, and that of Carranza in his later years, was disposed to be conciliatory. This did not prevent it from allowing (or encouraging?) the states to harass the clergy in order to keep it in suspense. This explains the kind of anticlerical guerrilla warfare which took place between 1920 and 1924, with zones such as Tabasco and Jalisco, where there was continuous fighting, and other zones which were peaceful, but with brief and localised outbreaks of violence, and periodic crises at the national level, as the Government reasserted its will.

This was not so much a new situation as the old policy of Díaz, now given fresh animation by the violence of the times and the ardour of the revolutionaries. There was a new factor, however, which made these tactics dangerous: after their victory in Jalisco in 1919, the Catholics had got the bit between their teeth – some of them, at least. Laymen and clergy were divided, as were the Government supporters, into radicals and moderates; these factions closed ranks whenever the enemy attacked. From time to time rallying signals were given on one side or the other – these might be appeals to conciliation or calls to arms.

The importance of the Catholic radicals was connected with the rise of an anticlerical pressure group in the course of the crises provoked by the problem of the succession to Obregón. The events of 1923 and 1924 were the responsibility of the supporters of Calles, whom the President had nominated as his heir, and especially of Luis Morones, the all-powerful boss of the state trade-union movement. There was a close connection between the hostility of Morones towards the Church and the dynamic social role played by the Church, which was devoting its efforts to mobilising the masses in the Christian labour movement. As long as Obregón was able to play the role of moderator, the crises never assumed serious proportions: in 1923, the expulsion of the Apostolic Delegate, Mgr Filippi, on the occasion of the laying of the first stone of the monument to Christ the King, did nothing to alter the excellent relations that Obregón maintained indirectly with Rome; the crisis of 1924 did not prevent him from making preparations for the establishment of diplomatic relations between Rome and Mexico City! When President Calles, who was involved in a much more difficult situation, took sides in the battle with all the ardour of his violent temperament, confrontation became inevitable.

CHAPTER 2

The Roots of the Problem

The Government: the Nature of Its Power, and the Objectives Pursued

Between 1920 and 1935 Generals Obregón and Calles, in one way or another, governed the country; they succeeded in resolving the problem of power, in establishing the rules of the political game in the form in which they have survived until the present day, and in creating the institutions needed for the growth of the modern state. They found themselves in difficulties on more than one occasion, and had to crush two serious military insurrections. They were obliged to ensure the goodwill of the United States at the price of important concessions, although their religious policy nearly destroyed everything else, for it provoked the great insurrection of the Cristeros. They triumphed, thanks to the control that they exercised within Mexico and to American support obtained from the outside.

To govern is to command. In what way is Mexico, a heterogeneous country, governable, and who exercises the *imperium*? The power of the state rested on the army and the labour unions within Mexico, and on American help outside Mexico. The army had been decisive in national politics since 1913; these Praetorians had only one weakness: they all expected to reach the presidency, and Obregón took advantage of this to eliminate them *en masse*. The rebellion of 1923–4 made it possible to liquidate the more popular leaders and to initiate, thanks to the faithful Minister of War, General Joaquín Amaro (1924–31), the domestication of the Praetorians. At the same time, efforts were made to achieve the professionalisation of the officer corps: all this, together with modernisation, the campaigns against putschists, and the corruption of the undecided elements, was an expensive process and, in an average year, consumed between a third and a half of the budget.

Calles made use of the army to maintain himself in power, and shattered it to avoid being overthrown by it, but he could not do this without the support of Obregón. It appears that the two men had an interest in the perpetuation of this alternating diarchy. However, Calles

17

feared, if not betrayal, then at least the weakening of this solidarity, and took precautions accordingly. Apart from the army, the trade-union movement (the CROM) was the only cohesive and organised group; its leader, Luis Morones, who had formerly been a supporter of Obregón, now served as a counterweight to his influence. From 1924 until the assassination of Obregón in 1928, Calles indulged in the difficult game of playing off the army and the CROM against each other.

The CROM had made Calles its president, and thus came to exercise a very great influence, controlling political life through its Labour party and economic life through the Ministry of Commerce, Industry, and Labour. Morones did not hesitate to employ any means, and simply got rid of opponents such as Senator Field Jurado. It was for this reason that the murder of Obregón was attributed to him.

The army and the unions were the twin pillars of the temple; the *agraristas*, a minority of farmers who had benefited from the agrarian reform and had been mobilised by the state, and also the bureaucracy, added strength to the Government. Armed after the threat of military rebellion had materialised, and mobilised against the Cristeros, the *agraristas* were demobilised when the campaign ended, and were always kept in subordination to the army, against which they might be used. As mere cannon-fodder, they played no part in politics, and were quite incapable of exerting pressure on the Government.

Obregón had had great difficulty in obtaining recognition from the United States and, after three years of tenacious resistance, had been obliged to come to terms as a result of the agreements of Bucareli. The United States, after securing the abandonment of Mexico's petroleum policy (in 1923, and again in 1927), began to show favour to the governments of Obregón, and later of Calles, after the crisis of 1926–7.

The personal friendship that existed between the remarkable Ambassador Morrow and President Calles was accompanied by close political collaboration. Morrow, in his diplomatic capacity, played an essential role in the settlement of the religious conflict, and, as a financier, he assisted his Mexican colleague. Thanks to his good offices, the Government was able to purchase directly from United States arsenals, after the 1929 rebellion, ten thousand Enfield rifles, ten million rounds of ammunition, and aircraft which took part in the battle of Jiménez with American pilots.

Calles was the great man of the age. He gave the nation the financial instruments of development and made it possible to begin the battle to increase agricultural production, the key to future development. The creation of an infrastructure of roads and of a national system of accounting, large-scale irrigation works and agrarian reform, were all manifestations of this policy of national reconstruction.

He solved the problem of succession and continuity, after the death of Obregón, by taking part in the creation of a single governing party, and by governing the country through his nominees until 1935, in the midst of continually recurring factional strife. He continued Porfirio Díaz's work of modernisation, giving the state control over all centrifugal and rival forces: *caciques*, warlords, state governments and legislatures, independent labour unions, the free press and, finally, the Church. A consequence of this process of centralisation, which left nothing in the Federal structure intact save the outward appearances, was the development of a bureaucracy that grew in proportion to the growth of the state. The state threatened to absorb every institution, including education and the clergy, so that Calles might well have uttered the famous dictum 'L'état c'est moi!'.

He fought against the two forces that opposed him: the army, which, thanks to General Amaro, he shattered and then rebuilt; and the Church, which he fought with ideological weapons and under the influence of his own personal hallucinations, but above all because he was the representative of the modern state, which was essentially an institution striving to achieve total power. This conflict, a manifestation of Regalism in modern guise, was the touchstone of his regime, its very essence. Two institutions confronted each other, the Church and the state; two political groups, the revolutionaries and the political Catholics, were struggling for power; two distinct worlds confronted each other, the people and its leaders, Old Mexico and the modern elites.

Calles was the protagonist of an attempt to achieve universal and absolute control over the country, using methods of an unprecedented modernity and efficiency which culminated in the creation of the PNR, the National Revolutionary party, inspired by the political methods of Mussolini. As an implacable champion of unity imposed by the state, with fire and sword, he was the incarnation, albeit a negative one, of the Mexican nation. Intensive propaganda destined for foreign consumption guaranteed the reputation of the regime, which was mobilising its energies against the forces of evil, which were always foreign: Chinese deported from the north-west, Red agents from Moscow, Black ones from Rome – all found themselves in the Islas Marías penal colony.

Modern nationalism, alien to the Hispanic tradition and modelled on North American values, was born in this period, as was the notion of

Mexicanidad. Rafael Segovia was right to discern, in this form of nationalism, the proof that the existence of the state precedes that of the nation. One of the aspects of this tendency, which inflated, modernised, and Americanised the cities, was the accentuation of the contrast between the city-dwellers and the rural population; the enterprise of modernisation was accompanied by tensions that found an outlet in violence and war.

By eliminating the landowning oligarchy between 1920 and 1940, the Revolution opened the way for the creation of a bourgeoisie possessing collective aspirations capable of mobilising the politically active population; this had been the one element lacking in Díaz's programme of modernisation. The official ideology took care to universalise, by means of education and as a result of historical evolution, the particular aspirations of this sector, and the Revolutionary hegemony was firmly based on the interventionist state. President Calles was the first to conceive of this system of domination, which was historically determined and may be described as an oligarchical hegemony, of which one of the keys was agrarian reform.[1] The state first disarmed the rural interests by distributing the land, and then took measures, to use Durkheim's terms, to increase the material and spiritual density of society; this was the origin of the two facets of Calles's policy, continued by Cárdenas until recent times – the great public works that contributed to geographical unity, and an educational system that forged the concept of Mexican nationhood.

Many instruments of domination had existed before 1910, but the Revolution overhauled the machinery of government and created so strong a state that Mexico has been directed, for the past fifty years, towards a system of domination that has been at least more efficient, more complete, and more universal than the old one. A hundred times more powerful (and technological progress contributed a great deal to this), benefiting from historical experience, perpetually on its guard, yet possessing flexibility, the State integrated the entire political class and controlled the masses.

Few things were able to subsist outside it, as idolatrous worship of the Leviathan-state grew to vast proportions. All power was concentrated in it so effectively that, in the civic liturgies, orators and teachers swung the censer before the altars where the people were led to adore the vain idols of the slogan 'effective suffrage, no re-election'.

Obregón was the first to concern himself with the ideological conflict, provoked by the full shock of the clash with the Church, the only power that escaped control by guns or money. It was then that the corpus of the official ideology was formed: this was a mass of ideas which was not a theory of government nor a reflection on the Revolution, but a verbal bombardment of the masses in an attempt to politicise them. The ideology contained elements of social Darwinism borrowed from those United States that Obregón admired so much, of liberalism, and of 'Christian' socialism; soviets were all the rage, and nationalism provided a justification for this harlequinade. Calles announced that the Revolution and the state were one and, in contrast to Obregón, who had declared the Revolution to be over, he made it eternal: it was to last as long as the Government's power. Nationalism was the 'backbone of the Revolutionary spirit', and it implied the condemnation of 'exotic doctrines' (those of Rome and Moscow). Calles was the founding father of the National Revolutionary party and of the 'socialist school'. The party was to be responsible for providing the regime with the justificatory ideology, which was to be propagated by the educators. Calles's 'Cry of Guadalajara' (1934) proclaimed this explicitly: it was necessary to create nationhood by 'forging the Nation', by means of the school, the factory, agrarian reform, the incorporation of the Indians, and by the state, the supreme arbiter which no one was to oppose, even by legal means.

This desire to absorb the whole of the individual led to a clash with the intellectuals; in 1929 the regime broke with the University, and Vasconcelos was a symbol of this separation. Nationalism, based on social psychology allied to a primary mobilising ideology, was not the monopoly of the state. In this field, there were clashes with the Church and with the forces of the Right. For the first time since the days of Maximilian, the Left was in a situation of inferiority as regards 'nationalist purity', for the agreements of Bucareli, United States military aid in 1924 and 1929, and the part played by Morrow in the solution of the religious conflict, all combined to make the task difficult. The conflict with the Church, a formidable rival, was inevitable in so far as the nation built by the state, like the Church of Rome, can admit no power to be superior to it.

Social Policy of the Church

'It is very strange that the Mexican clergy, generally speaking, has embraced the interests of the people as its own.'[2] One would understand only half of the concern that the Church provoked among the Jacobins of the new state if one were to forget that the Church possessed very great power, in proportion to its considerable will to power. This power, being no longer economic, was inevitably social in character, and also potentially political.

In January 1913, at the Great Workers' Diet held at Zamora (even Mexican social terminology was borrowed from the German Catholics), it was decided to undertake large-scale organisation of the Christian labour movement, which was to be independent of the state but not of the Church. The first real trade union, in the modern sense of the term, was founded the same year by Fr Méndez Medina in Mexico City, at a time when the World Workers' House, the *avant-garde* of anarchism, had not yet dreamt of organising trade unions. In 1915 the Great Workers' Union drew up regulations favouring the workers, and these were to a large extent incorporated into the Constitution of 1917.[3]

The bishops strongly encouraged this movement, and the statutes of the Catholic Labour Confederation were formally accepted in 1920. Two similar and rival projects could not fail to result in competition, if not in confrontation: the rivalry between the Catholic workers and the CROM foreshadowed the later confrontations between political Catholics and Morones, and between the bishops and the Government. The two movements developed simultaneously; in 1921 the CROM proposed a reconciliation between them, and Morones made use of the manual on labour organisation written by Fr Méndez Medina as a basis for the official manual of the CROM; by the end of that year, however, the Catholics had made such progress that Morones returned to the attack. In 1922 the CNCT (National Catholic Labour Confederation) represented 353 unions with a total of 80,000 members. If one bears in mind that the CGT had only 15,000 members and the CROM had 100,000 (though claiming four times that number), one can understand the concern of Morones, who had fought for a long time to impose his single confederation on the anarchist and Marxist dissidents, and now had to confront the supporters of 'Christian Restoration' as against 'Social Revolution'. Morones undertook to stop the progress of his opponents by any methods, and inevitably blood began to flow. As Marjorie Clark has written:

Unfortunately, nothing has yet been done to free the peasant from the politician. From this point of view it makes little difference to the peasant which of the many organizations he joins. He must take care to belong to the one which is strongest in his region, if he wishes to escape persecution ... he is promised land, money, tools, livestock if he supports one group; he is threatened with the loss of the land which he has already received, his crops are destroyed, his livestock killed, if he fails to comply with the demands of the political group in power. A tyranny equal to that of the *jefes políticos* of the Díaz regime has grown up.[4]

The CNCT concerned itself increasingly with the rural workers, who in practice were neglected by the CROM, and one often found peasants' unions under the guise of workers' unions. The Second Congress of the CNCT, held in 1925, made plans for the creation of a National League of the Middle Class, and also, which caused more disquiet to the Government, of a National Catholic Peasant League.

Labour organisation was the apple of discord between Church and state, and the agrarian problem was inextricably bound up with it. The concern aroused by the labour and agrarian activity of the Church, which was pressing for the unionisation of agricultural workers and the organisation of small properties according to the Raiffeissen system, was expressed by the deputies who, in late 1924, denounced the progress made by the clericals in this field.

The Church, contrary to the official version of events, had not sold itself to the big landowners, but it did have a project for agrarian reform which differed from that of the Government, and which threatened to attract the latter's political clientele. The two powers were fighting, without any intention of sharing the spoils, over what Calles rightly described as 'the spirit of the peasant'. It was for this reason that the Government attempted to impose a single trade-union organisation, and that the Church forbade Catholics to become affiliated to the CROM.

The Church engaged in a race with the Government to eliminate the big estates before the arrival of the representatives of the law, the politicians, and the surveyors. Its intention was to make agrarian reform unnecessary by cutting the ground from under the feet of its rival, thus preventing the latter from extending its control over the rural masses, which had never ceased to follow the priest in the areas where this was the traditional practice.

Drawing its inspiration both from German Catholic social thought and the teachings of Leo XIII, and from its own historic experience in colonial times, the Mexican Church, displaying a dynamic urge comparable to that of the Revolutionaries, was on the way to creating a system of Christian democracy before the term had been invented. Its underlying ideas, which were modern despite rhetorical survivals from earlier times, represented an attempt at an original solution, which was fundamentally opposed to the enterprise of construction of a new state undertaken by the Men of Sonora. The people, both the masses and their leaders, were the stakes in the dispute between the two powers. The revolution unleashed against the Díaz regime by the young neo-Porfirista heirs of an outmoded liberalism rapidly swept away the man whom they regarded as their adversary – Díaz; they then clashed with the clergy whom they believed to have died 'at Calpulalpán in 1860', and who had risen once more, also owing its deliverance to the revolutionary victory.

After a century of conflict between anticlerical liberalism and anti-Jacobin Catholicism, after half a century of liberal rule, everything was still the same. The only factors that had changed were the social groups behind the conflicting institutions and ideologies. The neo-liberals were faced with a Church which was no longer that of the 'top people'. The unpublicised labour carried out in the penumbra of the Díaz regime was now bearing fruit, and certain Catholics, behind the Church and by means of it, were asserting their willingness to take power. The vigour of that generation of laymen trained by the clergy after 1875 explains the violence of the clash of 1926. Modern-minded and radical, ultra-patriotic, confident in their strength, carried away by their enthusiasm, the Catholic militants threatened the revolutionaries in what the latter believed to be their exclusive stronghold – the workers and peasants.

The response of the Minister of Labour, Luis Morones, the absolute monarch of the CROM, the agent of the new state, took the form of the Schism of Soledad. From February 1925 onwards, the religious aspects of the conflict overshadowed all others, and what began in August 1926 was a war of religion. In that tangled web of contributory causes, political rivalries and disputes over the possession of political clienteles were evident factors.

The Sociology of Anticlericalism

The state was anticlerical because its own internal logic impelled it to be, because as a result of its own growth it clashed with the Church in every sphere. What social group was it that served the state and at the same time used it? The conflict with the Church was made even more inevitable by the fact that the revolutionaries were distinguishable by their geographical, and also their social and professional, origins. Northerners from the 'frontier', representatives of the still nascent middle class, they made their Jacobinism the vehicle for a pragmatic and very effective illustration of the theories of Max Weber. In their eyes, Protestantism explained the success of the United States, and they adopted as their own the Anglo-Saxon response to the Hispanic and colonial past of a Mexico which had fallen into decline through the fault of the Indians and the priests.

The importance of the part played by the army in the state has been mentioned; its leaders comprised the Revolutionary elite – in geographical terms they were Northerners, and in social terms, petty bourgeois. As elsewhere in Latin America, the middle classes had forced their way into political life through military *coups*, the standard expression of those classes that have no desire to make a social and economic revolution. Army officers occupied 60 per cent of government posts between 1920 and 1935, but they formed a new group of property owners, who joined forces with the *ci-devants*. They were improvised Croesuses wearing the mask of Spartacus; they opposed agrarian reform and protected their new-found social equals. This army, which shot the peasants, was also used for strike-breaking.

Overwhelmingly (90 per cent) Northern, the 'Revolutionary family' was of the same generation: Obregón and Calles, the oldest, were born between 1877 and 1881, and their ministers between 1890 and 1900. Garrido was a state governor at the age of twenty. All these school teachers, small businessmen, small farmers and minor employees, who had now become the masters of the state, were suddenly enriched, and formed a clan closely linked by business ties and marriage, before it became fused with the traditional ruling class surviving from the time of Díaz.

These people were to be found in the Masonic lodges, clubs and army messes, which were much more effective nuclei of social life than all the unions, leagues, and parties, until the foundation of the National Revolutionary party, which was to regroup this entire social sector and establish control over the factions that continually rent the ruling group.

The men from the northern frontier looked on themselves as the standard-bearers of civilisation, called upon to regenerate Old Mexico. This ideology was the radical and simplistic end-product of a long tradition that had existed on both sides of the Rio Grande, nourished by the United States Protestants with their 'Crusade' and the Mexican liberals of the *Reforma*. Anticlerical militancy sought for its roots in the past, and the moment of the expansion of the state served to stir up an old hatred, which now took a brutally violent form and found a fresh justification for itself in the opposition arising from the clerical party.

These anticlericals were often Protestants; they were also, under the same American influence, often Freemasons. These were two forms of religious expression which, combined with a third form, that of the truly fanatical zeal of the 'defanaticisers', especially the teachers and army officers, were to give birth, in the atmosphere of the war of religion, to the sombre creed of persecution.

These Northerners, born on the harshest of frontiers, outside the triangle of Indian and colonial civilisation, had a kind of doctrine of their own making that Roberto Pesqueira had formulated in an article entitled 'The Men of the North': the destruction of Hispanic culture and its replacement by North American culture.

They were the enemies of the Indian, of the peasant, of the priest of that Old Mexico which they never understood because they never belonged to it. They could all have said, as did General J. B. Vargas to the Cristero leader Pedro Quintanar: 'I should be very much in favour of the Catholic sect if it were national, that is to say, if you appointed your own Pope, a Mexican, and got rid of that immoral institution, confession, and of the celibacy of the clergy. I'm from the frontier, and in my village the Catholic Church is hardly known.' Thus spoke the man who signed himself 'The Free Man of the North'.[5]

Northern Protestantism was a logical development in a region empty of men until the end of the nineteenth century, and from which the Catholic Church, after the expulsion of the Jesuits, was to be absent for a long time. The sympathy felt by American Protestants for the Northern revolutionaries has never been denied:

When the Mexican Revolution began, the Protestant Churches threw themselves into it almost unanimously because they believed that the progress of the Revolution represented what these churches had been preaching through the years and that the triumph of the Revolution meant the triumph of the Gospel. There were some entire congregations who, led by their pastors, volunteered for service in the Revolutionary Army ... Many Protestant preachers are now prominent in the Mexican Government.'[6]

The man who spoke these words was S. G. Inman, a member of the Committee of the League of Free Nations.

This sympathy was repaid, for both Obregón and Calles favoured evangelical proselytism, and openly supported the YMCA and the missions. In 1922, 261 American missionaries were assisting 773 Mexican colleagues in 703 places of worship frequented by 22,000 faithful. In 1926, the Methodists had 200 schools and their bishop, George Miller, expressed praise for the co-operative attitude of President Calles. Thanks to the Episcopalian Bishop Moisés Sáenz, brother of the Minister of

Foreign Affairs, Aaron Sáenz, the missions were afforded every facility by the Government, and Protestants controlled the Ministry of Education, from which they had been removed by José Vasconcelos.

This proselytism, always based on the twin themes of the immorality of the celibate priests and the rapacity of the higher clergy who kept the parish priests at starvation level, was quite effective in the North and in the pioneering areas of the hot lands, but elsewhere it provoked reactions which were often violent, and which became increasingly frequent after 1926 as Protestantism grew in strength. To the Catholics, it was obvious that the Government was collaborating closely with the Yankee missions, and that it was working for the great 'decatholicisation' hoped for by Theodore Roosevelt as a prelude to annexation. The Catholic politicians would have given much to have been able to publish this telegram sent by the Episcopalian churches of Toledo, Ohio, and Taylor, Pennsylvania, to President Obregón: 'Millions of Americans feel for you and pray for you while you struggle to unloose the grip of the Roman Catholic Church upon your great country.'[7]

Freemasonry

Mexican Freemasonry has not really been studied adequately; nevertheless, this movement has played a very crucial role in Mexico, to judge from the words written by President Portes Gil in 1929: 'In Mexico the State and Freemasonry have been one and the same in recent years.'[8] This declaration was made at the end of the religious conflict; when it began, the Supreme Grand Commander of the Scottish Rite, Luis Manuel Rojas, had bestowed on President Calles the Masonic Medal of Merit: 'The Order over which I have the honour to preside has never before awarded this exalted honour; it has been decreed on account of the extraordinary merit which you have displayed as President of the Republic, solving so many problems in such a short space of time.'[9]

Freemasonry and the Government were, in fact, closely linked, so closely that it was necessary to be a Mason to be appointed to any important post. Portes Gil was Grand Master in 1933–4, and General Cárdenas was to establish the National Rite when he became President. And if the politician was, by the logic of the circumstances, a Freemason, the symbiosis between the state and the army led to officers being Freemasons: 'a large majority of the officers being members of the Masonic order [are] therefore resentful of the ban placed on that order by the Roman Church.'[10] There might occasionally be emulation between civilians and military men: Governor Zuno propagated Freemasonry throughout the state of Jalisco, through municipal presidents and teachers, while the generals established a second network of military lodges.

To form its cadres, Freemasonry also made recruits among certain popular sectors, but in such cases it became more like a corporation, as among the building workers and railwaymen. It was by no means restricted to one occupation, for in the North the *braceros* returning from the United States spread the Order among the smallholders in the rural areas. This particular type of Freemasonry arose in response to a need for professional efficiency (it preceded trade unionism and developed parallel to it, constituting a protest against the dictatorship of the official unions).

It is worth emphasising the sexual dimorphism that made Freemasonry essentially a masculine affair, in opposition to a religion that owed its survival to virtuous women. The woman, the mother, assured the continuity of Catholicism by insisting on the religious acts of marriage, baptism, communion, and Extreme Unction for all, and by transmitting these practices to her daughters.

Freemasonry, controlled and relegated to the periphery by Díaz, reassumed after 1914 the active role that it had played during the era of the Reform, and it supplied the Government with sorely needed organisation and cadres: municipal presidents, agrarian commissioners, labour leaders, and schoolteachers belonged to it, whereas the organisations embodying militant anticlericalism were subordinated to it, such as the Mexican Anticlerical Federation, founded in 1923 by Manuel Bouquet, the acting Governor of Jalisco who was swept away in 1918 by Catholic opposition. The ideology of this Latin Freemasonry reflected the needs of a state that was in conflict with the Church; those who belonged to the Order had one nightmare, the Roman clergy, the incarnation of evil in the world, and with which they were in continuous conflict. 'Under clerical domination these lodges [Jacala and Huejutla] had a short life; the fanatical and hostile atmosphere prevented the collaboration of Masons of standing.'[11]

The Freemasons did not conceal their intention of destroying the evil power of Rome, and they organised a 'public demonstration in support of the policy of religious intolerance, and the members of the regular and irregular lodges of the capital marched with their respective banners'.[12] The ideology of the zealots of reason and the 'defanaticisers' was thus defined by General Joaquín Amaro, the man whom the officers fêted on the day of his patron saint, in the Church of San Joaquín in Mexico City, with a parody of the Divine Office, complete with a sermon from the pulpit and champagne drunk from chalices:

The Apostolic Roman Catholic clergy, converted into a rapacious, obstructive, conservative, and retrogressive political party, has been the sole cause of the misfortunes which have affected Mexico from the days of the Spanish Conquest until our own time ... In the long series of uprisings and *coups d'état* which devastated our country for hundreds of years, the CLERGY HAVE BEEN THE STRONGEST INSTIGATORS AND THE MOST POWERFUL ELEMENT, due to their extensive material resources and their absolute identification with all the enemies of the Revolution.[13]

Amaro, who had a personal interest in the history of the religious conflict, established a library, which after his conversion he left to the Jesuits. He gave Colonel Ernesto Higuera the task of writing a report on the seditious activities of the clergy during the period 1926–9, which includes an analysis of the 'mystic neurosis' of the masses instigated by the priests, who draw their strength from 'the liturgical solemnity of the services, the magnificence of the priestly vestments, their age-old domination over untutored consciences ... The priests cleverly exploited their superstitious blindness and the idolatrous sentiments of the ignorant faithful'.[14]

During his term of office, Amaro took full part in the intense anti-clerical propaganda. 'His attitude is well known as being hostile to the hierarchy of the Church, and the publication in his office of *La Patria* and the issue from his office of the book *Iglesia Católica*, both bitter anti-Church publications, are evidence of his feeling towards the Church.'[15] *El Soldado*, a monthly magazine distributed to the troops, and filled with cartoons and anecdotes, depicted the Pope, bishops, priests, and monks as sexual maniacs. The director of *La Patria*, General Cristóbal Rodríguez, published a series of books and pamphlets along similar lines.[16] The speech made during the Cristero War by General J. B. Vargas to the people of Valparaíso (Zac.), was a synthesis of all the themes of the ideology of the 'defanaticisers':

The evil clergy, composed of traitors to the country, and taking its orders from a foreign leader who is always conspiring to provoke foreign interventions in Mexico in order to ensure his domination and privileges, is harmful because its mission is to brutalise the ignorant people so as to exploit it and make it fanatical to the point of idiocy, and deceive it by making out that the clergy are representatives of God, so as to live off the indolent and illiterate masses, which is where the Friar holds sway. It is enough to have some idea of the terrible history of the Inquisition for one to realise that priests and cassocks reek of prostitution and crime.
Confession is an industry invented to seduce maidens, to win over Catholic ladies and transform fathers and husbands into chaste replicas of Saint Joseph...

The Pope is a crafty foreigner who accumulates wealth in collaboration with the exploiting Friars who swindle the foolish people for the benefit of a country quite other than our own ... Nowadays, if Jesus Christ were to come down, the first thing he would do would be to hang them like rabid dogs.[17]

The literature published between 1914 and 1940 continually labours the same themes propagated by the Army, the CROM, and the National Educational System:

> The ox is the Indian
> The yoke the Cross,
> And behind walks the priest
> Pricking his rump
> In the name of God.

> The mines are Yankee territory,
> and the churches Roman territory,
> the American flag flies on the first,
> the Vatican flag flies on the second,
> raised by the Yankee engineers,
> raised by the Spanish priests.

These themes were repeated in the works in the series of 'anti-religious pamphlets' published by the CROM, those published by the state governments, the 'Catechisms of the Revolution' and those of the 'Socialist doctrines',[18] All those in power had simplistic and radical ideas which were nourished by the conflict between Church and state and which, in return, exacerbated that same conflict.

President Obregón, whose tolerance was based on scepticism, had appeared to counter these dangers when he addressed the archbishops and bishops in 1923; 'The present social programme of the Government is essentially Christian, and it is complementary to the fundamental programme of the Catholic Church.' Since the Revolution was Christian, then any conflict that might exist was a conflict between institutions, and the Church would be wrong if it failed to understand this distinction.[19]

The Root of the Problem

Obregón's letter might appear to suggest that the conflict might have been avoided if President Calles had not succeeded him. Violent persecution and war might have been evaded, but certainly not the conflict itself. Mexican anticlericalism, though the work of a minority, was that of a minority in power; it was establishing itself in this power structure at a time when the infant state had not yet armed itself against such an assault. The state then faced the threat of the political Catholics who had rallied behind the Church, the only institution existing outside it. Finally, at all points the hegemony of the state was challenged by the Church, a hegemony in the process of rigid, dictatorial construction, which rode roughshod over religious categories.

Obregón was right in reproaching the Church for engaging in institutional rivalry with the state, and in ordering it to confine its activities to the churches. His collaborators and his successors were wrong, although *a posteriori* they justify the Church, and when they entered homes, they tried hard to enter hearts and insisted that the state should be worshipped: 'We must take possession of the conscience of youth; because the young man and the child belong to our Revolution ... to the community, to the collective body.'[20]

Objectively, the Church was blocking the road of the state and denying it passage; objectively, the state was insisting on the abjuration of Christians, and was also denying free passage. Hence, one saw peasants refuse land distributed by the agrarian commission, and the *agrarista* leaders demanding apostasy in return for a plot of land.

Thus the conflict descended from the exalted spheres of Hegelian argument, and was incarnated on earth. An ideology inherited from past history found favour again and was reformulated; and the peasants, who, although they had suffered enormously for fifteen years, had played no direct part in this eminently political conflict, were suddenly affected by it and refused to suffer any more.

Valéry once said that customs are counter-revolutionary whereas the law is revolutionary; the truth of this is exemplified by these leaders, who hated the old Mexico and despised its traditions, looking down on both its customs and its faith. They would have discarded them completely in return for the least of the states of the Union. Modern Mexico has been formed by men who despised ancient Mexico; this was, to a great extent, the root of the conflict which set the nationalist Calles against the patriotic Cristeros; President Cárdenas (1934–40) was to have a foot in both camps – hence the paradox of the Freemason who was a friend of the priests.

The Revolutionary state, when it reflected on the means to secure its victory, was anxious to avoid being faced, like its predecessor, with uncontrollable forces. It took measures, therefore, to win over consciences, through the schools and the media of communication, beginning by muzzling the institutional Church, which enjoyed such power among the people. In addition to these more general motives derived from political theory, the Revolutionaries had other more particular and more personal reasons: as Northerners, as renegades from the seminaries (Álvarez, Zuno, Mújica, and many others) in the Centre, they were fighting their own war.

It would be puerile to suppose that this modern state was committed to anticlericalism for all time; it affected to hold clericalism as the sole enemy, but it never failed to compromise with it whenever it could. It believed it was hating the priests, whereas what it really hated was the land of the Christian peasants. After the *Cristiada*, it no longer harboured any hopes of destroying Christianity; this was still the hope of its school-teachers, labour leaders and intellectuals, who, after the conflict was over, still held impassioned attitudes towards it. The state no longer desired the conflict, once it had learnt that it could not do without the Church, and it initiated a new policy of conciliation with the Church in 1938.

Before reaching that point, however, history had to pass through the apocalypse of the *Cristiada*, a war that has continued to our own day and that has remained in the shadows, unperceived from outside, lived from inside, a war that demonstrates public ignorance of a religious phenomenon even when it is also a historical phenomenon. The historian feels surprise at finding this, just as the Mexican state did before him: he falls into it, so to speak, as into a hole in a badly kept road; the Cristeros have remained unknown, on account of the very originality of their enterprise and the irresistible human desire to reduce the unknown to the known – for example, explaining a religious conflict in purely agrarian terms.

CHAPTER 3

The Conflict Between the Two Swords, 1925–6

The Birth of a Crisis: the Aggression of 1925

During his election campaign, President Calles had not had any opponent, apart from the rebels, except General Angel Flores, a dissident member of the revolutionary family, supported by the National Republican party, which was the remains of the Catholic party but lacked both its audience and its aggressiveness. The Church never gave it the slightest support. The beginning of 1925 was not marked by any new event; Garrido Canabal, the Governor of Tabasco, continued to harass Bishop Díaz, and in Jalisco Zuno continued the persecution that he had initiated in late 1924. This was intensified in January 1925, and the contagion spread to the neighbouring state of Colima. Zuno, a young, well-educated and respected man, had opposed the candidature of Calles, and it was thought, rightly or wrongly, that he had sympathised with the rebels supporting De la Huerta in 1924. It seemed logical to interpret the fierce attack which he mounted against the Church as a desperate attempt to bring to a halt the political machine that had been mobilised against him. It would not be long before the Senate would sit as a Federal grand jury and depose him.

In Jalisco, the Catholics still had the recent memory of a resounding victory – that of 1919. They responded to Zuno's persecution by organising themselves for a long fight, under the leadership of Anacleto González Flores, nicknamed *El Maestro* on account of his earlier calling as a craftsman: the Unión Popular (UP) was inspired by the German *Volksverein*, and worked hard to become a civic and political organisation based on the masses. It was headed by a Directory of five members; the territory was divided up and organised into street blocks, zones, and parishes, each headed by a leader in close touch with his subordinates and his immediate superior. There were no ceremonies, solemnity, or protocol. There was no bureaucracy – it was a system based on direct contact and clandestinity. A periodical pamphlet, the *Gladium*, was published in an edition of 100,000 copies, and passed from hand to hand until it reached the remotest parts of the state. The prodigious success of the UP can be explained by its popular character, evidence of which was its low subscription rate (one cent per week) and the absence of bureaucracy and formalities. The leaders were selected for their activism and efficiency. Among the five members of the Directory, which was renewed frequently, there were two women, and the cell leaders were peasants or workers, depending on the locality or urban district. This feminist and proletarian character of the movement explains the misgivings of the better-off Catholics, who requested Archbishop Orozco, who was abroad from 1924 until May 1925, to abolish the UP or to curb its activities.

On 21 February 1925, at 8 p.m., about a hundred men, including several Knights of Guadalupe (the Order created by the CROM to replace the Knights of Columbus), under the leadership of Ricardo Treviño, the Secretary-general of the CROM, demanded that the parish priest of the church of La Soledad in Mexico City hand over the parish to them. When he refused, they drove him out, and handed the church over to Fr Joaquín Pérez. On Sunday, 23 February, the people of the district rose in rebellion, and there was bloodshed.

This marked the birth of the Mexican Catholic Apostolic Church, which, with the support of the Government, took possession of half-a-dozen churches. Since he could not, with propriety, leave the church of La Soledad in the hands of the schismatics, President Calles closed the church and installed the 'Patriarch' Pérez in the disaffected parish church of Corpus Christi. The schism went no further, and seven out of the ten schismatic priests were subsequently reconciled with the Catholic Church.

The incident had been arranged by Morones, the boss of the CROM, the minister and right-hand man of Calles, with whom he had concluded a pact when his relations with Obregón, which were never good, were threatened. Morones had several conversations with Pérez to plan the seizure of the church of La Soledad. Gilberto Valenzuela, who was then Minister of the Interior, has asserted that Morones was thus trying to canalise in the Government's favour the social and political forces based on religion. The part played by Morones cannot be seriously denied: Treviño was the son-in-law of Antonio López Sierra, the patriarch's secretary and later bishop of the schismatic Church, and the workers' leader Rosendo Salazar has written: 'It is a fact that they were physically present ... and it is also true that the services were attended by both men and women trade unionists, and also by the staff of the offices run by the Labour Party – they all played their parts as schismatic simulators of religious worship.'[1]

Why did Morones follow this policy, which, according to the unanimous testimony of trade unionists such as Salazar, of politicians such as Senator Caloca, and of Aurelio Manrique ('A Church is not founded like a trade union!'), led directly to religious conflict, to violent confrontation, to the Cristero War? Was it the desire to eliminate, or at least to weaken, a dangerous rival – namely, the Catholic labour movement founded by the Church? The CROM took part in all the conflicts, in all the provocations, from 1920 onwards; the bomb attacks against religious buildings, the red flags on the churches, the acts of symbolic sacrilege – these were all the CROM's doing.

It was not the first time that a Mexican government had tried the Gallican tactic. 'A scalded cat fears cold water': the Church saw, behind this attempt, the threat of overt persecution. In 1822 the Regalists had proposed the creation of a national Church, Gómez Farías and Comonfort had attracted the priests with the supposed advantages of such a Church, and in 1859 Melchor Ocampo had sought to create a Church which would 'render unto Caesar, without violent and interested interpretations, that which was Caesar's'. In 1868 Juárez, in turn, tried this tactic, and approached the American Episcopalians with a request that they provide the Mexican Church with a bishop. Carranza's followers had installed vicars to take the place of the fleeing prelates, and the Minister of the Interior, Manuel Aguirre Berlanga, used the services of a false priest, purporting to be a 'secret emissary of the Holy See', Mgr Riendo. The name of Joaquín Pérez was put forward at this time,[2] and the clergy were invited to 'get rid of the foreign priests, and tread underfoot the higher clergy who keep us in poverty ... become independent of Rome'.

Calles, as Governor of Sonora in Carranza's time, after expelling the Catholic priests from the state, wanted to replace them with priests willing to form a new Church; the semi-official periodical *Orientación* reported the arrival in November 1917 of Fr Ernesto Llano, who had come to take over the leadership of this Mexican National Church.

The Church had good reason to be suspicious of the Government. Did not the Soledad incident prove that Calles, as President, was the same man as the persecuting Governor of Sonora? On 14 February, a few days before the schism, had not the President reminded the states of their obligation to keep the clergy under surveillance – both as regards their activities and their numbers?

The Consequences of the Aggression in the Form of Schism

The Archbishop of Michoacán expressed the fear that 'the spark might kindle the fire . . . owing to the inevitable clashes to which popular passions are wont to lead. But I am still more afraid of these developments, on account of the natural distrust which must be provoked in the people by their failure to enjoy the guarantees to which they are entitled.'[3] Sharing the misgivings of Mgr Ruiz y Flores, the Catholics began to be alarmed and mounted guard on the churches. This spontaneous mobilisation opened up dangerous possibilities, as is shown by this fervent letter sent by the villagers of Santa Ana Chiautempán to President Calles:

Is it true that the Supreme Government attacked a church and wants to do the same to the Basilica? Here many people are already preparing to defend the churches with firearms. I already have over 3,000 men, and I believe that the women are greater in number; there are probably 7,000 altogether. We would rather die than allow the clergy to be persecuted.[4]

This reaction of the popular masses led, fifteen days later, to the foundation of the National League for the Defence of Religion (LNDR), the fulfilment of a long-standing project supported by Miguel Palomar y Vizcarra, who had been a militant member of the social Congresses, of the National Catholic party, and a propagator of the Raiffeissen Mutual Funds. The bishops had not been consulted, for in 1919 Mgr Orozco had expressed opposition to the first attempt to found the League. The League was a confederation of several Catholic, social, trade-union, and lay associations, for the purpose of legal and civic action. The League was founded on 14 March; on the twenty-fourth the Government condemned it, and on the twenty-sixth the Government insisted that the Governors strictly enforce Article 130 of the Constitution, allowing only the Mexican-born to exercise priestly functions.

On the twenty-eighth, tension increased as a result of the dramatic events at Aguascalientes: the Governor, Elizalde, rivalled in fervour his colleague in Tabasco, and had invited his political clientele to form the Order of Knights of Guadalupe, and had incited them to attack the church of San Marcos. The Catholics, who had been mounting guard day and night for a month, sounded the alarm, and the attackers, about a hundred in number, were obliged by the crowd to fall back. After being reinforced by 200 soldiers, with three machine-guns, they returned to the attack. The fight lasted until two o'clock in the morning, and resulted in many dead and 256 wounded. Four hundred people were summarily condemned and deported from the state. The only evidence of sedition submitted to the court were two pistols, some knives, and a sack full of stones. In this incident, too, the members of Morones's Labour party played an important part.

Mgr Vera y Zuria, the Archbishop of Puebla and a champion of conciliation, asserted, at the end of his 1925 pastoral visit, that 'the Catholic Faith is deeply implanted in the heart of the people'. The attitude of the martyr, the conviction that war was approaching, a prospect which the Archbishop himself rejected with horror, were evident in the speech of welcome made to him by a peasant in San Lorenzo Chiautzingo: 'Know, then, Your Grace, that if the moment comes to sacrifice their lives, they will die exclaiming "Long live the Pope! Long live the Most Holy Virgin of Guadalupe! Long live Christ the King!"'[5]

Rome favoured appeasement: a new Apostolic Delegate arrived in April on a mission of reconciliation; rebuffed by the Government, cold-shouldered by several prelates who considered him too timid, he left Mexico in May and resigned. But the march of events did not depend on Rome, and the conflict continued its course. In Jalisco, Zuno recommenced the campaign of persecution, and Mgr Orozco returned to Guadalajara after his stay in Europe; this meant that, to a certain degree, Rome was abandoning the policy of complacency, because Orozco symbolised the spirit of resistance. In July, the police in Guadalajara attacked several churches, and the Unión Popular mobilised: six hundred were wounded, and there were about the same number of arrests. Zuno closed the seminaries. At the end of the year, the grand jury that dismissed him concluded its list of indictments by asserting that by his campaign of persecution he had 'alienated from the rightful cause many workers and peasants'.[6]

In August the Minister of the Interior, Valenzuela, considered to be too lukewarm, was replaced by Colonel A. Tejeda, whom the French Legate described as 'one of the most implacable and terrible enemies of the Catholic Religion'. The year ended badly, with the clergy being expelled from Tabasco for refusing to get married and anticlerical measures being taken in all the states; representatives of the League, and later the bishops, went to Rome to say that moderation was no longer the appropriate policy and was based on erroneous information. In both camps, the supporters of a final confrontation campaigned to fan the flames.

The Conflict Between Church and State

The Rupture of 1926

The Participants: the Mexican Clergy, the Catholic Politicians, and Rome; the Factions within the Government

At this point will be repeated a highly critical opinion of the clergy and the Catholic associations; this critical attitude is a true reflection of the dynamism of those institutions. The testimony is that of Ernest Lagarde, a French diplomat, an expert on the Mexican religious question – the best, according to Dwight Morrow, the United States Ambassador and architect of the 1929 agreements – on excellent terms both with the bishops and the ministers. He supplied information, through his government, to Rome, which did not share the combative views of a sector of the Mexican clergy, and to the White House, which was directly interested. Lagarde, at the end of 1926, submitted to Briand a summarised report of a hundred closely written pages on the religious crisis in Mexico.

To Lagarde, as to all foreigners, 'Mexican Catholicism is overburdened with superstitious practices and has a definite tendency towards idolatry . . . Mexican worship is, in many respects, a grossly materialistic parody of the Roman Catholic religion.'[7] 'Even pious fervour is lacking [in 1924, Mgr Ruiz y Flores declared to the Apostolic Congress in Amsterdam that only 20 per cent were real Christians]. Mgr Crespi told me that in this country Peter's Pence, which is collected only because Rome insists, is not enough for the upkeep of the Apostolic Delegation.'[8]

'As the troops are, so are the generals,' Lagarde continued. 'The Bishops, not to mention the rest of the clergy, are tactless, narrow-minded, intransigent, deeply divided.' And he classified the bishops as 'moderate and conciliatory' or as 'Leaguers and impulsive'.

The real leaders of the Mexican Church are the Archbishop of Morelia, Mgr Ruiz, a notable theologian, a man of some energy who lives in a dignified style; de la Mora, of San Luis Potosí, a courageous and untiring organiser, both of whom have made their dioceses and their clergy the best in Mexico; Orozco, combative, ambitious, unreflecting, opposed to any conciliation, so much so that Rome has often had to reprove him; González, of Durango, who is very learned, but was made a Bishop too young, with the temperament of a political leader, but domineering, turbulent, excitable, inconsistent; Díaz, a Jesuit, intelligent, ambitious, prone to intrigue, intolerant, who as Secretary of the Committee of the Episcopate . . . tends to play an increasingly important part . . .; but all five are candidates for the succession, which is virtually open, to the appointment of Archbishop-Primate of Mexico City, and, because of this, they vie with one another in intransigence in order to make their influence felt.[9]

This analysis has been quoted at some length because, although biased, it is perceptive, not so much in its isolated assertions, which are often incorrect, as in the accuracy of its picture of the complexity of the institutional Church. One has become accustomed to speak of the Church as though the faithful, the clergy, the bishops, and the Pope formed one monolithic body. Lagarde subsequently reconsidered some of his judgements when events contradicted him, and when the popular reaction to the persecution surprised him, as it surprised both the Government and Rome.

A curious fact that emerges from the Lagarde report is that Rome lent more credence to the Mexican Government than it did to the bishops. This continued to be the case until President Calles reduced to impotence the policy of the Vatican, made up as it was of prudent compromises between interest and the dictates of conscience. Rome often regarded as obstinacy or idolatry conduct by its Mexican servants that was no more than fidelity to orthodoxy. Rome called to order the unruly bishops, condemning the 'incorrect behaviour' of 1923 (the Monument to Christ the King) and 1924 (the Eucharistic Congress) and offered reparations to Obregón.[10] The latter

authorised the stay in Mexico of an Apostolic Delegate who would be able to correspond in cypher with the Vatican; if serious problems arose, he undertook not to expel him, but would merely demand his recall. In return for these assurances, the Curia undertook to appoint to vacant episcopal sees only clerics who kept well away from political conflict . . . it inclined towards a policy of temporising, towards a tacit arrangement.[11]

The Vatican was afraid that fresh religious conflicts might encourage the rise of Protestantism, and that the Church's enemies might again provoke a schism. 'For all these reasons, the Curia regretted that the Mexican clergy, who supported the League and were imbued with a combative spirit, instead of seeking for a *de facto* compromise with the public authorities, maintained an attitude of overt hostility and flatly refused to have anything to do with the Government.'[12]

Rome persisted in its moderate attitude, and to the very end sought for that '*de facto* compromise' for which it was to continue to hope during the three years that the war lasted, and which it imposed on Mexican Catholics in June 1929.

In its confrontation with the Mexican Church and with Rome, the Mexican state was by no means one monolithic force; constantly changing, marked by crisis and expansion, it formed a combination of forces that were in no way monolithic, and at times counter-balanced one another: there was the army, the CROM and the Labour party led by Morones, and the followers of Obregón and Calles, all quarrelling over military districts, ministries, and governorships.

It has already been mentioned that this Government was seeking to create a state, the existence of which preceded that of the nation; it must not be forgotten that it was not really doctrines that were in power, but individuals and temperaments. President Calles was one of those personalities that leave their mark on a country. To date, there is still no good biography of this man, born in 1877 in Guaymas, Sonora, into a family of Spanish descent that seems to have played an active part in the history of the region in the second half of the nineteenth century; it produced judges, colonels, two Governors and the commander-in-chief of the army that fought the French invaders. Obliged to work at an early age, he was an assistant schoolteacher, then a schoolteacher, and finally a school inspector in the time of Díaz; at the same time he engaged in journalism, and was not ashamed of writing poetry. After fifteen years as a teacher, this energetic man became bored, and went into business, for which he certainly had little aptitude; he was behind a counter when the revolution of Agua Preta surprised him. He became a General, Governor of Sonora during Carranza's period of office, Secretary of Industry, Commerce and Labour, Minister of War, and finally Minister of the Interior under Obregón, who imposed Calles as his successor.

The testimony of his collaborators is unanimous: if a dictator is one who tolerates nothing outside his own will, then Calles was dictatorship personified. Calles, to reach his goals of 'order and progress', was ready for anything; he had decided to be 'master in his own house'. Ambassador Sheffield used this expression to explain the attitude of the President towards the oil question. In his conflict with the Church is also to be found this strong desire to be master in his own house.[13]

Calles was not an Obregón:

the *détente* which, thanks to the tactful approach of Obregón and the desire for peace on the part of the Holy See, had taken place in the relations [of the Government] with Rome, did not survive the coming to power of the new President ... Calles was a violent and passionate adversary of the Roman Church, not because he wished to prevent the latter from extending its influence and power, but because he had decided to extirpate the Catholic Faith from the soil of Mexico. What was so fundamental in his character, was that he was a man of principle, possessed of an energy which did not stop short of obstinacy and cruelty, and he was prepared to attack not only persons but also principles and even the institution itself, and that the system of government which, as a result of his philosophical convictions, he supported, condemned as economically and politically disastrous the very existence of the Church.[14]

Even though 'the authors of the Revolution had interests and ambitions which often conflicted', they were obliged, by the fact of the religious conflict, to follow that 'President with an iron will, who did not permit discussion, nor advice, nor half-measures, and who made his struggle against the clergy his own personal policy'.[15] When the conflict dragged on and took the form of the Cristero War, divisions again appeared within the Government camp and led to the solution of 1929. In the events leading to the rupture, the part played by the anticlerical pressure group (Tejeda, Garrido, Canabal, Morones, Amaro, Freemasonry, the Anticlerical Federation, and so on) was undeniable. Throughout the crisis, one continually finds the same men bent on causing the failure of the attempts at conciliation made by Obregón, or the Minister Pani or Lemestre. On the other side, the 'white radicals' among the Catholics were not afraid of an open fight, and rejoiced in the opportunity.

From Provocation to Rupture: 1926

January was a month of deterioration, and warfare on a small scale continued in the states. Calles promulgated a series of regulations to enforce Article 130 of the Constitution, and asked for extraordinary powers to reform the Penal Code by introducing into it measures concerning religion, which would thus reinforce the common law. The newspaper *Universal* conducted a campaign designed to arouse fervour, which culminated on 4 February with the publication of an 'interview' supposedly given by the Archbishop of Mexico City, Mora y del Río, in the course of which he was said to have asserted that the bishops did not recognise, and were prepared to fight against, Articles 3, 5, 27, and 130 of the Constitution. The violent reaction of the Government was followed by a denial on the part of the Archbishop, and an acquittal by the court appointed by the Minister of the Interior. It was all in vain: the opportunity was a good one, and the Government ordered the closing of Catholic schools and convents, the deportation of foreign priests, a limitation on the numbers of priests, as demanded by a strict enforcement of the Constitution. The resistance of the Catholics, mobilised by the League, infuriated the Government. After the death of seven Catholics as a result of the riots at the Church of the Holy Family in Mexico City on the 23

February, the Governors received orders to 'enforce the Constitution AT ALL COSTS'.[16]

From March to May, 'the President, enraged by the unpatriotic attitude which he attributed to the clergy and which he connected with the threatening policy of Washington, began to act with extreme rigour, abandoning all moderation'.[17]

In the states, official policy varied from friendly tolerance (Veracruz, Coahuila, Guerrero, Puebla, Oaxaca, Campeche, Guanajuato, Zacatecas) to outright persecution (Tabasco, Jalisco, Colima); in some places a tolerable arrangement gradually gave way to violent confrontation (Michoacán, San Luis Potosí).

There were as many different solutions as there were situations; the governors were as divided as the bishops. However, although the Government did not succeed in enforcing the law in a uniform manner, it did raise tension in the country to a dangerous level. Rome put a brake on the Catholics, ordering them to abstain 'scrupulously from any kind of political party'.[18] A new Apostolic Delegate, Mgr Caruana, arrived discreetly in March, and personally contacted Morones through his friend Frank Tannenbaum; expelled on 10 May, he returned home convinced of the futility of conciliation and, a changed man, advised the bishops to pursue the policy of resistance that Rome feared so much. On his advice, the Episcopal Committee was created; the prelates now had a combative organisation viewed with disapproval by Rome. The months of May and June saw a certain *détente*; a local agreement, based on the retreat of the Governor of Michoacán, made it possible for Mgr Ruiz y Flores to suspend the clergy strike in his archdiocese.

This was only a truce, and on 14 June Calles signed the decree which, published on 2 July in the *Diario Oficial*, was to provoke the rupture. Known to historians as the 'Calles Law', it reformed the Penal Code by virtue of the full powers granted in January to deal with infringements of Article 130. The bishops, surprised by this sudden measure, tried to discover the final objective of the Government. Was it merely an attempt at intimidation, or was it true that the Government was trying to suppress completely the Church and the Catholic religion? There was still a majority of the Episcopal Committee in favour of temporising, since according to Rome even the registration of the clergy with the Ministry of the Interior was not contrary to canon law.

Cardinal Gasparri announced that Rome desired 'to seek, by means of direct conversations, the possibility of an arrangement'.[19] Lagarde served as the intermediary, despite his scepticism, and he was present at the conversation between Tejeda and Mgr Tito Crespi, who was in charge of the Apostolic Legation. On 23 July the prelate made further concessions, only requesting the 'attenuation' of the enforcement of the law. The Minister of the Interior was unbending. 'In fact, it was too late ... on both sides, tempers had been so aroused that any attempt at a compromise was viewed with suspicion.'[20]

The part of the Calles Law that most irritated the bishops was Article 19, which decreed the compulsory registration of the clergy, for it allowed the Government to hand over churches to the schismatics. The directors of the League and their Jesuit advisers were in favour of resistance, but the Episcopate, although it was now convinced of the necessity of resistance, was divided as to the action to be taken. Some of them feared that the suspension of religious services might provoke people, who were already highly alarmed, into violence born of despair: Guízar y Valencia of Veracruz, Orozco of Guadalajara, supported by Banegas (Querétaro), Vera y Zuria (Puebla), Fulcheri (Zamora) and Ruiz y Flores (Morelia), were in favour of passive resistance by the clergy and, if necessary, their martyrdom. Rome was silent, being reluctant to impose a course of action on the divided bishops. The League took advantage of this situation to mobilise large crowds throughout the country; the ease with which it did this made it lose its sense of reality. If, in reaction to the suspension of religious services, the people arose as one man, the Government would be obliged to capitulate, the leaders of the League were now maintaining, and their success impressed the bishops. Mgr Crespi was alone in his view, and on 11 July the Episcopal Committee, in the absence of Mgr Orozco, who had returned home to calm his flock, decided to suspend religious services, subject to the agreement of Rome. Thereupon, the Episcopal Committee approved the proposed economic boycott submitted to it by the League. Rome did not reply until 23 July, after the defeat of Mgr Crespi: 'The law is condemned, as is any act which may signify or be interpreted by the faithful as an acceptance or recognition of the said law. The Mexican Episcopate is to adhere to this principle in its actions, so that it counts on majority support and, if possible, unanimity, and give an example of concord.'[21]

On 24 July, the Committee decided that religious services should be suspended as soon as the Calles Law came into force – namely, on 31 July; the last hesitations of the bishop had been swept away by the attitude of the President 'who had become so violent on the religious question that he had lost his temper every time anyone has mentioned the subject in his presence. His face became flushed, and he thumped the table to express his hatred of and his profound hostility towards religious practices.'[22] The prelates Mora y del Río and Díaz had already been prosecuted, and the leaders of the League arrested.

On 25 July, the Episcopate published a collective pastoral letter justifying the suspension of religious services, and stating that the churches would remain open and be guarded by the faithful. The Public Prosecutor was immediately retained by the Government, while crowds filled the churches to receive the sacraments. The President was right to declare: 'I believe that we have reached the moment when the lines of battle are definitely drawn; the hour is approaching for the decisive battle; we will see whether the Revolution has triumphed over reaction or whether the victory of the Revolution has been ephemeral.'[23]

The Significance of the Rupture

'President Calles has decided this time to go the whole hog and force a complete cessation of religious cult through the country, calculating, as he told his friends, that if once the habit of church-going could be broken, the Indians would forget it.'[24] The words of this British diplomat, who held his appointment in Mexico City in 1926, described correctly the intentions of the Government. On 26 August, Lagarde met Calles, who told him that

every week that passes without religious services will lose the Catholic religion about 2 per cent of its faithful ... He had decided to finish with the Church and to rid his country of it, once and for all. At times, President Calles, despite his realism and his coldness, gave me the impression ... of approaching the religious question in an apocalyptic and mystic spirit.[25]

Tejeda, the Minister of the Interior, expressed himself in the same way: 'The Church has exceeded our wildest hopes in decreeing the suspension of religious services, nothing could be more pleasing to us ... We have got the clergy by the throat and will do everything to strangle it.'[26] At the moment of the rupture, each side fell back on the past and invoked historical precedents from the eighteenth and nineteenth centuries. The Government's argument was simple: religion was part of the state, and the Church with it; everything, therefore, must be subjected to regulation by the state. With what right were the clergy refusing to render to Caesar that which was Caesar's when the United States was threatening the country?

Calles resented, as though it were evidence of treason, the chronological coincidence between the religious conflict and the difficulties with the United States that arose in January 1926.

To the Government, the collusion between the Church and the foreigners – that is, the United States and the oil companies – was so glaringly obvious that it was pointless to look for proof of it. Oil explained everything, even the creation of the new dioceses of Huejutla and Papantla.[27] In fact, the battle was decisive: the social question was relegated to second place, and the American problem was resolved after 1926 when Kellogg chose the path of conciliation and sent Ambassador Morrow. There remained the problem of the place of the Church in a society which the new state wished to embrace entirely, since Church and state were to be found in all spheres of life. These anticlericals, the agents of the state and of its nationalism, where the heirs of the Caroline tradition of the 'légistes' who, ever since the time of Philip the Fair, had fought Roman imperialism and never ceased to dream of a national church subject to the state. In the interval before they could abolish 'fanaticism' by means of education, they wanted to put an end to the separation of Church and state in order to shatter 'the Roman bloc'. This was the abandonment of the liberalism of Díaz's time for the neo-Regalism of the modern state that was on its way to becoming totalitarian. Liberalism had expected the laws of the Reform to shatter the Roman bloc into a multitude of petty sects; but separation had merely consolidated the Catholic Church. It was, therefore, necessary to abandon the old tactics: this was the significance of the Schism of 1925, of the Calles Law, of Circular 103 of the Ministry of the Interior; of the creation of parish committees responsible for running the churches, while all awaited the disintegration of the Church. Díaz Soto y Gama, the theorist of the Revolution, dreamed of a Christianity directed by the state, leaving to the priest the role of cultivator of the moral virtues. The law of 2 July, which was juridically unsound and even harmful to the interest of the civil power itself, had an obvious spiritual significance: it showed that the Government was confusing passion with its theory of the state, without any possibility of conciliation with reality. It went beyond the defence of the interests of Caesar, to indulge in the Jacobin terrorism of hostility to religion itself and to unleash a war of religion.

In the Revolutionary camp, apart from opportunistic moderates such as Obregón and Pani, some denounced the policy of the Government, whom they accused of fabricating a conflict in which the people would be shattered. The law threatened the Church with death, they reasoned, so how could the Church accept it? In every parish it could, with a semblance of reason, denounce the injustice of the law, preach resistance to it and, perhaps, justify rebellion. The National Peasant League, at its Congress held in November 1926, considered this question, and refused to support the criminal Government, which 'is trying to take from the people, through violence, its most treasured religious sentiments'. Aurelio Manrique denounced 'the present religious conflict, artificially provoked' by the Government and its 'devious policy over the religious question'.[28]

The bishops were in agreement in protesting against the condemned articles of the Constitution, especially against Article 130, the source of the Calles Law. In practice, the measure of their agreement did not go beyond this, and it needed all the energy of a politician like Calles to unite them in a movement of resistance, which was temporary and never without reservations. Apart from the great, vague majority of the undecided, there were unconditional followers of Rome who were waiting for Rome to pronounce on the matter (in fact, Rome did not do so until June 1929), the supporters of Cardinal Gasparri and conciliation at any price, and, finally, those whom one might call the nationalists, who had no clearly defined policy but were convinced that a great part of the trouble stemmed from the ignorance of Rome regarding the country. This group believed that the Apostolic Delegate should be a Mexican, and they proposed the name of Pascual Díaz.[29]

The prelates who favoured conciliation, who were not necessarily the same men as those who arranged the peace of 1929, searched until the very end for a solution to the problem, despite the hostility of the members of the League, who denounced them to Rome, and of the Government, which for the moment refused to make any concession. A proof of the fact that one must proceed with great caution in describing the attitude of the different prelates is the difference already observed between what Mgr Orozco actually did and what has been said about him. This man, reputed to be a firebrand, a Templar-bishop, the *bête noire* of the Government, was not only categorically opposed to the suspension of worship, but even authorised the Catholic schools to remove the crucifix from their walls.

Since 1914 the great dilemma had been whether to repudiate the Revolution entirely, or to try to reconcile it with the Church. This had been tried between 1919 and 1925, and was to be tried again in 1929, and later under Cárdenas, but in 1926 Calles put an end to all hopes in this direction. Mgr Díaz, who in 1929 was to play the most important part in establishing peace, asserted in 1926 that the registration of the clergy was 'the symbol of the subjection of the Church to the state in the spiritual sphere ... a secession'.[30] The registration of the clergy was a deliberately hostile measure, as Calles confided to Lagarde; it was the prelude to an attempt to establish a constitutional church, and was a threat to the sacraments because the non-juring priests would be proscribed and the others would be schismatics. It was not surprising that the Church saw a trap in the Calles Law, which aimed at 'an enslaved Church in a tyrannical state'.

Finally, the situation was unacceptable to the laymen, who were exerting pressure on the bishops; these were the laymen whom the bishops had spent a generation in training, and who now wished to participate in the social and economic development of Mexico. In the excited Mexico of Revolutionary times, the Church and the Catholics were no longer quiescent; their audacity and their rash behaviour were symptoms, sometimes imprudent ones, of dynamic adaptation to the new circumstances. The restructuring of the administrative cadres showed their consciousness of insufficiency, their impetus and their strength. In 1926 Mgr Orozco wanted to avoid conflict, and later opposed armed resistance, because he was optimistic about future developments and did not want to commit himself. Among the laity, however, there were many impatient men who believed that it was necessary to commence 'the reconquest', because 'the so-called sovereign people has come off worst. First it has been proclaimed King; then it has been crowned with thorns.'[31]

From July onwards the Catholics and the bishops tried to make full use of legal methods, and demanded the reform of the Constitution, which was the last road left open, according to President Calles. This solution, however, was unthinkable; one might just as well have asked the Revolutionaries to surrender and voluntarily abandon power. To the Church, it appeared that the Constitution could easily be modified, and in this it was completely mistaken – as mistaken as the state, which asserted that the measures taken did not affect religion. Both sides pretended not to realise that to give way on the letter of the law was a spiritual surrender, a capitulation.

There remained one unknown factor of which nobody spoke, and which nobody appeared to remember, which everybody under-estimated, at least – the attitude of the Christian people. In the course of the summer of 1926 it was the people who, little by little, came to the forefront of events, while behind the scenes the Government and the bishops continued their negotiations.

CHAPTER 4

The Conflict Between the Two Swords, 1926–9

The Cristiada[1]

From the day when the Episcopate announced its decision to suspend public worship,

people began to go to put their consciences in order, even though it was a time when there was plenty of work to be done. With every day that passed, the crush of people increased in the village; people came from all the surrounding homesteads; one could feel sorrow in every breast, every face was pale, every eye was filled with sadness and throats were constricted as people pronounced words, and it was always the same question: 'Why is this and why are they closing the churches, what is happening?' and the only answer was 'Who knows? I don't know'.[2]

The nightmare of 31 July, the last day of worship, and the traumatic experience suffered that night were the immediate causes of the insurrection; more than one person, on his knees in the dark as the Blessed Sacrament passed by, came to his own decision. On the following day Aurelio Acevedo put out his horse to graze 'so that it could put some fat on and be able to withstand the hard labour which would face it when the rains ended'.[3] This 'hard labour' was the war which Aurelio Acevedo saw approaching and for which he was preparing without further delay, visiting all his companions in the peasant union of Valparaíso, Zacatecas.

The rallying of morale, which had first begun in 1925 on account of the Schism, gained momentum around Easter 1926, when in most dioceses people did penance to ask for mercy. As one witness described it: 'Penance and more penance, prayers in public and songs of penance; but He remained insensitive to all the Catholics did and requested – it only increased his Satanic rage. This was a dirty trick on the Government's part; we Catholics already felt ourselves hating it as much as Satan himself. The scourge was upon us.'[4]

When, at the end of this period of tension, the suspension of worship took place, that seemingly inexhaustible patience was suddenly broken; it was not the patience of the Church, but that of the Christian people, of the poor. *Patientia pauperum non peribit in aeternum.* The war came as a surprise to the state and the Church, which had not bargained for this eventuality. In August there were six insurrections and many riots; all the acts of the Government, whether well- or ill-intentioned, were resented as acts of aggression: the closing of the churches for stock-taking, the arrest of priests or laymen who refused to form the cultural associations provided for by the law, and preventive measures (the dispatch of troops to villages that had never been garrisoned, and the commandeering of arms and horses), were the ultimate reasons why men took up arms in August. The mobilisation of the army, the religious persecution that began, and the repression that accompanied it in accordance with its own blind logic – these did the rest.

Thirteen new centres of insurrection appeared in September, and a score of others in October, and the Federal army began to realise that the business would be less easy than it had supposed; then General Ismael Lares was killed at Durango, and half a regiment annihilated with him. In November and December insurrection spread throughout the central plateau; at the end of December the 59th Regiment, commanded by General Arenas, was annihilated near Colotlan in Jalisco. In the state of Jalisco, at the end of the year, 20 municipalities out of 118 were in a state of insurrection, despite the opposition of the archbishop, who forbade the Unión Popular to have recourse to armed force. The leader of the UP, overwhelmingly encouraged by his troops, took the decision to fight, because people were saying:

Better to die than deny Christ the King, without fearing martyrdom or death, in whatever form it might come! Sons, do not be cowards! Up and defend a just cause! That is what mothers were saying to their sons. At the same time, everybody was repeating in chorus the cries of 'Long Live Christ the King!' and 'Long Live the Virgin of Guadalupe!'[5]

Anacleto González Flores could no longer expect prudence and moderation from these people, and he had to abandon his dream of a 'revolution of the eternal' and of a people of martyrs who died on their knees, in order to follow his men who, deliriously, with exasperation and heroism, ran towards the battle. For the people it was clear enough: patience, penance, and prayer of the period from May to December had been of no avail, for 'the heart of Calles had been hardened'. Rather than the unconvincing slowness of the civil struggle, the populace, its nerves shattered by the suspension of services, preferred open war, without realising what that would mean in terms of horror and, also, of slowness.

Initial Engagements

After 1925 the League, led by the young militants of Catholic Action, recruited from the middle classes, which supplied the state with its organisational cadres, had carried on an intensive campaign of agitation and mobilisation, encouraging legal action, economic boycotts, and non-violent actions. The course taken by events during the summer of 1926 surpassed their hopes, and from thenceforth, they thought in terms of a seizure of power rather than constitutional reforms. The numerous spontaneous risings in late summer and autumn precipitated this change in their political tactics. Consulted as to the theological legitimacy of a war of this nature, the Episcopal Committee, referring to the classics on the subject, answered with a prudent expression of assent that the Leaguers interpreted as unconditional support. Strengthened by this support, the directing committee of the League gave the order for a general rising for the first days of January 1927, thus demonstrating its military non-existence and its political irresponsibility. The insurrection, which was psychologically possible after the earlier risings, was massive and unanimous throughout the Western Centre, where the rural masses who supported the UP, which had given the battle-cry, tried to re-enact the capture of Jericho. Coming from all the villages and all the hamlets, men, women, and children gathered together to make the Government capitulate by this display of force. Everywhere the crowds elected new municipal councils; their euphoria bore no relation to the war that was approaching.

The Government's response was purely military: what could crowds armed with sticks and stones do against regiments and battalions? At the first clash, the corpses were left strewn oh the ground and it was an utter rout. Of the thousands of pilgrims, all that was left was a handful of insurgents who took to the bush. The generals were able to telegraph Mexico City: 'It is not a military campaign, it is a hunting party', and President Calles considered the business to be concluded after five weeks. However, the report of General Ferreira, Commander-in-Chief of the Western Centre, ended with these words: 'The rebels are protected by all the inhabitants.'

By this time, the League had lost the game politically because, even before it had lost prestige in the eyes of some bishops who had been favourable towards it, it had ruined its representative character. From being the mouthpiece of the Catholic people, it was now reduced to a faction of conspirators who had deceived the leaders of the civic resistance movement, such as Anacleto González Flores, by leading the masses to the slaughter. With rare exceptions, the insurrections owed nothing to it – in any case, they received neither arms, nor money, nor organisation, which was lacking everywhere – not even that of the Federal District, since the former Zapatist General Manuel Reyes had been persuaded to take up arms by a nun of Tlalpan, 'Madre Conchita'. Only one insurrectionary movement can be attributed to it, that of General Gallegos, which took place in October 1926 in Guanajuato; even in this case, the League was content to get in touch with the man and make him all sorts of promises, which were never kept and which obliged Gallegos to carry out his insurrection under very unfavourable conditions.

If in the Western Centre, from León to Colima and Tepic, the insurrection was the unanimous act of thousands of men, this was because the UP, and not the League, had for a long time controlled the population. Elsewhere, those movements of 1926 that had survived grew in strength. Everywhere, the order for the insurrection had the catastrophic effect of provoking an immediate rising when nothing was prepared. After the massacre, one might have thought that the League had ensured the definitive victory of the Government.

The considerable resources of the Federal army made it possible for it to crush separately the isolated centres of insurrection in 1926 and then, in early 1927, the Altos de Jalisco region and the Sierra Gorda. However, because of the popular character of the insurrection and the enduring nature of its underlying motives, risings occurred again as soon as the flying columns withdrew. From June 1927 onwards, there were many men who, after fleeing to the United States, returned to the country with a rifle and ammunition purchased north of the Rio Grande, and money saved after some months of work. The untiring activity of the Minister of War, General Amaro, who, combining the use of trains, lorries, aviation, and cavalry, endowed his army with considerable mobility, was condemned to perpetuate itself in vain. It was a colonial war, carried on by a colonial army against its own people, and followed the course of all wars of this type: the harshness of the repression, the execution of prisoners, the systematic massacre of the civilian population, scorched earth, looting, and rape, all left in the wake of the Federal troops the germ of fresh risings.

The Insurgent Movement and its Leadership

In May 1927, Amaro was promising victory by Midsummer Day, but on the latter date he was obliged to triple the number of units operating in Jalisco (from four to twelve), and to double that of those operating in Michoacán (from four to seven); and all the time he had his back turned on Colima, and Guanajuato was astir with trouble again. Between the 18th and 22nd parallels, from Aguascalientes to Iguala, there were concentrated twenty reinforcement units, some brought down from the North, and others brought into a state of readiness hastily. It was not arms that were lacking but men to carry them; a month later, twenty more regiments and battalions were brought from the Yaqui territory (Sonora), which had been decisively pacified after the last Indian War in 1926: these included the five victorious units with their aircraft and their mountain artillery, and five battalions of Yaqui warriors conscripted after their defeat.

The military machine, despite its desire to conquer the Cristeros in order to settle accounts with the Church, was not adequately equipped to deal with this resistance. Ignorance of the degree of popular exasperation (although there had been quite enough evidence of this), and the facts of strategic geography and the shortage of troops to deal with popular guerrilla warfare covering a vast territory – these factors determined the course of events. The Federals, at the height of their strength, never had a numerical superiority of more than two to one: 100,000 of them against 50,000 Cristeros.[6] The war, therefore, went on. Its character will be described later.

The combatants dispersed in January had become guerrilla fighters; in July 1927, there were already 20,000 of them, operating spontaneously and without any organisation, always short of ammunition and with no money, but already well-mounted and armed with rifles captured from an enemy worn down by *piquyhuye* (hit and run) warfare. The American military attaché noted the absence, remarkable in Mexico, of any supreme leader. Villism, Carrancism, and Zapatism were so called from their leaders, whereas here such personalism was lacking. The insurgents were called the *Populares* in the areas controlled by the Unión Popular; elsewhere they called themselves the Defenders or the Liberators. The Government, in disparagement, called them the Christ-the-Kings, and later the Cristeros, calling them by the name of Him whom they regarded as leader.

The League had given up all hope of directing the movement, but did not cease to interfere with it and, to control it, it looked for a technical director who would be both competent and obedient. It believed it had found him in the person of General Enrique Gorostieta, a man of forty, a career officer, a gifted artilleryman who had left the army when the troops of Díaz were disbanded. Disheartened by civilian life and detesting the new government, he expressed sympathy for the resistance of the rebels, with whom he had nothing in common. As a Northerner, he was a liberal, a Jacobin, and a Freemason. The League sought him out and · offered him the opportunity of avenging himself, while cashing in on an adventure which promised well for him. A somewhat mysterious character, capable of great enthusiasm, he embraced the cause of the Cristeros without sharing their faith. He still had his half-pay from his service as a mercenary, and suddenly history gave him his chance. Like Felipe Angeles, another cadet, another artilleryman, he had the grit and ambition needed to reach the Presidency. Like him, he became a changed man through his association with the combatants.

As a soldier and as a man, he was won over by the Cristeros; he who had so often cursed the mediocrity of the Federal army, who had only known inefficient officers bullying miserable troops, was astounded by the miracle he was witnessing: soldiers in sandals and dressed in white linen, still filled with the communal spirit of their village, of their field, of their private undertakings, of their family, held steady under fire, did not hesitate to respond to supreme demands, and before his eyes crossed that line beyond which one no longer loves oneself, beyond which one no longer thinks of preserving one's life. He saw them stand up and march calmly to the battle, hurl themselves machete in hand on the Federal machine-guns, and scale heights at the summit of which simple peasants begin to appear to us as great warriors.

A career general, a technician of sophisticated weaponry, at the age of forty he discovered for himself, guerrilla warfare, of which later he became a notable theorist and practitioner. Gorostieta, the agnostic Freemason, who had become a Christian after his own fashion in the midst of those Cristeros whom he admired without any trace of indulgence ('With Tlaquepaque mud one can't make Sèvres porcelain'), was working for the destruction of the regime. Did he want power? He would not have been the first general to sit in the presidential chair, and when victory seemed near, in 1929, everybody hurried to make political overtures to the man whom the American military adviser called 'a formidable fighter'.

Consolidation of the Movement

The consolidation of the Cristero movement was an accomplished fact in July 1927, and its renewed expansion had not waited for Gorostieta; the latter established contact, understood the nature of the war, and put his methods to the test in a small region from September 1927 to February 1928. After this long process of maturation, he was able to extend his influence swiftly to the six states of Jalisco, Nayarit, Aguascalientes, Zacatecas, Querétaro, and Guanajuato, and then become the supreme leader of the insurrection. The League had made a lucky choice, it is true, but so much good fortune only confirmed its inefficiency, and Gorostieta was able to say of it:

I have already said my last word on the subject, and I am waiting for their answer, so that I can withdraw or carry on the work . . . I am now responsible to YOU [the Cristeros] for the final success of our struggle and our efforts, and if I am responsible . . . I must have full powers to do everything that accrues to our advantage.[7]

In autumn 1927, when the Federal army was obliged to concentrate its efforts on Mexico City, after the Gómez–Serrano political crisis, and campaign in Veracruz against Gómez, the Cristeros were so strong in Jalisco that the Government had to withdraw its protection from the haciendas and the foreign-owned mines. At the end of January 1928 Amaro, who had just led the campaign in Colima, asked for more troops, aircraft, and money. There were 35,000 insurgents in twelve states, from Durango to Tehuántepec – that was the situation in March. In May the Cristeros of the South Jalisco Division, commanded by General Jesús Degollado, were capable of mounting two months in advance an attack on the port of Manzanillo, which necessitated the combined movement of several units. By the middle of the year it was clear that the rebellion could no longer be crushed and that the war was going to drag on forever, for the Government, supported by the United States and in control of the towns, the railways, and the frontiers, could last out indefinitely.

In July 1928 Obregón, the successor of Calles, was assassinated, and the growing division between the faction of Obregón's followers, cheated of their victory, and the Calles faction, which held firm against wind and tide thanks to the political genius of its leader, operated in favour of the Cristeros.

The isolated centres of resistance declined, were extinguished, or were rekindled intermittently in Coahuila, San Luis, and Veracruz; the rebellion was marking time in Guerrero, smouldering in Puebla, and spreading in Oaxaca, Mexico City, and Morelos. In the three large regions where the Cristeros were already firmly established, they continued to nibble at the Federal army, and on the 'smallpox-chart' of the General Staff the black spots ran together and covered the whole of the Western Centre from San Juan del Río to the Pacific. The big offensive launched in the winter by the Federal army did not succeed: in January 1929, it was no longer possible to follow the war from day to day:

You will have gathered from the Press that things have begun to boil up in Guanajuato and in Querétaro ... here in the Altos I have nothing left to do ... The Gómez Loza Regiment has increased in size to such an extent that I have been obliged to form a second Gómez Loza Regiment and put Fr Vega in command of both of them ... We are now fighting almost in the outskirts of Guadalajara ...[8]

The Federal officers recognised that the 'situation is very serious for the Federal troops who are constantly on the defensive and are often defeated'.[9]

For the big offensive of December–January, the army assembled the maximum number of troops, artillery, and aircraft on the Jalisco: thirty line regiments, six regiments of mountain artillery, and three squadrons of aircraft; they had recruited intensively, and had brought troops from faraway Chiapas, Yucatán, and Tabasco, to guard the railways and thus free the combatant units for battle. After clearing the area of the Altos of its civil population, the army launched the attack and found the enemy area empty. The Cristeros had been preparing for a long time and had stored away the harvests of all resettled peasants, issuing them with receipts. The army once again looted the civilian population, which underwent indescribable sufferings from the cold, hunger, and epidemics. The spirit of resistance, far from being broken, grew in strength, and resettlement 'drove more men into rebellion'.[10]

In February the Government was obliged to cut by 30 per cent the salaries of its officials, in order to finance the campaign, and the American Military Attaché noted: 'The revolution is growing more serious.'[11] From 2 to 23 February there were 123 battles in the state of Jalisco alone.

For the first time, some politicians expressed misgivings about the future:

We have spent two years fighting the insurgents and we have still not finished with them. Are our soldiers incapable of fighting peasants, or is it that we do not want to finish the rebellion? Then let us say so at once, and not keep throwing more fuel on the flames. Don't forget that if three more States really rise in rebellion, with the three that are already in revolt, then the Public Power is in danger of collapsing![12]

The American Consul in Guadalajara accurately described the problem, and it was fully understood by Ambassador Morrow, who noted: 'It seems unlikely that the State can be successfully pacified in spite of every effort on the part of the President and the local military authorities until the settlement of the religious question.'[13]

The Apogee of the Cristero Movement: March–June 1929

At the beginning of March 1929, Generals Manzo and Escobar rebelled against the Portes Gil–Calles Government. The North-western bloc (the three rebel units in Veracruz were crushed by the ten loyal units) could count on 25,000 men, or one-third of the Federal army. The Praetorian Guard composed of Obregón's followers, who had now risen in rebellion, had waited for too long, since they had been the masters of the political game in July 1928, after the death of their leader. They had allowed themselves to become isolated geographically and politically, and their movement, condemned by the United States, never had a chance. They therefore tried to rally the Catholics, by repealing Calles's legislation, and the Cristeros, by concluding a pact with Gorostieta. Gorostieta made a calm analysis of the situation: unscrupulous generals, discomfited politicians, whose unthinkable victory would only aggravate the situation in the country, were offering him the chance to enter the Federal arsenals and obtain ammunition, the lack of which had, until then, prevented victory.

On their side, the supporters of Escobar believed that they could manipulate the Cristeros, and could not resign themselves merely to equipping them. Not only did Escobar devote all his time to robbing the banks in the Northern region, not only did he allow himself to be bought by the Government, but, above all, faithful to his caste until the end, he never delivered a single cartridge to the Cristeros, when he might have given them train loads of ammunition.

Calles, the Minister of War, abandoned the West to the Cristeros and sent 35,000 troops to the North to crush the rebels, who were bombed by American aircraft at Jiménez.[14] In order to do this, it was necessary to scrape the bottom of the depots and conscript improvised troops: *agraristas*, regional militias, veterans of General Cedillo's army, convicts, the unemployed, workers from the trade unions, everybody was pulled in as in the good old days of the press-gang.

Gorostieta was pessimistic as regards the future: certain of the defeat of the Northern rebels, he predicted that 'after their defeat the Turk [namely, Calles] will turn on us. He will come with a great number of troops, with high morale and pride in their victory, against our men, who lack supplies as usual.'[15] He therefore ordered an immediate offensive, and between 3 March and 15 May the Cristeros defeated the auxiliary troops (30,000 men) and the few troops of the line (about fifteen units) left in the West. The entire zone, except for the biggest towns, was falling into their hands. The arrival of Cedillo's troops was not sufficient to restore the situation, and General Amaro for the first time despaired of the situation, telling President Portes Gil that it was essential to arrive at a compromise with the Church. In June, despite the return of the victorious troops from the North, the Cristero movement was at its zenith. Having beaten General Cedillo in a pitched battle, the Cristeros were proving that they could manoeuvre above the regimental level. At Tepatitlán, on 19 April, three regiments commanded by Fr Vega, 'Pancho Villa in a cassock', enveloped six Federal units in a pincer movement.

In the West there were 25,000 men armed and organised in regiments, usually operating as guerrillas for lack of ammunition. In the rest of the country, there were 25,000 Cristeros, more or less well-organised, feeling that they had the wind behind them, at a moment when the Federation was in difficulties. Gorostieta kept calm: without money, without ammunition, how was he to counterbalance the financial, military, and political support of the United States? He confided: 'I don't know how this is going to work out, the Government cannot finish us off as long as worship is suspended; and we cannot defeat it, so that there is an equilibrium.'[16] He regarded the Presidential elections fixed for the autumn as a possible way out: in January, he had contacted Vasconcelos, the independent and popular candidate. Vasconcelos sent him a message that action would be taken on the day after the elections; first he wanted to demonstrate the Government's deceitfulness. Then the Cristeros would supply him with the necessary military force.

On the Government side, there was a realisation of the seriousness of the situation, and recourse was had to the only possible solution, the resumption of public worship, which would disarm the Cristeros and consequently Vasconcelos. Gorostieta tried to dissuade the bishops, telling them to be on their guard, and threatening them, when negotiations between Rome and Mexico City in May, through the United States as intermediary, were making rapid progress. But he knew that once peace was concluded, he would have to give in, because he knew his men and the reasons why they were fighting: 'As soon as they open the churches, you will all leave me.'[17] Speaking of the bishops, he told a friend, on the day of his death, which had occurred in strange circumstances, some days before the peace: 'They are selling us out, Manuelito, they are selling us out.'[18]

The Diplomatic Conflict: the Genesis of the Modus Vivendi

Table I below sets out the relationship between the events of the war and the diplomatic initiatives that strove to control it.

TABLE I   *Diplomacy and the war*

The diplomatic conflict	The war
1926 *31 July*: suspension of religious services	
21 August: conversations between Calles and the bishops	*August*: first risings
September: rejection of the petition of the bishops	
1927	*January*: insurrection of the entire Western Centre
March: Calles approaches Coolidge to settle the oil question	Suppression of the movement
April: expulsion of the bishops	
	June: renewal of the insurrectionary movement Total number of Cristeros, 20,000
July–August: United States changes its Mexican policy; meetings in San Antonio between the bishops and the Government	
October: Gómez–Serrano crisis	Situation serious in the Western region
November: oil question resolved; arrival of Ambassador Morrow	
1928 *January*: Vatican agents meet Morrow and the Mexican bishops in Cuba	Total number of Cristeros, 35,000

TABLE I *continued*

The diplomatic conflict	The war
27 March: agreement on oil	
29 March: letter from Fr Burke to Calles, Calles's reply; interview of Ulloa	
15 April: apology at Celaya, official speech; the Nuncio replies favourably through Mgr Díaz	
17 May: interview between Mgr Ruiz and President Calles; Mgr Ruiz leaves for Rome	*May*: attack on Manzanillo
1 July: Obregón re-elected President	Hostilities suspended for a month
17 July: Obregón assassinated	
Rome waits for the power problem to be resolved between the factions	*December–January*: biggest Federal offensive
1929 *January*: relaxation of persecution	
February: Portes Gil sends an emissary to Gorostieta to discuss peace terms	*February*: Cristero counter-offensive
Overtures to the bishops	
March: rebellion of Escobar and Manzo	*March, April, 1–15 May*: Cristero offensive
19 March: Portes Gil wants peace before the Presidential elections	
May–June: conclusion of the agreements	*15 May to 10 July*: Federal offensive
21 June: public announcement of recommencement of public worship	Total number of Cristeros, 50,000

Between 22 June and 20 September all the Cristeros laid down their arms.

The principalities and powers continued their negotiations for three years, and for three years war was a continuation of policy by other means. The war had surprised the state, which considered religion to be merely an activity for pious women, and President Calles said that 'Jalisco is the henhouse of the Republic', because in that state the

Catholics were so fervent. The war was also a surprise for the Church. The two powers profited from it to raise their demands, while the war was for a long time the life and death of the Cristeros.

While the people arranged things in their own way, the Holy See and the Government were trying to reach an agreement. These two processes might interact on each other, as is suggested by the chronological table above, without ever becoming confused, except at the beginning and at the end of the war.

The continuity of the negotiations (six conversations at the highest level in three years), and the mutual interaction of the factors in the situation, were the characteristics of that chapter of diplomatic and political history, which witnessed the following participants in action: the supporters of negotiation and peace (any kind of peace), General Obregón, who was working to make peace coincide with his return to the Presidency, with him in the Government camp politicians such as Mestre and Pani, and also Obregón supporters loyal to their master; bankers like Echevarría, the Legorreta brothers, and the men who exercised their good offices in the quarrel between the Government and the American oil companies. After the tragic death of Obregón, Calles and President Portes Gil were to adopt this political line on their own account. On the side of the Church, the partners were powerful: Rome, which never abandoned its hope of finding a *modus vivendi*, and its emissaries, the American Frs J. Burke and E. Walsh, the Mexican prelates Mgr Ruiz y Flores and Pascual Díaz, who controlled the majority of the Episcopate (thirty-one out of thirty-eight).

Facing each other, and opposed to any kind of compromise, were the radicals on both sides. On one side was the Morones-Tejeda bloc, which in 1926–7 succeeded in virtually controlling President Calles and obliging him to adopt an increasingly hostile attitude towards the Church; on the other was the Obregón-Pani bloc. At that time Calles's biggest problem was Obregón – an Obregón intent on winning laurels as a peacemaker. This group, drawing its strength from Calles's collaboration succeeded in making the attempts of 1926 and 1927 fail by barring the path of Obregón.[19] When Portes Gil, in May–June 1929, finally succeeded in concluding the 'arrangements', the belligerent lobby, its strength diminished by the political ruin of Morones, on whom had been laid the responsibility for the death of Obregón, had no further power: Calles, rid of Obregón and Morones, no longer had to walk a tight rope and could decide his own policy.

On the other side, the League mobilised the 'white radicals' behind

Ceniceros y Villareal, an old militant of the Catholic party, who had once been elected Governor of Zacatecas, and, above all, Miguel Palomar y Vizcarra, the Catholic deputy from Jalisco and representative of the political youth movement. The League, which at first enjoyed the sympathy of the Episcopate and of Rome, had alienated every man of good will by the end of 1927, when only three prelates were favourably disposed towards it. This had made it possible for it to denounce on several occasions to Rome the 'treason' of the negotiators: in August 1926, March 1927, and August 1927. Its later interventions had no more effect on Rome than those of the radical anticlericals on the Government. From the day when the Powers had no longer any need of their extremists, they worked in the greatest secrecy to prevent defections: the League was no longer to be kept informed, and to prevent the 'Leaguer' bishops from frustrating this measure, they themselves were to be kept in the dark; on its side, the Government followed similar tactics.

At the end of August 1926, General Obregón had arranged for a meeting between President Calles and Bishops Ruiz and Díaz. Having for a long time weighed his desire to conquer the Church with his sense of political reality, Calles had agreed to the meeting in order not to break with the moderates. The violent reaction of the radicals had swiftly brought him back to his personal position, and he had sent the bishops away, saying: 'the only solution open to us is the chambers [of the Congress] or arms'.

In February 1927 *The New York Herald Tribune*[20] reported rumours of a negotiated agreement having been achieved through the good offices of Frs Burke and Walsh and Dwight Morrow. These persons were to play a decisive part in the conclusion of the 'arrangements' thirty months later. In March, without any positive results, Obregón met the bishops in Mexico City.[21] Priests, friends of Obregón, Mestre, and other officials had served as intermediaries.

Calles had little sympathy for these activities of Obregón, and in April, using as a pretext the Cristero attack on the Barca train, he deported all the bishops from the country.

Obregón refused to be discouraged and, after announcing that he was a candidate for re-election, in June, he continued his negotiations with the bishops in San Antonio and Washington. Calles, who had reached an agreement with his formidable friend over the Presidential question, facilitated his task by putting a brake, if not on the war, then at least on religious persecution: the Leaguers were released from prison, and those who had been sent to the Islas Marías were repatriated. The Minister of Foreign Affairs, Aaron Sáenz, went to Texas, with the agreement of Calles, to engage in serious negotiations. The publicity that this received in the Mexican press obliged the Government, to save its face, to deny the existence, indeed the very idea, of any negotiations.

In November 1927 Obregón's position was strengthened by the arrival of the new American Ambassador, Dwight Morrow, who in under six months solved the vexed petroleum conflict between the two countries and at the same time sought the settlement of the religious question. In both spheres, he persuaded the protagonists to withdraw from their theoretical positions in order to reach a *modus vivendi*. Morrow had a brilliant mind and, before becoming interested in Mexico, had read the classical works on the relations between Church and state: Stubbs, Creighton, Lord Acton, and others; 'the temptation to see the Mexican business as a problem of applied history was almost irresistible.'[22]

Rome immediately understood the importance of Morrow's attitude: in January 1928, in Havana, Fr Burke found Caruana, the Apostolic Delegate, Morrow, and Bishops Mora y del Río and Tritschler.[23] Calles, the sceptic, agreed to form part of this scenario once it had been set up. A first attempt came to nothing, because *The New York Herald Tribune* reported it, which annoyed Calles. On 27 March agreement was reached on the oil question and, profiting from the euphoria of the moment, Morrow embarked on his second operation. An exchange of letters between Fr Burke and President Calles was immediately followed by a meeting in the fortress of San Juan de Ulloa.[24]

On 15 April the Government gave an indication of good will: the Minister of Education Puig Casauranc, in the presence of Obregón and Calles, made an open overture, to the bishops, appealing to their common devotion to the Virgin of Guadalupe, the mother of Mexican nationhood. This was the famous *mea culpa* of Celaya. At Morrow's request, the State Department suggested to the Nuncio, who passed the message on to Mgr Díaz, that a gesture should be made in return. This was done. Mgr Díaz y Flores became president of the Episcopal Committee and met Calles on 17 May: he was the only bishop to be privy to the conversations held at Ulloa. Agreement was reached on the preliminary arrangements for peace talks, and Mgr Ruiz left for Rome.

On 1 July Obregón was re-elected President, which caused Rome to favour a compromise. *L'Osservatore Romano* had already reminded its readers on 8 June that the Pope had never given his blessing to the Mexican Catholics who were at war with their Government. On

17 July, at 5 o'clock, Obregón had a meeting scheduled with Morrow to discuss the affair, but a few hours before he was assassinated by Toral, a fervent young Catholic, who was acting on his own account, but was nevertheless manipulated by people of Morones's faction.

Peace was postponed until a more favourable time, and Calles had first to survive the terrible crisis provoked by the disappearance of Obregón, which put an end to this kind of alternating diarchy modelled on the Lower Roman Empire that had seemed capable of giving the country political stability. This is not the place to recount the victory achieved by Calles, the speech of the Testament of September 1928, the foundation of the National Revolutionary party, the elimination of Morones, and of the interim Presidency of Portes Gil, after the political and military liquidation of the Obregón faction (as a result of Escobar's rebellion). It will suffice to say that Calles had some problems to resolve before returning to the question of the Church, and that Rome did not wish to reach any agreement before the regime was definitely established in power.

Portes Gil and Calles delayed for as long as possible the inevitable rebellion of the Obregonist generals, and they tried to crush the Cristeros, so as not to have to fight a war on two fronts. After the defeat of the great offensive of December 1928 to January 1929, emissaries were sent to Gorostieta to negotiate an alliance against the future putschists. At the same time, there was a suspension of police and judicial measures against the clergy and Catholics who were infringing the Calles Law. After the bishops had condemned the Escobar rebellion and congratulated President Portes Gil on his escape from the dynamiting of his train, the moves towards a negotiated peace continued more intensively than before.

The victorious Government was urged to finish the business, in order to avoid a relapse into civil war if the Cristeros were still in rebellion at the time of the Presidential elections.[25] Rome, at the behest of Morrow, sent Fr Walsh, SJ, who had worked for the Vatican in Russia during the Revolution, and it used the good offices of Miguel Cruchaga Tocornal, a Chilean diplomat, who acted as intermediary between Mexico, Germany, and Spain. Both these men had spoken to the Pope, as had Mgr Ruiz y Flores and Mgr Díaz. Events moved more quickly after an interview granted by the President to the American Dubose on 2 May. At the end of the month, Mgr Ruiz was appointed Apostolic Delegate, and on 5 June, at St Louis, Missouri, Morrow attached his carriage to the train in which Ruiz and Díaz were travelling and, as far as the Mexican frontier, the three men prepared the ground for the negotiations.

Everything was done in the greatest secrecy; no bishop was received in audience, and Tejeda was no longer able to have his protests published in the press. From 12 to 21 June the bishops, the President, and the mediators worked without interruption, and on 21 June the 'arrangements' were published. Morrow had drawn up the written views of both sides and had persuaded their respective adversaries to accept them. Now all that was lacking was the approval of Rome, which was received on 20 June, and this made it possible for the bishops and Portes Gil to sign the agreements published in the press on 22 June. They were based on the negotiations of May 1928, and had the approval of Calles: the law was left as it was, but it was no longer to be enforced in a manner hostile to the Church. Public worship could begin again. Rome had spoken, Rome, as always, had chosen the path of prudence, as in France and England and Italy. In 1925 Rome had forbidden Catholics to take part in politics, from 1926 to 1929 it had negotiated, and in 1929 it accepted the *modus vivendi*.

One can understand why the Church had approved the 'arrangements', because this was consistent with its usual policy, but what had driven the Government to compromise?

> My lords Bishops,
> prolong my life
> which the Cristeros are cutting off,
> and I offer you in return
> anything you ask.

Thus sang the Cristero bard, at the end of a war which had cost the lives of 90,000 combatants and an uncounted multitude of civilians.

To put an end to the war by warlike means was clearly out of the question, and whereas the Cristeros could not hope for a military victory in the foreseeable future, the Government, too, recognised the impossibility of achieving complete victory. To enter into negotiations with the Church in order to make possible the resumption of public worship was the only way to end the war. Escobar's putsch was defeated, but it paved the way for the financial catastrophe prepared by the economic crisis, which had become permanent since 1926: political uncertainty, the petroleum crisis, the textile crisis, the war, the boycott, the suspension of public works, credit and investment, the withdrawal of sight deposits, and the run on the foreign banks – these factors were aggravating the situation with every day that passed, and it was necessary to import cereals and haricot beans. Servicing of the foreign debt was suspended after August 1928. What prevented collapse was the financial, political, and military support of the United States, increased domestic taxation, Draconian economies and the expansion of agricultural exports:

TABLE 2 *Agricultural exports, 1924–9 (in million pesos)*

1924	59·9
1925	72·0
1926	79·9
1927	78·6
1928	92·0
1929	71·5

Source: MID 2515 G II/9, 24 May 1932

Table 2 makes it easier to understand why, in March–April 1929, Ambassador Morrow was so concerned about the fate of Pacific coast tomatoes, the exports of which were prevented by Escobar's rebellion. One can also understand why peace was achieved at that moment:

the commercial and financial situation is now at its worst, there is virtually a moratorium as far as the payment of debts are concerned. . . It is the general opinion among the better class of Mexicans here that unless the Mexican government is able to exterminate the marauding bands of 'Cristeros' which infest the surrounding country, *or come to some agreement with the Church whereby religious services may be resumed*, the possibility of a return to normal conditions is very remote.[26]

Moreover, at the most dangerous moment of the Escobar crisis, Morrow telephoned the State Department to say that his greatest worry was the Cristeros, with their 12,000 men concentrated in Jalisco and Guanajuato. He asked the Department to contact Montavon, the intermediary with Rome, and tell him 'that it would be wise to act as quickly as possible'.[27] His haste was due to the fact that he considered the Government to be threatened by something much more serious than a Praetorian putsch. In 1929, everyone expected to see the end of the interim Presidency of Portes Gil and the automatic election of Calles's official successor. The candidature of José Vasconcelos, Obregón's Minister of Education, threatened to upset this system of permanent political stability that the State Department favoured. The Obregonists, beaten in open battle, saw this as an opportunity for revenge; the Catholics saw it as a deliverance;

and the people saw in Vasconcelos a new Madero, to whom the students and the women were burning to devote themselves.

The presence of the Cristeros made the rigging of the elections a problem, and their collusion with Vasconcelos's movement, which had the effect of mobilising the urban middle classes, posed a threat. The political, and consequently military, weakness of the Cristeros derived from their isolation and the absence of urban allies. Vasconcelos's movement would provide them with these allies, and receive in exchange an army. It was necessary to demobilise the Cristeros before the autumn and, to achieve this, to come to terms with the Church. Once more Church and state moved their pawns: in 1928 Obregón had said to the war-weary Cristero leaders, 'No, wait a bit longer ... wait until the Turk leaves office and I am President.'[28] Now the Church snubbed those who expressed misgivings as to the purely verbal nature of the guarantees given by Portes Gil to the combatants: 'I don't know, and I'm not interested in knowing, in what conditions you are going to be left ... The only thing I must tell you is that you must now lay down your arms ... the banner for which you were fighting has ceased to exist now that the arrangements have been made.'[29]

As the Cristeros had not been consulted in the course of the negotiations, it took the whole of the month of July for the Government and the combatants to organise the laying down of arms, which took place in August and September. Only a third of the combatants came forward to lay down their arms and receive a safe conduct.

Part II The Cristeros

CHAPTER 5

Church Folk and Townsfolk

The Bishops, Rome, and the Armed Struggle

The bishops, when they chose the path of resistance to the Government, were counting on the fidelity of the Catholics, and their hopes were not betrayed. The collective pastoral letter of 21 April 1926 contained the words 'the moment has come to say NON POSSUMUS', and that of 25 July asserted that 'it would be criminal on our part to tolerate such a situation'; on 12 September, when the conflict had begun in earnest, a further letter exhorted the faithful to 'imitate the constancy of the early Christians ... who died like good men, and their blood was the seed of new converts'.

At the same time, the bishops made it clear that they did not desire any form of resistance that was not passive and peaceful. The impetuous Mgr Manríquez, who was later to become a supporter of the Cristeros, three times in the period 1925–6 forbade recourse to violence, and the other bishops did the same. It was, in fact, the episcopal decision to suspend public worship that unleashed the Cristiada, but the bishops were not formally responsible.

In the face of the *fait accompli* of the Cristero rising, the Church reacted with the utmost prudence, and did so at first in the theological sphere. Many of the insurgents had first consulted their parish priests as to the legitimacy of the insurrection; the parish priests in turn consulted the bishops, who handed the problem over to the theologians. On 1 November 1926 the Episcopal Committee again stated that the Episcopate had never said that what was happening in Mexico was a case of legitimate armed defence on account of the exhaustion of all peaceful methods of struggle against tyranny.[1] At the end of the month, however, the Episcopal Committee gave an affirmative answer to a theological inquiry from the League, which was asking it to 'form the collective conscience ... in view of the fact that it is a case of a licit and laudable action, deserving legitimate armed defence'.[2]

Mgr González y Valencia, Archbishop of Durango, summarised the

67

feelings of some when he issued his famous pastoral letter of 11 February 1927: 'Outside the Flaminian Gate', in which Rome was not brought into the discussion: 'We never provoked this armed movement. But now that this movement exists, and all peaceful means have been exhausted, to our Catholic sons who have risen in arms for the defence of their social and religious rights . . . we must say: be tranquil in your consciences and receive our blessing.'[3] Mgr Manríquez, Bishop of Huejutla, was the only one to side openly with Mgr González. The others remained silent, as did Rome.[4]

Rome's silence was never broken, except to deny that any blessing had been given to the combatants; furthermore, the Pope had dissolved the committee of Mexican bishops in Rome and asked Mgr González to leave the city, stating that both bishops and priests should abstain from giving moral or material assistance to the insurgents.[5] The attitude of merely waiting on events adopted by the Vatican in the course of the summer of 1926 gave way to opposition to the armed rising, because it was hampering the negotiations being carried on first with Obregón and later with Calles. Ambassador Morrow was not exaggerating when he cabled the Secretary of State: 'It is unnecessary to observe that the remarks of Gorostieta do not have the support of responsible Catholic leaders [the Bishops] in Mexico.'[6] The Nuncio, Fumasoni-Biondi, even wanted the bishops to condemn publicly the League and the Cristeros. Mgr Ruiz y Flores replied that he realised the importance of such an act in hastening conclusion of peace, but he found it impossible to take such a step.

In practice the majority of prelates were undecided, and left the faithful in complete liberty of action, declining to reply to their requests for guidance. Twelve out of thirty-eight denied that they had the right to rebel, while three, those of Huejutla, Durango, and Tacámbaro (Mgr Lara y Torres), congratulated them on their action. The two last bishops, reprimanded by Rome, obeyed the orders of the Nuncio and ceased to support the movement. The obstinate Manríquez, who dreamed of setting off to die with the combatants, refused to yield, and was deprived of his diocese.

Some, who had not encouraged the movement or given it material assistance, defended it by their words or their presence (Mora y del Río, Valverde, Méndez, and de la Mora); those who were closest to the Cristeros, without it ever being possible to reproach them for collaboration with them, were the old Bishop of Colima, Amador Velasco, and Orozco y Jiménez, Archbishop of Guadalajara, who led clandestine lives, throughout the three years, to administer their dioceses.

The opponents of armed action drew strength from the fact that they were acting in obedience to Rome: Echevarría of Saltillo, Uranga of Cuernavaca, Rafael Guízar of Veracruz, Antonio Guízar of Chihuahua, Vera of Puebla, Banegas of Querétaro, Corona of Papantla, Fulcheri of Zamora, Martínez of Morelia, and finally, Archbishop Ruiz y Flores and Mgr Pascual Díaz. The Bishop of Chihuahua solemnly forbade the insurrection in his diocese, in January 1927, even wielding the threat of excommunication. At once, his diocese was spared persecution, and he himself, strengthened by the esteem in which he was held by the Government, played an important role in the Vatican. As the Bishop of Zacatecas put it: 'The tyranny of the authorities justifies the resolution of the Catholics to defend themselves by armed force ... however, it is not absolutely clear that all Catholics have an obligation to employ this ultimate recourse ... non-violent methods would have led to the same result.'[7]

Ruiz y Flores and Díaz, the most important figures, who represented Rome's view, had only one criterion in mind – efficacy. Against the United States, everyone in Mexico was powerless. Since the Government had American support, it was with the United States that one should negotiate; in these circumstances, the Cristiada was at best a 'sterile sacrifice' and the Cristeros misguided people who could be reproached for interfering in politics.[8] Ruiz y Flores expressed himself in less exaggerated terms than Díaz: 'Armed defence has had the glory of being a live and effective protest, of keeping the religious question alive, and of, we hope, obliging the Government to look for a solution.'[9]

It is interesting to record that Cardinal Garibi, then Secretary to Mgr Orozco, asserted, echoing the words of Díaz: 'The Cristeros were worse than the Government men. What disorder! And to think that they nearly became the government! At least the Federation is made up of people on the side of order. It was providential that there were Cristeros, and providential that the Cristeros ceased to exist.'[10]

The Priests and the War

The overwhelming majority of the bishops and priests, displaying a criminal degree of conformism, wallowed in an accursed inertia, all expecting sheer miracles from Heaven to give liberty to the Church. They were all content to give exhortations and say a few prayers. The priests, more strict than ever, mostly had recourse to theology and, without further consideration, announced the illicit nature of the violent struggle in defence of the Church.[11]

Fr Arroyo, vicar of Valparaíso, who spent the entire war in the company of his parishioners in arms, understandably spoke with some bitterness. While the great majority of the clergy withdrew from the rural areas and sought refuge in the big towns under the control of the Government, and only a handful of priests chose to remain with the Cristeros, a considerable minority shared the hostility of certain bishops to the armed struggle as such. General Gorostieta justifiably complained to Archbishop Ruiz y Flores: 'one of the biggest problems is to counteract the fatal effect in the minds of our people caused by the acts of our Bishops, and the more direct activities of disorientation carried out by certain priests who are acting on instructions from the Bishops.'[12]

In Oaxaca, Guerrero, Guanajuato, Querétaro, Michoacán, Coahuila, Chihuahua, Veracruz, San Luis Potosí, Puebla, and Zacatecas, most, if not all, priests employed all means to combat the insurrection. In Jalisco, when Luis María Castañeda went to inform the parish priest of Santa María, Pancho Acosta, of his decision to join the rising, the latter reproved him harshly and condemned the Cristero movement, saying in conclusion 'that the Government gave the orders, and that was all there was to it'. Fr Jesús Pérez, of Tenamaxtlán, and also old Fr Salvador Ocampo, of Lagos, were both hostile to the Cristeros, whom they received at the time of the peace of 1929 by calling them openly and in church 'cattle-thieves'.[13] Fr Luis Sánchez, of Bolaños, preached sermons against the Cristeros, thus justifying the Government clan of the Guzmáns, for 'the good father said that we should not believe in the Cristeros, that we should not listen to those cattle-thieves'. Frs Gómez of Tlacuitapa, Pablo Hernández of Jesús María, Román Tavares, and Francisco Gómez also engaged in propaganda against the Cristeros.[14]

In Zacatecas, the Cristero state *par excellence*,

at once we came across one obstacle which we would never even have imagined: the very Fathers forbade us to fight for Christ, for the religion our fathers taught us and then reaffirmed for us in baptism, confirmation and our first communion. And this was when we were fighting chiefly to defend them. You must not have recourse to violence, they would tell us; a Christian must be humble and patient, and let himself be struck. He should always turn the other cheek, Jesus was as gentle as a lamb, that's why He let them crucify Him. What is more, ever since Moses we have had the Fifth Commandment, which forbids us to kill. To take the life of our neighbour, even if he is persecuting us, is something which can only be done by the Lord of Life – God. And so on. Even the nine that fled to these mountains and valleys with our families! We rebels wanted to know why, if it was true that the only path open to the soldiers of Christ was to turn the other cheek, they were not going to surrender so that they could die like martyrs straight away. This was another mystery for us rebels.[15]

It was, indeed, a mystery if one remembers that the entire propaganda of the Government centred on the idea of 'turning the other cheek' and obeying the Fifth Commandment. The Cristeros replied to the priests: 'without their permission and without their orders we are throwing ourselves into this blessed struggle for our liberty, and without their permission and without their orders we will go on until we conquer or die.'[16]

The overwhelming majority of the priests, whatever their personal views might be, worked passively against the Cristeros, simply because they abandoned their parishes, fleeing abroad or to the big towns where persecution took only mild forms. They spent three years in a situation which was at times uncomfortable, but more often comfortable enough, staying in the houses of well-to-do Catholics, or even those of the persecutors, celebrating Mass in private. In the big cities where they still remained, 'the priests don't want to get mixed up in anything, they don't take sides or anything like it'.[17]

Anxiety to be conciliatory sometimes went too far: in the dioceses of Zamora and Morelia, in July 1926, the bishops had ordered the churches to be handed over to the committees organised by the Government, and the priests carried out this order, despite the fact that it conflicted with the instructions given in the collective Pastoral Letter. In 1929 registration with the authorities, which had been rejected in 1926, was accepted by certain bishops, thanks to a subtle logical distinction being made, and 2,600 priests and five bishops registered with the Ministry of the Interior in February.[18]

The Government handled this situation as best it could; since the beginning of the conflict it had considered the priests to be an extremely dangerous element, and in February it ordered their arrest in the Western states affected by the mass rising of January. Later, it was content to resettle them in the towns, obliging them to report regularly to the police. Underlying this policy, one found situations of complacent conciliation: an ecclesiastic would complain of the Cristeros, who considered him as a coward, and praise the kindness of a Federal general who had given him lodging in his house to please the pious womenfolk. General Roberto Cruz, the Chief of Police, had a priest dining at his table at the moment when Fr Pro was shot. While at Tepatitlán Fr Tranquilino Ubiarco was being hanged, Fr E. Salinas was protected by his godson, the municipal president, Quirino Navarro. And rumour had it that, if priests captured in the open country were hanged while in the towns they were living like lords, the reason was that 'the generals would go to any lengths to have the priests with them. The latter were very well off, looked after by the generals themselves'.[19]

The Government took steps to demonstrate the advantages of coming to terms, which were obvious enough in the 'shop-window' states where persecution had ceased: Yucatán, Chiapas, Oaxaca, Puebla, Guerrero, Veracruz, San Luis, Coahuila, Chihuahua, and Sonora.[20] Tolerance, which was possible in these outlying states either because Catholicism was weak there (for example, on the Northern frontier), or because of the isolation of the Indian South and East, which were of little geopolitical importance, never led, however, to the schism which the Government so keenly desired: in Tamaulipas two priests celebrated Mass in public, a few others in Guerrero and Puebla, and one priest in Oaxaca, all with the authorisation of their bishops.[21]

The incident of Fr Pro, executed without trial after the assassination of Obregón by the Catholic Toral, did nothing to change this policy of indulgence, practised on condition that the priest was or was prepared to become a city-dweller. At the same time the Government shot priests captured in the countryside. The Government, which was on the lookout for a guilty party, thought that by leaving the peasants on their own, it would swiftly extinguish the rebellion. By shooting priests in this way, it obliged the latter to take refuge in the towns, where in practice they were left in peace. As far as the clergy was concerned, this calculation was accurate enough: after the first executions, in February 1927, the bishops ordered the priests to leave their parishes, and only volunteers were left behind. The latter category totalled about a hundred priests, who refused to abandon their flocks at the moment of persecution and when faced with the threat of death, priests of the Archidiocese of Guadalajara and the diocese of Colima were inspired by the example of their bishops, Mgr Orozco and Mgr Velasco. They did not all join the Cristeros, and, if they helped them at all, it was by administering the Sacraments. Harassed by the army, they were running a great risk, and many of them perished. They worked ten times, a hundred times more than they had done before the war, spending the entire day christening, marrying, and hearing confessions. 'Now that the priest has left, the only priest in the Valley of Jérez and Tepetongo was Fr Félix de la Castañeda in Juanchorrey, and the faithful came from all over the region, coming by night in caravans.'[22]

Of these hundred priests, fifteen were in fact chaplains to the Cristeros, twenty-five were more or less involved in the movement, while five actually took up arms. The Church consistently refused to provide the Cristeros with the military chaplains whom they requested. The bishops had refused this request in the case of the League, and always refused it to the combatants. Miguel Gómez Loza deplored the fact that 'the Fathers in these parts do not approach our soldiers; they say it is because they do not want to commit themselves or they are afraid of their superiors. Those who have the most right to, and the most need of, spiritual succour are the most abandoned'.[23]

When, in March 1929, General Manuel Michel lost the priest who was accompanying his soldiers, his cousin Fr Guadalupe Michel, he had the greatest difficulty in finding a replacement for him, because, as Fr B. Santiago said to him: 'In all this region, there is not one of my profession who will accompany you in your adventures. Those whom I have approached do not want even to talk about it, because they do not want to have anything to do with you.'[24]

Some priests had, on an individual basis and against the orders of their bishops, already taken their decision; Fr Encarnación Cabral reasoned thus: 'I am fulfilling the orders of my Bishop not to abandon my parish, if I accompany Trino [Trinidad Castañón, a Cristero Colonel].' And he was speaking the truth, because nearly all the men in his parish were soldiers in Castañón's regiment.[25] Of these chaplains, some belonged to the Quintanar Brigade, such as the parish priests Fr E. Cabral, and the curate Fr Buenaventura Montoya, who had been punished by his parish priest because he had greeted the entry of the Cristeros into Huejuquilla in August 1926, commenting on the Gospel for the day: 'Let your light shine before men.' The son of poor parents, and loving arms and horses, he was greatly loved, and 'they never found fault with him, although they tried hard enough to'.[26] The San Gaspar Regiment (operating in the Altos de Jalisco) had the parish priest Fr Santana García with it; Fr José C. Cabral marched with the 'Free Men of Jalpa' Regiment, Fr Federico González with the Cristeros of San José de Gracia, Michoacán, Frs Sánchez Ahumada and Miguel Guízar Morfín with those of Jacona and Cotija, Michoacán. Fr F. Escoto was chaplain to the group from San Diego de Alejandría, while in Colima Frs Enrique Ochoa and Emeterio Covarrubias accompanied the combatants. The South Jalisco Division, as chaplains for its nine regiments, had Frs Lorenzo Placencia, Ramón Pérez, Pedro Rodríguez, Guadalupe Michel, and José María Espinosa.

Without deciding to accompany the Cristeros, some priests who sympathised with them continued to lead their clerical life under their protection: Sedano, parish priest of La Punta, Colima, José Cabrales of Nochistlán, José Quesada, the parish priest of Encarnación, Toribio Romo, Fr Casas, and half-a-dozen others in Jalisco and Michoacán.

A score of priests took an active part in the movement, helping with its organisation and contributing a useful element of prudence to its actions: among these were the chaplains mentioned above, Pedro Rodríguez, R. Pérez, L. Placencia, and Santana García. The parish priest of Puerto Vallarta, Fr Francisco Ayala, whose *nom de guerre* was 'Don Wences', worked in broad daylight in Guadalajara, with false papers, a uniform, and an official car. Pedro González, the parish priest of Jalpa de Cánovas, Guanajuato, was the organiser of the insurrection of 1927; and Isabel Salinas, known as the 'mad priest from León', had the *nom de guerre* of Claro de Anda. Epigmenio Hernández, the parish priest of Juquila, Oaxaca, was, apart from Don Wences and Claro de Anda, the only one to occupy himself with material matters. Only Fr Federico González (San José de Gracia, Michoacán) and Fr José María Martínez (Coalcomán, Michoacán) could really be considered as leaders, in contrast to their five colleagues who were combatants.

Two military leaders and three soldiers came from the ranks of the clergy, which on the whole respected canon law on the subject. The two who reached the rank of general, Frs Aristeo Pedroza and José Reyes, were both of the Indian type physically, but they had nothing in common except their unflinching courage. Those who knew Pedroza revered him as a saint *sans reproche*; of Vega, 'the infamous Father Vega', 'the Pancho Villa in a cassock', it was said that he had Villa's military genius and his ferocity. A black-hearted man, a murderer, a skirt chaser, he had the spark of genius, that inspiration on the spur of the moment which the cold intelligence of Pedroza lacked. A strange priest, who had been forced into Holy Orders, he was accompanied by an impetuous family: two brothers who died in the attack on the Barca train in April 1927, a mother who worked with the direct action groups in Guadalajara and who handled a dagger, and a sister who was as tough as her brothers.

The three others were 'Pérez Aldape, the fool, he was fond of firing off shots, of killing, he got drunk on *pulque*',[27] suspended by Mgr Orozco, Fr Carranza, parish priest of Tlachichila, and Fr Leopoldo Gálvez, known as the 'Little Father', who fought with the men of San José de Gracia (Michoacán).

In summary, therefore, it may be said that in January 1927 there were 3,600 priests in Mexico, after the departure of the 400 foreigners. Table 3 shows the disposition of priests towards the Cristeros.

TABLE 3 *Relationship of Priests with the Cristeros*[28]

Priests actively hostile to the Cristeros	100
Priests actively favourable	40
Combatant priests	5
Neutral priests (helping the Cristeros with alms)	65
Priests who abandoned their rural parishes and those living in the big towns	3,390
Total	3,600

TABLE 4 *Priests executed in the Cristero rebellion*[29]

Jalisco	35
Zacatecas	6
Guanajuato	18
Colima (diocese)	7
Elsewhere	24
Total	90

Except in the archdiocese of Guadalajara and the diocese of Colima the clergy, acting on the orders of their bishops, withdrew. The minority that stayed behind paid a heavy penalty. The purely military contribution made by the priests was so insignificant that one cannot describe them as the military leaders or maintain that they were the cause of the insurrection. However, the presence of a bishop in Colima, and of an Archbishop in Jalisco, even if they had no contact at all with the insurgents, represented priceless moral support. Above all, this handful of priests prevented the Cristeros, who were shocked and then angry, from becoming new Donatists. At the time of the 'arrangements' these priests, speaking against their own convictions, were able to persuade the Cristeros to give their obedience, and thus prevent a schism, which was all the more of a threat because those who had negotiated the 'arrangements' belonged to the clerical group which was hostile to the combatants.

The National League for the Defence of Religion (LNDR)

Originating in a defensive reaction in 1925, the League immediately became a political movement, carried forward by the march of events and intoxicated by its own prodigious growth, before it became a clandestine and subversive organisation.[30] Having some resemblance to the generation of social Catholicism, of the National Catholic party, and of the combative youth movement of the ACJM (Catholic Action of Mexican Youth), and finding itself at the head of a vast crowd of supporters only too easily stirred into action, it then passed from the defensive to the offensive, with the firm intention of seizing power and exercising it alone. In contrast to the National Catholic party of 1911, it affirmed an uncompromising radicalism. It had to face, in 1926, the same problem as Latin American left-wing movements forty years later, that of whether to have recourse to armed struggle in order to seize power. The radical Catholics were to face this problem as late as 1940, when the Sinarquista movement on the one hand, and National Action (AN) on the other, made recourse to violence unthinkable. In 1925 and 1926 the League was carrying on a non-violent legal struggle inspired by the *Kulturkampf*, by the resistance of Alsace to the measures imposed by Herriot, and the struggle of Gandhi against the British. But Calles was not Bismarck, and did not change his policy under the influence of public opinion; and it was now that the spontaneous risings provoked by the suspension of public worship gave the League the hope of overturning the Government by organising and controlling a movement that had arisen outside its ranks.

Recruitment and organisation[31]

At first the League was a heterogeneous coalition composed of the Knights of Columbus, the Catholic Ladies, the Congregation of Mary, the Nocturnal Adoration, the Catholic trade unions and the Acción-Católica de la Juventud Mexicana (ACJM). Finding no support in the upper strata of society (the Knights of Columbus and the Catholic Ladies soon left the organisation), the League recruited all its cadres among the middle classes, those which provided the social base of the revolutionary régime. The difference between the supporters of the League and those of the Government was not social but ideological; in consequence, ambiguity was a characteristic of both groups. Culturally and socially, the Leaguers were first cousins, hostile brothers of the revolutionaries, and they lived in a world which had no connection with that of the Cristeros or the followers of Zapata.

Lawyers, engineers, doctors, civil servants, men of the Church or closely connected with the Church – such were the cadres of the League,[32] and they were assisted by some officers of the old Federal army, and strengthened by the activities of the young men of the ACJM, who took part in the direction of the movement and controlled all its middle and lower levels. Among the leaders, there was only one businessman,

Bartolomé Ontiveros (alias J. M. Delgado, alias Lencho, alias Juanito), the owner of the tequila distillery in La Herradura, a traditional and provincial business. Lawyers were prominent among the principal leaders: Rafael Ceniceros y Villareal, the president, Palomar y Vizcarra, the vice-president, and also Mariano Ramírez; Capistrán Garza, the president of the ACJM and the first commander-in-chief appointed by the League.

All these cadres were of urban origin, and the majority, at the national level, came from the provinces, even though they had lived in Mexico City for years. In this, they were no different from the Revolutionaries; there was, however, one important difference: the provinces from which they had come were invariably in the traditional Mexico of the high plateau, whereas the Revolutionaries had come down from the North. In political terms, the past of these leaders (when they were old enough to have a past) was characterised by support for Madero and later for the PCN, in the case of the civilians. At the side of the old PCN militants one finds the brother of President Madero, Emilio Madero.

All these men – except Ceniceros, who was born in 1855 – were young, and save for Palomar (born in 1880), very young. They were between twenty-five and thirty-five years of age, and all the students of the ACJM were under twenty-five. The majority were young men, unmarried, and with only their salaries to live on.

The League was controlled by a Directing Committee (CD), the number of members of which varied; between 1926 and 1929 Ceniceros and Palomar, the president and vice-president, were the only permanent members; they were joined in July 1928 by José González Pacheco (alias José Tello), whose signature is found on all the documents issued after that date. After the discomfiture of 'General' Capistrán Garza, who in 1926 was promising the support of the White House and the oil companies, and the taking of Ciudad Juárez on 1 January 1927, the CD made a Special Committee (CE) responsible for military matters; this was successively headed by Ontiveros, Luis Segura Vilchis,[33] Dr A. Ortega, and Jesús Rebollo.

At the higher level the League was short-handed: one example of this will suffice. José González Pacheco was simultaneously vice-president, secretary, and responsible for propaganda, the press, and finance. A few overworked men (González Pacheco and Luis Segura Vilchis had to work in their offices during the day) had to do everything. Segura, head of the CE, personally directed the commandos. Most of the staff were paid, but nobody made his fortune. Money, of which the League

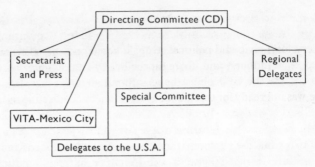

Fig. 1. Organisation of the League

was always short (which did not prevent it from squandering its funds), came from bonds, subscriptions, and gifts (Mgr Manríquez collected $1,000) and from the Cristeros, who sent money to buy ammunition. Being short of money, the League often used the Cristero subsidies to finance its activities. This gave rise to the belief that the leaders of the League were thieves who led a luxurious life in Mexico City with the money of the combatants who, owing to shortage of ammunition, were obliged to fall back before the Federal army. The material penury of a movement supported by the middle classes and without support from abroad (one has only to contrast the sums of money which passed through the hands of the Carrancists, the Villists, or even the Felicists) explains the lack of effectiveness of the League from the military point of view. It was incapable of providing the Cristeros with arms, munitions, and organisation. It did give the Cristeros General Gorostieta, but it quarrelled with him almost immediately.

The Leaguers

The League established itself in the Federal District, and later in the provinces, making use of the organisations already existing, the trade unions and the ACJM. It recruited hundreds of thousands of supporters, although in many cases their participation did not go beyond the signing of a form and the payment of a minimum subscription. The petition for the reform of the Constitution was signed by two million people, but when the League chose the path of armed struggle these urban masses were of no further use, and the lack of organisation, of militancy, made itself felt to a disastrous extent.

The League did not have the strength or the effectiveness of Anacleto González Flores' Unión Popular, and it was partly for this reason that it chose, as the easiest solution, armed struggle, following the example given by the Cristero peasants. Anacleto González Flores had set out on a very long civic and political struggle based on day-to-day activity, inspired by Windhorst and, more especially, by Gandhi. He was able to do this because the UP mobilised and inspired an entire population. The League was not ready for this labour of training, of clandestine militancy, of mobilisation in depth. It preferred war, as did all the Mexican Revolutionaries, because it preferred to move swiftly; it wanted power, and at once! It chose this path because it was the easiest, because it was incapable of acting differently. Reliance on the volunteer spirit and a distrust of the masses were as characteristic of the Leaguers as of their cousins who supported Calles. Finally, there was a universal appeal to force.

Its justification was that it allowed itself to be carried away by a favourable and unexpected current of events, and that it became inspired by the wildest hopes. In 1925–6 it was supported by the bishops and priests: there were 36,395 members of the League on 25 June 1925; 800,000 in September 1926, of whom 500,000 were women. The League became firmly established in a triangle formed by Orizaba, Ciudad Madero, and Colima; it was, above all, strong in Mexico City and the big towns. In the West, when the archives contain references to the League, one should take this to mean the Unión Popular, for the League was unable to establish itself as long as Anacleto González Flores refused to place his organisation under its authority. When he did so, it was at the request of the bishops. The only state where the League emerged from the towns and took roots as an autonomous organisation was Chihuahua, where there were no Cristeros.

The young men of the ACJM were the most fervent propagandists and were the leaders at the local level; they were militants who, when the time came, would be prepared to die for their cause. At that moment these young men, students often drawn from the middle classes, were to discover the peasants, and the shock was to be considerable. In photographs, one can see, in symbolic form, the difference between the Leaguers of the ACJM and the Cristero peasants. The first group have city haircuts and moustaches, boots and buttons, and are dressed in khaki; they look like the brothers of the dashing officers on the Government's General Staff. Those in the second group have no uniform; they are long-haired peasants, wearing sandals, with jutting beards. The city encounters the countryside, and it is not easy to make contact. More than once, repelled by the distrust of the Cristeros whom they had too often approached with the arrogance of the city-dweller, they fled from privations of guerrilla life and returned to the towns.

The Action of the League

From 31 July 1926 onwards, the League conducted a campaign of economic boycott which certainly had sufficient impact on economic life to exasperate the Government, but not sufficient to impel it to come to terms. The boycott was very effective in the provinces, and much less so in Mexico City; it worsened a situation already affected by the bad harvests, the fall in petroleum production, the slump of henequen in the world market, and the fall in the price of silver. 'Coming when money is scarce this is all the more effective': economic activity fell by 75 per cent between August and December, under the combined effect of these factors.[34] In order to oblige the Government to come to terms, the boycott would have had to be thoroughgoing and overwhelming in effect; but those who were enforcing it were the great mass of the people, who were unable to reduce their purchases significantly, because they had never been able to buy more than what was strictly necessary for subsistence. An organisation like the UP was needed to persuade the rich people of Jalisco to take part in the struggle. Elsewhere, whether they were Catholics or not, the rich were horrified by the idea of the boycott, and they succeeded in persuading the Vatican to share their view. 'I shall not give a cent, I want the régime established by the Men of Sonora to be maintained. To it I owe the six million pesos I have made.'[35] The wealthy Catholics achieved, through Rome and certain leaders of the League, the abandonment of the boycott. The tobacco company El Buen Tono, which was on the verge of bankruptcy, persuaded Fr Araiza to intercede with Ceniceros, while the French shop La Ciudad de México, in Guadalajara, used the good offices of the Knight of Columbus Efraín González Luna.[36]

The interests of the wealthy Catholics led to their solidarity with the Government; this explains the presence of Manuel Gómez Morín, the future founder of the PAN, at the head of the State Bank founded by Calles, and the conciliatory role played by the big Catholic bankers, and also opposition of influential Catholics to civic or armed resistance.

The decision to go to war was taken on the spur of the moment, without discussion or preparation – it was a sort of headlong flight forwards. Some had considered war as early as August, and were thinking of making contact with General Estrada, a revolutionary who was in exile in the United States; in October, after the first risings, people were talking openly of war; and in November they consulted the bishops, after the decision had already been taken. In December the wildest hopes were entertained: Palomar announced that the American 'Home

Missions' would donate a million dollars,[37] and Capistrán Garza, sent as an emissary to the United States although he spoke no English, allowed the wish to be father to the thought, and demanded an immediate and general insurrection for the first week of January. He personally was to enter the country at the head of an invading army. Who was the most guilty, the loud-mouths or those who naïvely believed them? In December the League gave orders for an insurrection within a week. It took four months for it to dismiss Capistrán Garza.[38]

From that time onwards the League, except for two or three bishops, lost the support of the Episcopate. Its leaders, rather than open their eyes, preferred to let themselves be carried away by their feelings of hostility, and they accepted the version of events supplied by Capistrán Garza, according to whom the man responsible for all the setbacks was Bishop Díaz, who had prejudiced the American Catholics against them. With a singular ignorance of the facts, they carried their attacks on him as far as Rome.

They displayed the same obliviousness in the military sphere. The League did not learn the lessons of the criminal disaster of January 1927 and, not content with having sent its people to be massacred, set out to molest the Cristeros in every possible way. Infuriated by its inability to control the organisations that constituted the strength of the movement in the West, it attacked the Unión Popular, the secret organisation known as the 'U', and the Women's Brigades, which supplied the Cristeros. It denounced the 'U' to Rome and succeeded in getting it condemned, together with the Brigades, as secret societies falling under the ban of the nineteenth-century encyclical.[39]

The League never ceased to play a double game with Gorostieta; it was jealous of his prestige, and created every kind of difficulty for him. At the end of this process, the League witnessed a gradual shrinking of its area of influence, which finally was confined to the Federal District and its immediate surroundings. As for its interventions in the military sphere, these were either ludicrous or criminal. The facility with which it distributed generals' insignia was only equalled by the incapacity of those whom it appointed. Less amusing was its appointment of two generals to the same command so that they nearly caused bloodshed in Michoacán and Colima,[40] the squandering of the Cristeros' money, and the perpetual conflict with their organisations.

The members of the League, who knew nothing of the world of the Cristeros, confined themselves to waiting for three years while the

Cristeros pulled the chestnuts out of the fire for them. After that, the Leaguers and their friends wrote the history of the war, for peasants are not historians.[41] The Leaguers were reproached for not having seized power, although history has treated them harshly, only finding explanations for their failure. The League, like every revolutionary, subversive, clandestine movement which has been defeated, and is therefore incapable of forging its own history, offers the spectacle of its weaknesses, defects, and crimes. It was necessary to write this history because the League itself had fabricated its own version of the Cristero War, which it appropriated as its own. According to this theory, which is classic because it is commonly accepted, because both Church and state found it advantageous, the League was indissolubly linked with the war and the Cristeros were its troops.

CHAPTER 6

The Recruitment of the Cristeros

Geographical Background

Every geographical account of an insurrection has an element of ambiguity: rebellion develops both where men wish to rebel and where they are capable of doing so. Abstention is difficult to analyse, because it may stem from a lack of willingness or a lack of opportunity; finally, the negative factors may prove insufficient to deter men from the moment when the desire to fight has become strong enough. One must, therefore, bear in mind that recruitment is not the same at the beginning as it is at the end of the rebellion, that it fluctuates over the course of time. The near-unanimous participation characteristic of the beginning, which is more in the nature of an assembly than a rising, is replaced by a process of individual commitment that varies according to local circumstances. Thus one sees recruits, in growing numbers and in regions as yet only slightly affected, overcoming measures of intimidation which are already proving effective, because everybody knows that the war is terrible and that it will be long.

Participation in the insurrection is not only governed by geographical, historical, and social factors, but also by psychological considerations. The Federal general Cristóbal Rodríguez, who commanded the Querétaro zone, declared that 'the same fanaticism' reigned everywhere; nevertheless 'the perfidious efforts of the Clergy did not achieve the same results in every place'.[1] In his conclusions, he emphasised the warlike character of the men of Jalisco and Michoacán, and the submissive nature of those of Querétaro. It is true that it is possible to confuse a military vocation and religious faith, and that these do not always coincide; military action demands greater efforts from the Indian who marches on foot, commanded by half-caste *caciques*, than from the free peasant of the Altos region.[2] One cannot deduce differences in the intensity of individual commitments or participation on the basis of a smaller number of men under arms, even if the only dependent variable at one's disposal is the number of insurgents in each region.

It is true that physical geography is a factor, but a less decisive one than may be imagined. Who, indeed, would think of taking to the *maquis* around Celaya, or in the Cañada, Michoacán, in the approach to Zamora? There were men, however, who left their region of origin and joined the combatants in the Agustinos or the Sierra Tarasca. The Altos de Jalisco, the symbol of the Cristiada, did not lend itself ideally to guerrilla warfare, in contrast to the mountains of Durango or Coalcomán. Surrounded by a belt of plains and valleys, these plateaux, gently undulating and broken only by low hills, were on the whole open and easily accessible, thanks to the railways which bordered them on three of their four sides and to the roads which crossed them. This high land, densely populated with numerous villages every ten kilometres, with innumerable smaller settlements which filled the links of the network, proved to be impregnable, and it was there that the army carried out the first measures of resettlement, thus proving that war was a function of population rather than of topography. Although, in the mountains of Michoacán, the Cristeros might go for a long time without seeing a single Federal soldier, the plateaux of Zacatecas were quite unsuitable for guerrilla warfare, and the Cristeros were able to say: 'We know that from now on we are going to win by running away,' for it was impossible to fight for more than fifteen minutes in one place without being outflanked or surrounded.[3]

At times, all the factors militated against insurrection: in the state of Puebla the first risings were quickly overwhelmed. A region held under harsh control for centuries, a land of *caciques*, a fief of the Ávila Camacho family, flat country lying under the gorge of Puebla and overshadowed by Mexico City – here ethnic divisions, economics, and geography had their effects. The railways between Mexico City and Veracruz and Mexico City and Oaxaca made it possible to fan out troops in every direction, but this was less important than one fundamental fact: the passivity of the central plateau from the Conquest to the present day, and its failure to participate in the great events of 1810, 1865, and 1910; rebellion broke out often, but it was crushed and took root only in the mountainous areas and the periphery, the Sierras of Zacapoaxtla and Zacatlán, the axis of volcanoes running from Orizaba to Toluca and the mountains of the South.

Finally, a distinction must be made between a military zone characterised by the more or less active sympathy of the population towards the rebellion – the entire region lying to the west of a line drawn from Durango to Tehuantepec – and a constellation of much smaller insurgent areas.

TABLE 5   *Geographical distribution of Cristeros under arms, May 1929.*

State	Number of combatants	Total area (in hectares)	Number of men per sq km
Michoacán	12,000	1,000,000	17
Jalisco	10,000	1,200,000	13
Aguascalientes	1,200	130,000	15
Colima	1,000	80,000	14
Guanajuato	3,000	1,000,000	39
Querétaro	1,000	250,000	21
Nayarit	2,500	170,000	6
South Zacatecas and border areas	5,000	200,000	5

In May 1929, there were 50,000 Cristeros under arms. Table 5 shows their distribution.[4]

Economy and Society

The results of a questionnaire organised by the author[5] show that of the combatants only 14 per cent were small proprietors, and of these half owned under five hectares. Fifteen per cent, farmers or share-croppers, had a similar economic and social status: men working freely and on their own account land which they owned or rented.

Sixty per cent lived by manual labour, by the strength of their arms. These labourers were agricultural workers, muleteers, craftsmen (potters, carpenters, bakers, masons and so on), workmen (miners, drivers, smelters), or were engaged in various occupations ranging from charcoal-manufacture to music. Sometimes a plurality of occupations was the rule, even among the small proprietors and the share-croppers. The remaining 10 per cent was composed of the *agraristas* (the beneficiaries of agrarian reform), and the well-to-do, and included one priest, nine *rancheros* owning from 100 to 300 hectares and one big landowner, who was the exception confirming the rule (he owned 300 irrigated and 800 workable hectares).

Table 6 is based on research at the regional and village levels, by consulting archives and by direct inquiries, especially in San Franciso de Asís (Altos de Jalisco), Coalcomán (Michoacán), and Valparaíso (Zacatecas). Studies by Luis González and Paul S. Taylor shed light on the problem in the cases of San José de Gracia (Michoacán) and Arandas (Jalisco).[6]

As a result of this inquiry, it is possible to reject as false one dual

TABLE 6 *Economic and occupational status of cristeros under arms*

Occupation	Total number	Occupation	Total (%)	
Priest	1	Manual workers (agricultural workers, craftsmen, etc.)		60
Landowner	1			
Administrator of *hacienda*	3	Farmers and share-croppers	15	
Ranchero	9	Small proprietors	14	29
Small proprietors[a]	51	*Agraristas*		4
Farmers and share-croppers	63	Well-to-do farmers (landowners, *rancheros*, and administrators)		4[e]
Agraristas	16			
Agricultural worker	79			
Workman, craftsman[b]	44			
Other manual workers[c]	60			
Muleteer[d]				

[a]Thirty owned from 1 to 5 hectares, 10 had less than 1 hectare, and 11 owned from 5 to 15 hectares.

[b]Workman, craftsman: miner, baker, leather-worker, stonemason, potter, etc.

[c]These included a wide variety: charcoal-burner, lime-burner, hatter, gardener, wax-whitener, rocket-maker, singer, ditch-digger, etc.

[d]An artificial category: the *arrieros* all had a second occupation and all except six of them worked on the land. Three were *agraristas*, 8 were proprietors, and the others had several simultaneous occupations.

[e]The total is less than 100 because the figures have been systematically rounded downwards.

86

socio-economic correlation, according to which the Cristeros were small independent proprietors threatened by agrarian reform, or agricultural proletarians used by the big landowners to protect the haciendas from expropriation. These theories have been sufficiently widely accepted to make it necessary to consider them seriously. Is it true that the Cristeros were small proprietors like the inhabitants of the Altos de Jalisco?[7] This was not the case in the rest of the country or in the rest of Jalisco, and it was only relatively true in the very heart of the Altos. Finally, the theory of a conspiracy by the big landowners who were making use of the Cristeros, that is to say their peons, as 'White Guards' does not stand up to an examination first of their attitude to the Cristeros and second of their attitude to the Government. A socio-economic gulf is quite apparent: the rich sided with the Government and denounced the Cristeros as 'shirtless ones, sandal-wearers, cattle-eaters, down-and-outs'.

Small properties certainly existed in plenty in the Altos, and it is worth remarking that, although on an average 15 per cent of those who answered the questionnaire were small proprietors, the figure is 25 per cent for the people of the Altos. There, as elsewhere (though to a somewhat lesser extent), the haciendas continued to control the most numerous and the best lands.

Table 7 shows that there were 777 properties of over 1,000 hectares each, covering an area of 2,600,000 hectares, or 33 per cent of the area of all rural private properties, and 43 per cent by value.

TABLE 7 *Rural properties in Jalisco*

Hectares	Number of properties
Less than 1	40,413
1–5	55,241
6–10	14,729
11–50	24,205
51–100	4,260
101–200	2,233
201–500	1,528
501–1,000	621
1,001–5,000	614
5,001–10,000	120
Over 10,000	43
Unclassified	516

Source: 1930 Census

TABLE 8   *Number and area of haciendas of over 1,000 hectares in Jalisco in 1930*

Canton	Number	Area	Area of canton	Percentag
Guadalajara	76	288,434	563,500	51·2
La Barca	92	202,194	841,200	24·0
Ciudad Guzmán	113	582,055	1,083,400	53·7
Lagos	72	468,345	558,000	83·9
Teocaltiche	39	84,617	526,100	16·0
Autlán .	96	407,559	1,062,800	38·2
Sayula	69	303,482	321,400	94·4
Colotlán	19	71,498	940,700	7·6
Ameca	52	144,804	254,700	56·7
Ahualulco	62	222,021	481,600	46·1
Mascota	131	699,027	1,238,700	56·4
Chapala	35	80,836	196,200	41·2
Total	856	3,554,872	8,068,300	44·1

The 1930 Census, based on units of agricultural exploitation rather than rural properties, recorded 50,000 units of over 1 hectare, which may be classified as shown in Table 8. This census took account only of land under exploitation – namely, 68·5 per cent of the area of the state. Of this exploited area, units of over 1,000 hectares accounted for 1·7 per cent of the units and 60 per cent of the area. If one adds the *ranchos* of between 100 and 1,000 hectares, this category would include 12 per cent of the units and 86 per cent of the area covered by the census. This is confirmed at the level of municipalities: in Mazamitla, 43 proprietors owned 10,000 hectares, and 288 owned 1,311.

There was, therefore, an agrarian problem in Jalisco, and this explains the presence of nearly 25,000 *agraristas* concentrated in the Sayula-Chapala sector – that is to say, on the best land, near the roads and railways. This reform was only partial in character, because it did not affect the canton of Lagos, where the haciendas of over 1,000 hectares constituted 84 per cent of the total area, nor those of Autlán, Mascota, and Ciudad Guzmán. In all, only 2·99 per cent of the total area had been redistributed, whereas 44 per cent still belonged to the properties of over 1,000 hectares.

The peculiar feature of Jalisco was that, in the region of the Altos and that of Cañones, which stretched as far as Zacatecas, very small properties existed side by side with the haciendas. There were more pro-

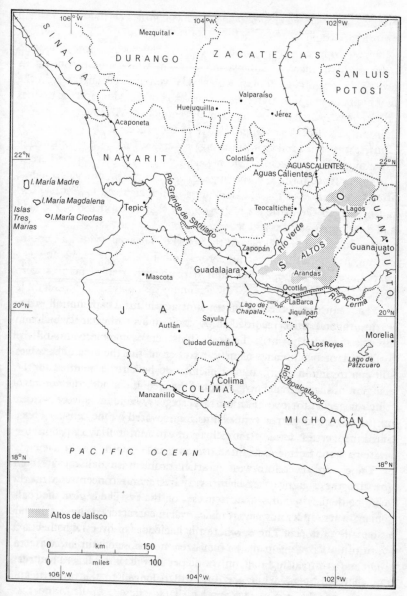

Jalisco

prietors than elsewhere, but the great majority of these very small proprietors could not make a living on their own and took employment as share-croppers and engaged in other simultaneous occupations to increase their income. Subdivision of land, which was a continuous process in the region, took place on relatively narrow surfaces, in the mountainous and hilly parts, on the plateaux of the Altos and the ravines of Cañones, which were very densely populated. Although such subdivision was effective enough relative to the *ranchos* and the communal lands, it was of no avail against the big properties, which were continually expanding. The problem of the big landholding did not appear here in its most intense form, but the appearance of a swarm of small tenants, after the collapse of the old structures in the eighteenth century, had not prevented the existence of large units that controlled the best land and distributed pasture and leases.

The volcanoes of Colima and the south of Jalisco provided a Cristero contingent (5,000) that was numerous both in absolute terms and as a percentage of the population, but here the agrarian structures were very different. In this zone the communities played a considerable economic role until the end of the nineteenth century. From 1870 onwards, the offensive carried on by individuals who had come from elsewhere tended towards the destruction of the communities and the formation of big haciendas. In the course of that process, which was still continuing in 1920, a few rich men despoiled the members of the communities and transformed them into peons. In a second process, which began in the twentieth century, the very big estates were divided up, and worked partly by administrators, partly by share-croppers. Small properties were practically non-existent. All types of labour relations were to be found there: the immense, centuries-old hacienda of Trojes, in the south-west of Michoacán, was abandoned by an absentee owner and worked by virtually free share-croppers who, once a year, paid him in hides, soap, cheese, or honey. The region of Coalcomán, surrounded by mountains, was characterised by a similar system. Besides this, there was the haciendas already established as a result of the dividing up of a bigger estate, around which there gravitated *comuneros* crowded together on the slopes of volcanoes, farm-labourers and share-croppers, while the first *agraristas* were making their appearance (in the region of Zapotlán, Tuxcacuesco, Apulco, and San Gabriel); finally, there were the capitalist plantations of the recently colonised zone of Colima where, as a unique phenomenon, the big haciendas continued to expand between 1920 and 1926.

Cristeros were recruited everywhere: Indian *comuneros* of Jiquílpan, Jalisco, despoiled by the Pinzón family of the Buenavista hacienda, peons from the San Pedro Hacienda (near Tolimán, to the south of San Gabriel), and the share-croppers joined the movement in droves, as did that other marginal group, the *salitreros*, hunters who lived in the old crater of the Nevado and sold the hides of cattle that had run wild.[8]

Michoacán probably provided the most numerous contingents: small proprietors and share-croppers from the north-western fringe, living in conditions similar to those of the Altos; *comuneros*, share-croppers, and peons from the South and the hot lands, where the Italian, Dante Cusi, was intensively exploiting vast haciendas; Indian communities from the lake, valley, and the Sierra Tarasca, who were in conflict with the *agraristas*; *comuneros* and peons from the North and the East, on the borders of Guanajuato and Mexico City. In this state the big property reigned supreme, while the communities, already pushed back to the higher ground, were resisting their new enemies, the timber companies and the *agraristas*.

In Guanajuato and Querétaro small proprietors were a rarity, and the Cristeros were drawn from the peons of the big cereal-growing haciendas of the Bajío Real, a few share-croppers and craftsmen. Quite near the Altos, in the valley between San Julián and Arandas, the hacienda of Jalpa de Cánovas, which in 1910 had only peons, transformed one-third of its employees into share-croppers, because of the difficult economic circumstances. In Aguascalientes, all the Cristeros were peons, like their leader José Velasco. Haciendas covered the flat lands, and handed over some land to share-croppers on the borders of Jalisco.

In Zacatecas a distinction must be made between the zone of Cañones, identified with the old canton of Colotlán (Jalisco), small in area and densely populated, and the valleys and river basins dominated by the great haciendas dating from the Conquest which, towards the semi-arid north, gave way to the enormous estates of Chihuahua. In the first region, small properties were gradually abolished, while the well-to-do *rancheros* swiftly expanded their domains and thus reconstituted considerable holdings, which lasted for another generation; examples are the Valdéses, and the Robleses at Mezquitic, Totatiche, and Villa Guerrero. Monte Escobedo, on account of its poverty, preserved its democratic egalitarianism, escaping from the grasp of the powerful who already (through three or four families) controlled Huejuquilla, enjoying everywhere a monopoly of commerce and cash.

Away from the high ground, the haciendas monopolised the land, and the beds of the Cañones de Colotlán, Tlaltenango, and so on, belonged to them. Huejuquilla was surrounded by the big estates of San Juan Capistrano, Abrego, and Lobatos (where General Justo Ávila had raised his division in the time of Pancho Villa). Fourteen haciendas owned all the land of Valparaíso, where only one independent property survived – Potrero de Gallegos, which had remained undivided since time immemorial. Peons and share-croppers from these haciendas, small proprietors from the highlands, all were Cristeros except for the better-off *rancheros* and the *agraristas* recently settled in Valparaíso and Jérez.

In Durango, peons from the big estates near the town and half-castes or Indians from the mountains joined the rising. The *comuneros* lived from the labour of their lands and forests; their enemy was no longer the hacienda, which had already despoiled them,[9] but the timber company that came to take away their wood.

In Nayarit and Sinaloa small properties were almost non-existent, and one finds the most diverse types of tenure and exploitation, from the Huichole Indian community, which took part in the war, to the tobacco plantations passing through the colonisation projects at Rosario and Escuinapa attributed to the Revolutionary veterans of General Ángel Flores.

At the opposite extreme from the modern peasant communities of the West, the Indian South (Morelos in the mountains, Guerrero, Oaxaca, and Puebla) is comparable to the highlands of Durango and Nayarit: there was communal property and exploitation of the land by family groups, and resistance by the communities to the offensive of the haciendas, which were expanding rapidly under the direction of their proprietors, who were Spaniards – a double anachronism! Livestock was the only exportable commodity of these dispossessed *comuneros* who had become peons and shepherds; the others, from whom the famous *chiveros* were drawn, jealously defended their communal pasture lands and were formidable fighters.

The history of the Mexican rural areas has still to be written, but it must be affirmed that the Cristeros cannot be identified with a single social and occupational category. The presence among them of *rancheros* and big landowners is the exception that confirms the rule: all the rural sectors took part in the Cristiada, except the upper stratum and the *agraristas*. The big landowners among the Cristeros were so few in number that one can name all of them: J. Jesús Quintero, of Los Reyes, Michcacán, who owned 300 hectares fit for irrigation and 800 hectares of arable land and pasture; José Guadalupe Gómez of Tenamaxtlán, Jalisco, with 10 irrigated hectares and 500 hectares of arable land and heath; Manuel Moreno, of Unión de Tula, Salvador Aguirre of Tequila, and Luis Ibarra of Cocula, Jalisco had less than 200 hectares; Filomeno Osornio and his sons worked 10 irrigable hectares, 30 hectares of arable land, and 300 hectares of heath, where there were five horses, forty-five cows, seventeen mules and three hundred goats. With the Osornios of Santa Catarina (Sierra Gorda, Guanajuato), one reaches a category of modest stock-breeders who appeared to be rich men in poor regions: this was the case with Pedro Quintanar (Huejuquilla) and Justo Ávila, the one-time general in Pancho Villa's army, to whom the Revolution had not brought a fortune, for he had only twenty-five cows on his ranch at Monte Escobedo; or with Aurelio Acevedo who, as the eldest brother of an orphaned family, worked 60 hectares with twenty cows. Rodolfo Loza Márquez of Zapotlán del Rey, Jalisco had 5 irrigated hectares and 45 hectares of arable land. Gregorio Espinosa of Coeneo, Michoacán, belonged to that small group which did not carry much weight in the total: one really big landowner, with a total of 1,100 hectares, three *rancheros* with about 500 hectares each, a dozen *rancheros* owning from 50 to 200 hectares, most of the time in extensive stock-breeding.[10]

Not all the inhabitants of the rural areas lived from working the land, whether as landowners or proletarians. In a world that had still not been transformed by roads, the muleteers (*arrieros*) played an essential role as intermediaries between commerce, craft industry, small agricultural industries (cheese, honey, soap, alcohol, and so on), and agriculture. The workman, the craftsman, and the small shopkeeper were often themselves peasants.

Armed participation in the insurrection was, therefore, the work of all sorts of peasants and country dwellers, to whom one cannot ascribe a common or uniform economic motivation. The inhabitants of the towns, except for some workmen who were still close to the countryside (leatherworkers in León, drivers in Guadalajara, miners, and others), and some students (of whom a majority were seminarists) born in the villages, were absent from the battlefield. Their absence, which was compensated by their activities in the urban networks of espionage and supply, did not have the same negative implication as did that of the rich landed proprietors, who were hostile to the movement and often, with the help of the Government, directed the local opposition to the Cristeros.

Many have thought that the peasants should have supported a government which was carrying out agrarian reform (without asking themselves what kind of agrarian reform it was), and explain their attitude in terms of their status as small proprietors or their dependence on their employers. In the same spirit, an attempt has been made to present the movement as 'a conservative response to change'. The Cristeros, some maintain, recruited their forces above all in regions unaffected by modern trends and the market economy. This is to return, by another road, to the prejudices of the Government of the time, which saw the rebellion as a product of backwardness, obscurantism and fanaticism. But although it is true that the Indian communities, eminently an example of living tradition, often sympathised with the Cristeros, it was in the most modern places and those most affected by urban ways that the movement was the most strong, unanimous, and organised.

The most enlightened peasantry was to be found in Jalisco and the Western Centre in general, in a region endowed with a remarkable network of small towns; these served as relays for trade between the regional capitals, but themselves blended into the surrounding countryside. Perhaps too much emphasis has been placed on the contrast between the towns and the countryside; this antithesis, however true, does not constitute the basic underlying tendency which is to be found in the history of the rural areas of the West. There was a continuum from the farms of the Altos as far as Guadalajara (a town which was proud of the nickname Rancho Grande) or León, passing through Ayo el Chico, Arandas, and Ocotlán. Colima lived in a close and continuous physical relationship with the country, as did Querétaro, Guanajuato, Durango, and even Oaxaca. Moreover, this made it possible for the Cristero peasants to go into the towns without being noticed.

Those rural communities where the peasant element predominated varied from one region to another, but the Cristiada was strong in the places integrated into the national market, political life, and the media of information. Arandas, Tepatitlán, Sayula, Valparaíso, Sahuayo, and Zamora were thus integrated, and it was the Western Centre, which posed the greatest military problem for the Government, whereas the traditional peasantries of the *pulque* zone did not stir at all. The high density of the population of the Altos, a tight network of large villages with a surprisingly urban appearance completed by a sprinkling of hamlets and farms, numerous means of communication, an enterprising and equestrian peasantry, were all so many favourable circumstances facilitating the supply of resources, itself a cause of commitment to the Cristiada.

TABLE 9   *Distribution of settlements by population, c. 1921*

Size of grouping	Structure of settlement (percentage)	
	Western Centre*a*	Eastern Centre*b*
Less than 500 inhabitants	40	31
500–2,000	19	35
2,000–4,000	8	17
Over 4,000	33	17

*a*Aguascalientes, Colima, Guanajuato, Jalisco, Michoacán, Nayarit, Querétaro (3,900.000 inhabitants)
*b*Hidalgo, Mexico City, Morelos, Puebla, Tlaxcala (3,000,000 inhabitants)
Source: 1921 Census, corrected with the help of the 1910 and 1930 Censuses

Sex, Age, Marital Status

The history of the Cristiada, that of the battles at least, assigns the most glorious role to the men who went off to the fight, urged by their wives, mothers, and sisters, and who would never have been able to hold out without the work of the female spies, suppliers, and organisers, on whom fell the brunt of the work of logistics and propaganda.[11] The women, it is true, presented quite a problem: there were the young girls who applauded the Liberators and whom Gorostieta feared like the plague, and there were those whom the soldiers would find in a village as they passed through and who pleased them. Aurelio Acevedo testified that arms attracted them as a magnet attracts iron. Anatolio Partida, who was reproached for the amorous successes of his soldiers in the Altos, far from their native region of Michoacán, replied: 'I am bringing men, not pansies.' On the whole, however, their lives were austere, and they soon made amends for any irregularities. The wives of the Federal soldiers who were killed in an ambush begged the Cristeros of Durango and Zacatecas to take them with them; they rejected the temptation, except for Ignacio Serrano, the leader from Sombrerete, who thus brought bad luck on the Quintanar Brigade, until at length he expiated his sin and repudiated the woman.[12]

The activities of the womenfolk were not conducive to the repose of the warriors: they were the first to declare war and were the worst enemies of the Federal troops, who exacted vengeance on them and raped them systematically. In August 1926 the women had been the most enthusiastic partisans of mounting guard on the churches, and everywhere, at Cocula, Guadalajara, and Sahuayo, the men played the role of timid supporters, who confronted the Government and its soldiers only to defend their womenfolk. The heart and soul of the resistance in Huejuquilla was María del Carmen Robles, who held her own against General Vargas, her executioner; María Natividad González, nicknamed Generala Tiva, was the treasurer of the Quintanar Brigade, while the indefatigable Petra Cabral, not content with giving her sons to the cause, took supplies to the Cristeros under the nose of the Federal troops. Agripina Montes (La Coronela), whom the Federals imagined to be commanding the troops in the Sierra Gorda, was not, perhaps, a military leader, but she organised the rising of Manuel Frías at Colón and spread it throughout the region with the energy of a soldier. 'How magnificently the women behaved! They used to follow us with their little children. Oh, how the poor girls used to help us! They were running so many risks!'[13]

Everywhere there were such women as Lupita Chaire, as at Victoria, Guanajuato, to replace the civilian leader who had fallen, and this exceptional participation had the force of an explosion: the institutions and behaviour of the sexes were, in normal times, sharply differentiated, and in more than one respect, as far as Mexico was concerned, one could quote Germaine Tillion in *Le Harem et les cousins*. A woman's place was in the house, in the kitchen, and in church on the epistle side; the *paseo*, the serenade and the *vuelta* made for the solidarity of the sexes, but they led only to the intimacy of lovers. Whereas the men made money and smoked as they talked, the women, except for the old ones who displayed a formidable independence, would meet together at the shop, at the water-fountain, and at the place for washing clothes. Theoretically, *amour propre* and courage were masculine values, yet shame (*vergüenza*) was felt with such violence by the women at the moment of the religious crisis, that it was often they who took the decision to engage in first resistance and then rebellion. Was the woman more strongly attached than the men to the Church, which gave her substantial responsibilities (the administration of the resources of the parish, of the priest's personal affairs, of certain religious fraternities)? The factor that relegated her to an inferior position (her non-participation in political affairs) in normal times – did it, perhaps, give her superiority in that it made possible for her a unanimous and immediate rebellion? How many wives of generals and politicians struggled, like so many Penelopes, to undo at night what their husbands had done during the day? How many were there, like the wife of General Amaro, and a certain close female relation of President Calles, who attended clandestine worship, intrigued against the Government, and cared for the orphans of the Cristeros? This happened to an even greater extent among the popular sectors. The women obliged the men to shoulder the burden of their responsibilities, and Anacleto González Flores was able to pay tribute to the women as the principal driving force behind the Unión Popular. This feminist sentiment, which arose all of a sudden, even led the Women's Brigades to want to direct the war by placing each regimental commander under the 'protection' of a woman colonel. Gorostieta was repressing a great deal of fervour when he restricted the women to the essential tasks of supply, finance, welfare services, propaganda, and supplies; but one found some women's groups making explosives, teaching men the art of sabotage, and even taking part in direct action. Miguel Gómez Loza, the Civil Governor of Jalisco, emphasised that their role was decisive and often first in importance. In fact, despite appearances, a matriarchal system held sway throughout the Bajío Real, in Jalisco, Zacatecas, and Michoacán; in this land of *machos*, the married man continued to obey his mother and did not touch his wife's possessions; was *machismo*, perhaps, the expression of a mother-fixation, an effort at counteracting that state of eternal infancy? There was real obedience on the part of the men, and not merely outward respect. The worst insult consisted of implying that someone was not really a man or, which meant the same thing, of telling him to 'fuck his mother'; in 1926, the woman was telling the man that he was not a man because he accepted such an atrocity. A sister was telling her fifteen-year-old brother that he was not as good as the defenders of God's cause, and thus many villages were left almost without men, and women worked in the field to feed the soldiers and followed them into the mountains, taking their children with them. This combination of faith and ferocity, apparent in both sexes, was one of the structural factors which caused the explosion.

By means of the questionnaires and the military records of the Quintanar Brigade, which have all been preserved by Acevedo (they give details of 2,000 men), one can analyse the age and marital status of the combatants. Table 10 shows the percentage of men in each age group.

Sixty-two per cent of the combatants were married men, and 90 per cent of them were fathers. The young men were very young indeed, for 18 per cent were under 20, and the average recruit in Colima would have been between 17 and 27 years of age. There were cases of boys of 10 whom the military leaders refused to enlist, and of whom they got

TABLE 10   *Ages of Cristeros, from sample of 2,000 men of the Quintanar Brigade*

Age	Percentage of the total	
11–19 years	18 }	49
20–29 years	31 }	
30–39 years		39
40–49 years		8
50–59 years		2
Over 60 years		2

rid by imposing conditions of enlistment which they supposed impossible. And then, one day, the boy would return, complete with the horse or the rifle that had been demanded. In many cases the boy was an orphan or intent on avenging the death of his brother, or even a child sent by his mother, who had already lost all the men in the family.[14]

Participation in the Cristiada was, in sociological terms, an exceptional activity, because it did not respect sexual and family structures, and overturned the barriers of convenience and discretion. The type who, traditionally, kept apart from a *bola* (brawl) – the very young man, the father of a family, and the old man, the woman who always disapproved of adventure and reproached the man for his inclination towards violence, and who no longer fulfilled her stabilising role in this period of history – all gave the Cristero movement a remarkably broad dimension, for it included both the supporters of order and the old revolutionaries,[15] and the people whom sex, race, or culture had relegated to a marginal role.

The Ethnic Background: the Indian

Without embarking on an otiose discussion of the definition of the term 'Indian', and confining one's consideration to those groups which considered themselves Indian, one finds evidence of their participation in this war from Sonora to Tehuantepec. Although the Yaquis, crushed in 1926–7, did not join the movement (they took part in it in 1935–6 after the *Secunda*) the mountain peoples – Coras, Tepehuanes, and Huicholes from Durango, Zacatecas, Nayarit, and Jalisco – were mostly Cristero sympathisers; sometimes they were neutral or, more rarely, pro-Government; they were participating, for the first time since Lozada's rising in the nineteenth century, in a historic event of national importance.

With a strong admixture of white blood, and having continuous labour and commercial relations with their half-caste neighbours, the Tepehuanes (numbering between three and five thousand in 1926) were Catholics. The existence of pre-Christian elements in their religious practices – for example, the *mitotes*, or May and June festivals, connected with the rain, the sun, and the fertility of the soil – does not contradict this assertion; these symbolic ceremonies connected with the soil were similar to those found among Roumanian peasants. Those of Huajicori (Nayarit), Mezquital, and Huazamota flocked to join the Cristero leader, the *mestizo* Dámaso Barraza, after the great rising of January 1927. Federico Vázquez was followed by the men of San Lucas, San Pedro Jicora, San Francisco Tenaraca, San Miguel Yonora, San José Joconoxtla, Santa María Huazamota, Taxicaringa, and Temoaya. Juan Cifuentes led the men of Santa María de Ocotán, Morohuate, Cerrito Gordo, and other places. Valente Acevedo and Trinidad Mora, like Vázquez and Barraza, were acculturated Tepehuanes, and their troops were men who had been acculturated or had just ceased to be so. In the entire sierra, the only *mestizo* villages were Huazamota and Mezquital. In Mezquital, after the death of the great Barraza, the Government established a garrison of Coras and Tepehuanes. At Huazamota, the half-caste local chieftains, the Muñozes, chose to support the Government, and provoked a violent conflict among the half-castes, with the support of only one Indian chief, Chon Aguilar, who had been the first to admit the timber companies to the communal forests. The Cristero Tepehuanes of this region followed the half-caste Florencio Estrada, who was married to a woman of the Muñoz clan.

Sixty per cent of the Tepehuanes were Cristeros, and two-thirds of the Huicholes. A people endowed with a strong personality, and influenced by the Jesuit missions in the eighteenth century, they professed Christianity for the most part, while preserving previous practices such as harvest festivals. The activity of Fr Magallanes, who was the first to re-establish contact with them after 1914 and was struck down by the Federal troops, increased their awareness of the crisis of 1926. San Sebastián supported the Cristeros, San Andrés was at first neutral and later supported them, and Santa Catarina disowned its leader, Agustín Carrillo, in order to observe absolute neutrality.

The Coras (living in Mesa del Nayar, San Pedro Ixcatán, Jesús María, San Juan Carapán, San Juan Peyotán, and Santa Teresa) were the least Catholic of the three peoples, and had no leaders to rally them to one side or the other. After the arrest of Mariano Mejía, the Cristero leader of Jesús María, they took part in the war on an individual basis, some following the pro-Government Tepehuanes Aguilar and Flores, while others joined the Cristeros under the command of Andrés Soto, Chano Gurrola, and so on. The participation (or non-participation) of these Indians, known by the generic name of Poblanos, is part of the more general problem, considered below, that of the *caciques* whose decision to support the Government caused divisions in the communities. Such a decision carried much weight, but it was never absolutely decisive.

In Jalisco, the Indians, whether in the minority like the Teules of the north, or in the majority like those of the south and Colima, did not react differently from the *mestizo* or Creole peasants to the Cristero movement; where the cultural situation was so similar, the ethnic factor was of no importance. All the villages supplied their contingents to the Cristero army, except Suchitlan, Colima, and San Lucas and Mexticacán, Zacatecas. In these three places the Indians had become *agraristas* in order to recover their lands.

All the Indian areas of Michoacán, whether Tarascan or Nahuatl, supported the rising, except in the places where there was a militia formed by the *agraristas*. In places where there was an agrarian committee (Cherán, Nahuatzen, Charapán, Ciudad Hidalgo, and Naranja), there were attempts, successful or otherwise, to overturn it. Massacred at Cherán and expelled from Charapán, the *agraristas* were the victims of resentment that had been building up for years, and the explosion of violence merely succeeded an urge to violence which had been reduced to impotence for too long. By the end of the war, the Tarascan communities had practically expelled the *agraristas* from the mountains and the plateau: they had moved to the valley or emigrated to the United States.

It was in this region that the confrontation between Cristeros and *agraristas* was most bloody; the war provided the traditional communities with the opportunity to settle accounts with the agrarian committee which threatened them. The problem surpassed by far the bounds of the land question, and became one of political anthropology; the community, when its possessions, its functions, and its institutions were attacked, overwhelmingly identified itself with the Church, which was another victim of the Government. The religion of the Tarascans, which was basically Catholic, without any degree of syncretism, gave them the strength and the means to resist a process which they had passively suffered until that time.

From Tarascan territory one passes to Mexican territory: Guerrero, Mexico City, Morelos, Taximaroa, Tlalpujahua, Zitácuaro, Jungapeo, and Tuzantla. In the three states of Guerrero, Mexico City, and Morelos, like the regions of Puebla, Tlaxcala, Veracruz, and Oaxaca, all affected by the Cristero movement, belonged to a Mexico which was more Indian and at the same time more varied: one observes the entire gamut of historical developments, from the groups shattered by the Mexican state to the Indo-colonial clans of the still unsubdued mountains of Zacapoatxla, with the villages of Morelos in between. Zapata had recruited troops there, and the Cristeros were numerous; they gathered together from all parts, old Zapata followers and men from villages which had resisted Zapata, because he had permitted his troops all kinds of licence outside Morelos. From Pómaro, Michoacan, to Tehuantepec, Oaxaca, and thence to Zacapoaxtla, Puebla, one finds Cristeros inspired by a primitive form of Christianity, a blend of Hispanic and Indian culture, which was to give many headaches to the organisers of the Socialist educational system ten years later.

It would be difficult to find, except perhaps in 1810, a comparable movement in the history of Mexico: marginal groups, defined as such by the degree of their lack of participation in a history of which they were the victims, groups which never stirred except under the stimulus of private interests and purely local motivations, took part in a movement which, like a bursting dam, carried all waters mingled together before it: the Cristiada.

Society and Politics

The political system at the level of local relationships, derived from comparative wealth and power, was based on the powerful men, the village leaders, the rich shopkeepers, the politicians who united all these activities and who were known as the *caciques*. A society is not defined merely by an analysis, expressed in percentages, of age, sex, and income, but by a study of its structures, the combinations of interdependent sectors, its activities and institutions. The *cacique* was at the heart of the system. In considering the distribution of land, mention has been made of the weakness of small properties in the face of the grouping of fortunes in units of medium size, more closely attached to local patterns of dominance than the very big estates.

The really important person in this context was the rich man, Don Fulano, the only man who could employ and help those whose system of tenure was insufficient to provide an adequate income; from him they expected the establishment of the conditions of a mortgage, a monetary loan, an advance in kind, any favour. Clienteles were formed around him, and he was the apex of a pyramid of hierarchies, for the craftsman and the farmer rarely enjoyed adequate income and security. Class relationships had lost all their paternalistic overtones, and the hard times accentuated this process: in the Altos and the Cañones, the democratic appearance of a society in which there were numerous small proprietors was an optical illusion; in consequence, antagonisms were more violent there than elsewhere.

The rich man was not resented, and if he placed his power at the service of the community who would complain? Nobody considered him to be superior: God had placed him in that position, and woe betide him if he forgot Lazarus! But he was obeyed, because he distributed rewards and punishments, by means of his money, or by means of the law of which he was often the enforcer. There were murmurs against the rich, against their way of making money which did not appear to them to be bad. The good *cacique* escaped these murmurings and curses, for money could establish a personal relationship which might make it possible to seek the common good and, through it, friendship. Too often it was said that 'we don't deserve anything from these great persons; he who is full does not remember the man who is hungry'.[16] According to the proverb, 'the rich look on every poor man as a thief'.

In a land of clienteles, a land of *caciques* where the state was the boss and the *agraristas* the clients, the Government and the powerful local men rubbed shoulders, and it is not surprising to see them making common cause against the Cristeros. Even the control exercised by the parish priest over his flock was part of this system of patronage, and there were always pretexts for conflict between the Church and the *caciques*, and particularly at village level. It has been said that the crisis of 1926 was largely due to this rivalry for the possession of clienteles. Whether they were murderous *caciques* or honourable patriarchs, whether of the right or the left, they made no move in 1926–7, and mobilised all their forces in the service of the state.

However, they owed their integration into the local system to a situation which the crisis threatened to change fundamentally: from the moment when they ceased to be intermediaries, and became the servants of a state which was now hostile, from the moment when they ceased to render a service to the community whose religion was attacked,[17] many of their clients abandoned them and even tried to overthrow them. The *caciques*, as a class, were solidly opposed to the Cristeros, who at first, trusting to these relations of patronage, had counted

on their support. Genaro Ramos of Miahuatlán, the Muñozes of Huazamota, the Guzmáns of Bolanos, the Bugarins of Atolinga, the Robleses of
Mezquitic, the Valdéses of Totatiche, Concepción Barajas of Ahuijullo,
Quirino Navarro of Tepatitlán, among others were all Cristeros at first,
and remained so for long enough to know about the conspiracy, and then
handed their friends over to the Federal troops. Often they were trying to
save their position and their wordly goods, and sometimes they sincerely
desired the good of all and wished to spare their villages the horrors of
war. Their attitude explains the delays suffered by the insurrection, the
setbacks, the divisions, the lack of participation.

The *hacendados* (big landowners) were only one case in point, and the
war made it abundantly clear that their interests were not those of the
people. 'There is another bad element, namely the rich Catholics: for
example, Señor Manuel Urquiza [a member of an extremely wealthy
family of Querétaro], the owner of haciendas ... They do not give any
help to our troops, but rather go to some lengths to help the Government agents; there are others who openly show their enmity towards us.'[18]
They received the Cristeros with rifle-shots, sent messengers to warn the
army, and invited the senior officers to set up their headquarters in the
haciendas. Protected by detachments of Federal troops, these men, who
were indispensable to the national economy, were spared the hardships
of resettlement; when the army was no longer capable of guaranteeing
their safety, it provided them with arms, in July 1928 in Guanajuato
and Colima, and in December 1928 in Jalisco and Michoacán.

The *cacique*, a rich man supported by the other rich men, in order to
mobilise his clientele, made use of a structure which, in practice,
turned out to be ambivalent and ill-equipped to resist the shock of the
religious crisis – namely, the clan. The body of relations was formally
defined by ties of kinship, but only functioned effectively in common
action. Cutting across economic and social structures, the clans divided
the rural areas into vertical groupings, which were sometimes allied, like
the Guzmáns of Bolanos and the Muñozes of Huazamota, to assert their
domination over a region. Sometimes the *cacique* was merely the head
of the victorious clan, and sometimes he owed his strength to a coalition
of several family groups; often the defeated side would aspire to revenge.
The revolutionary crisis reawakened feuds between clans in several
places, between 1913 and 1925, overturning the ancient hegemonies and
constituting others, and the Cristiada exacerbated these conflicts, sometimes partaking of their bitterness.

The partriarchal families lived in groups of homesteads, and often recently established villages considered themselves as owing their foundation to two family groups which had become confederated. Thus, in San José de Gracia, Michoacán, the ties of kinship overspilt into the neighbouring village, La Manzanilla, and the two villages treated each other as cousins. These structures, which protected the individual, guaranteed mobilisation: this was especially true in the *ranchos*, where the father governed the family household until his death; there were frequent cases of three generations living together and working the land in common. Eminently functional, this organisation made it possible to bring into production the pioneer zones of the west and south of Michoacán in the nineteenth and twentieth centuries.

At the time of the rising, entire *ranchos* took collective decisions: the Barajas and the Galindo *ranchos* of Tepatitlán, the Dueñas *rancho* of Atotonilco, those of Alvarez of San Francisco, and Flores of Tapalpa mobilised three generations of men and women.

A new social constellation had just made its appearance, often composed of strangers to the region, but sometimes linked to the family structures – the group of the *agraristas*, clients 'nourished' by the state and local *caciques*, who were now recruited from the agrarian committees. A comparatively privileged class, these kulaks displayed a tendency to crush their brethren who had not been so fortunate and to violate traditional norms.

These factors explain the divisions within the villages and the opposition between one village and another. The importance of parish-pump quarrels and personal rivalries sheds light on many surprising decisions, and the peasants were often absorbed into this endless war of all against all. Villages often paired off in opposition to each other: San José de Gracia against Mazamitla, and La Manzanilla against Pueblo Nuevo. There were factors at work other than ignoble psychological motivations: Teul felt inclined to bully Florencia, which was growing in size, whereas Atotonilco was reluctant to see San Francisco de Asís escape from its control and achieve autonomy. The *agraristas* of Jomulco wanted to impose a municipal president of their clan on the *agraristas* of Jala. When Pedro Franque, the leader of the men of Jomulco, approached with his militia, declaring that he intended to capture the parish priest, Fr Ledesma, at the same time the *agraristas* of Jala appealed to the Cristeros for help. This happened just after the beginning of the war, and provoked an increased intensity of it in the zone.[19]

In a fragmented world, where the segmented structures of family, clan, and village militated against overall unity – for the benefit of the *cacique* and in favour of civil war – it might be supposed that it would be impossible to comprehend the geographical background of the insurrection, which appears inextricable. There is a great temptation to say: such-and-such a village was Cristero because another one was not, but the converse might have been true. Indeed, study of the history of each particular insurrection demonstrates the forces at work: most of the time, abstention from the conflict did not signify active support of the Government or antagonism to the Church: it reveals merely the will of the *caciques* and the effect of the clientele system. It was, in effect, the breakdown of those ties of family and political solidarity, an unprecedented refusal to follow the *cacique*, that made the war a civil war at the local level.

The patronage system was, therefore, breaking down, at the same time as the community and the family, while the division in the heart of the countryside was becoming attenuated. San Pedro and Ihuatzio, rival Tarascan villages, became momentarily reconciled, as did Coalcomán and Aguililla. The Guzmán clan fell apart, after its leaders decided to support the Federal side, and the Campos family of Chimaltitán fought their brothers-in-law and their maternal uncles. Old Francisco Magaña, to the great astonishment of the Federal troops, ordered the shooting of his little son Chon Moreno Magaña of Cotija, because he was a Cristero. Emilio Valdés, the son of the *cacique* Don Juan Francisco Valdés, who was a Cristero against his father's wishes, was nicknamed the Madman as a result. Old Don Juan Francisco, with his other sons, organised an armed group against the Cristeros, while one of his bastard sons, Isidro, formed a Cristero group in the ravines of Bolanos.[20]

The desertion of the *caciques*, whose role was everywhere called into question, the abandonment of the cause by the rich, who denounced the movement as *La ratería* (banditry) and the Cristeros as the 'shirtless ones', meant that the movement derived no benefit from the existing cadres and had the effect of pitting the people against the state and the rural micro-bourgeoisie. Can one speak of the 'people', in referring to the Cristeros? It is possible to do so, because it was a movement exceptional in its intensity, its geographical extent, and the number of combatants mobilised; and because it involved all the rural groups, except for the highest stratum, and cut across the existing structures. Those who could joined the insurrection, and those who were not free did not do so – the passive Indian in the areas where he was subject to domination, and the *agrarista*, who was the Cristero's worst enemy.

The Agraristas[21]

During the war, 25,000 *agraristas* served permanently as auxiliary troops in the Federal army and fought the Cristeros, whether in self-defence groups which made possible the partitioning of the country for search operations, or in properly formed battalions which campaigned far from their bases. Finally, in 1929, the Government mobilised all available *agraristas* for military service, and they were obliged to shoulder the burden of the campaign in the Western Centre and the West, while the regular troops went up to fight General Escobar's rebels in the North. In the course of this offensive, they suffered severely and were annihilated as a fighting force. Dissensions which caused misgivings to the Government took place in Durango, where the leader J. Guadalupe Ramírez had to be shot, and in Zacatecas, Guerrero, and Colima, where the *agraristas* changed sides and became Cristeros.[22]

Almost exhausted by 1929, the *agraristas* had been harshly treated for three years by a Federal army that made use of them but despised them. They were not, perhaps, very good soldiers, but, besides the fact that they fought on foot against the Cristeros who were excellent horsemen, they were fighting against their will an absurd and disastrous war. They were made to march, as a disorganised rabble, in the vanguard, as a shield, to face the first shots the moment battle was joined, and they were always abandoned when there was a retreat.

Although they lacked enthusiasm, they were considered as formidable enemies by the Cristeros, because like them they were peasants and knew the country and its inhabitants. In economic, social, and cultural terms, they hardly differed from the Cristeros.[23] It is a striking fact that they were practising Catholics just as devout as the Cristeros; those of Ahuijullo hid their parish priest, and never breathed a word about the presence of Mgr Velasco, who was in hiding in their region. Those of Jalisco did the same in the case of Mgr Orozco, while at Jungapeo, Michoacán, some of them were shot for refusing to take up arms against the Church.

This explains why, at the beginning of the war, the Cristeros had counted on their support. Why could they not contribute their military organisation and their arms? This hope, which soon proved unfounded, explains the naïve manner in which the conspirators invited the *agrarista* leaders to rise in arms with them; this behaviour often led to denunciation and disaster.[24]

In such circumstances, the tragedy was bound to be bloody, and it was so because the *agraristas* were caught between two fires, the Government and the Cristeros; as the popular saying put it, they were 'pecked by the cocks and hated by the hens'. It was all the more a tragedy because families were divided: Aurelio Acevedo was present at the execution of a relative of his who was an *agrarista*; the brother-in-law of Trini Castañón was an *agrarista*, and there were many similar cases: an *agrarista* father and a Cristero son, or the other way about, and brothers on opposite sides. Although in Zacatecas executions of prisoners took place only exceptionally (five in three years), as a consequence of friendships,[25] it was not the same story elsewhere. All *agrarista* leaders who were captured were shot, as were soldiers in general, although the regular Federal troops were spared.

The Cristeros made a distinction between the religious and the agrarian problem: 'We are not against the *agraristas*, we are in favour of the redistribution of land, but we are against the *agraristas* when they become soldiers.'[26] José González Romo, the Cristero leader in Coalcomán, wrote to Jesús Morfín, the *agrarista* leader in Ahuijullo: 'Tell the *agraristas* that we are not fighting them because they are *agraristas*, but because they support the tyrant who is trying to wipe out the religion of our country and hand us over to the Protestant Gringos. We will resolve the agrarian problem, but without deception, giving title immediately to lands which are occupied.'[27]

Against *agraristas* – peasants, Catholics, and relatives – who were nevertheless 'our inevitable enemies who, with the rifle in their hand and impelled by the rifle, never failed to do us some harm',[28] the anger of the Cristeros was unleashed.

The Government had always made use of the *agraristas* for the purposes of political control, for rural policing, for military action, both before and after the Cristiada, because they were the best placed to exercise surveillance over the peasants: 'For the bulls of Jaral, horses from the same place!.' The division among the peasantry provoked by the agrarian reform was all the more exacerbated when those who often came from elsewhere or were drawn from the marginal sectors suddenly became privileged by the grace of the state, and became its clients and its policemen. This favoured minority felt ill at ease in the midst of a peasantry which described them as 'thieves' before calling them, after 1926, 'traitors'. The Government took advantage of this division, and cleverly used it to dissociate those two rural passions, land and liberty, which, when combined, led to uncontrollable explosions. It therefore used a kind of blackmail with the land, which had brought the *agraristas* into its grasp, and thus provoked hatred of that 'well-fed' group; the hatred was all the greater because this blackmail obliged the others to turn away nostalgically from that land of which they dreamed.

One must, therefore, understand in this political and military sense the renewed distribution of land which took place between 1927 and 1930, when it had ceased before the Cristiada, and was to cease immediately after it.[29] In order to win over these rebels, to recruit new adherents and restrict popular support for the Cristeros, distribution was accelerated, particularly in the zones where the rebellion was strongest. This phenomenon, of which the answers to the *agrarista* questionnaire give an idea (one-third of the grants were made between 1926 and 1929), has been expressed in quantitative terms after the examination of the records of the Land Department and is shown in table 11.

In short, in 1926, 375,762 peasants had received 3·5 million hectares of land, after ten years of agrarian reform; during the three years of the

TABLE 11 *Distribution of lands, by state, to* ejidatarios, *1915–26 and 1927–9*

State	1915–26		1927–9	
	Hectares	Ejidata-rios	Hectares	Ejidata-rios
Aguascalientes	67,732	5,805	33,425	2,574
Colima	27,788	1,100	—	1,419
Durango	160,995	7,433	46,764	2,559
Guanajuato	28,736	4,730	60,646	8,513
Guerrero	71,481	7,871	82,876	8,277
Jalisco	135,670	21,072	167,567	16,822
México	120,290	30,930	148,853	33,255[a]
Michoacán	83,106	12,872	119,405	16,108
Nayarit	52,783	5,209	20,334	1,928
Morelos	65,375	7,114	227,000	17,380
Puebla	182,932	29,304	183,390	22,137
Querétaro	25,181	2,966[a]	37,178	2,781[a]
San Luis-Potosí	546,103	19,229	617,639	23,379
Tlaxcala	34,995	14,226	11,023	4,532
Veracruz	74,707	13,939	51,837	8,619
Zacatecas	265,980	14,580	70,496	2,141

[a]This was a special category – 'collective use' – and therefore does not strictly refer to *ejidatarios* (owner-workers of communal lands). In Querétaro, in 1929, there were only 2,100 true *ejidatarios*; the rest was 'collective use'.

Cristero War, this figure rose to 592,544 *ejidatarios*, installed on 5 million hectares. President Portes Gil alone distributed 1 million hectares in 1929 to 127,000 heads of families. Figure 2 shows the importance of this phenomenon and its limitation in time.

Cristeros and *agraristas* were bitter enemies, both during and after the war; with the exception of the *agrarista* leaders, it should be pointed out that the hatred of the Cristeros for the *agraristas* was stronger than the *agraristas'* hatred of them. The *agraristas*, when they were convinced that they were in the right and acting in good faith, at worst saw the

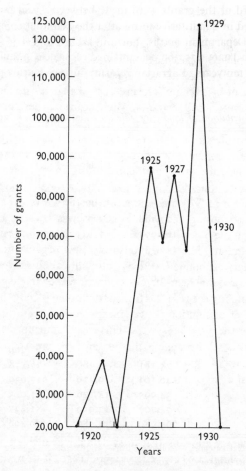

Fig. 2. Land grants

Cristeros as bandits and rebels; only the cadres considered them as 'White Guards' in the pay of the Vatican and the landowners. The Cristeros, however, regarded the *agraristas* as the incarnation of evil, of all evils: they were heretical, impious, sacrilegious, servants of Antichrist, of the persecuting Caesar, having begun life as thieves. It is true that it was for those who had profited from the Revolution that the insurgents reserved their most virulent hatred and their cruellest ill-treatment (those who profited from the agrarian reform which had harmed the majority were only a minority), but it was not agrarian reform that provoked the Cristero insurrection. The problem is not to find out why some *agraristas* decided to fight for the Government, for this question is meaningless. The possibility of choice no longer existed as soon as the *agrarista* was issued with a rifle, the symbol of his function as a guard dog; if economic determinism played a part in this, it was a negative influence, because the *agrarista* was not able to ask himself the question, tied as he was to the Government by his land. The presence of an *agrarista* militia controlling a community (as at Naranja, Michoacán) is, therefore, a negative correlation, in so far as insurrection had been made impossible.

In fact, outside the ranks of the rich and the *agraristas*, relatively privileged men enjoying a privileged position, there were no anti-Cristeros in the rural areas, and, constituting an example of great symbolic significance, the old followers of Zapata fought under the banner of Christ the King. Why was there this hostility towards a government which was distributing the land, unless it was because there was no identity among the objectives pursued? The agrarian reform, aside from its setbacks and its defects, established a new organisation, a modern one, with partly economic but above all political objectives. And it was here that the shoe pinched: the Government was trying to gain partisans and recruits among the refugees from a traditional society that was either on the verge of dissolution or was incapable of integrating them after the collapse of the agrarian system. This rural lumpenproletariat, which was recruited not only among the peasants (before 1930 one-third of the beneficiaries of agrarian reform had never touched a plough), was exploited by the Government for political ends.

Structures and the Combination of Circumstances

Only fragmentary and unsatisfactory data are available for the study of economic development between 1910 and 1930. It is, nevertheless, possible to discern the principal characteristic of this period: by means of nationwide statistics, the historian is enabled to forget history. What a paradox! Here is a land where the countryside is ravaged day after day between 1914 and 1920, and then again after 1924, yet which records figures for a growth of agriculture commensurate with that of the gross national product. The wave of destruction so painfully suffered by the rural masses of the Old Mexico of the central plateau was offset by the almost complete immunity enjoyed by the modern enterprises of the dynamic sector established under Porfirio Díaz, the plantations and commercial agricultural undertakings; livestock were slaughtered wholesale, cereal harvests were lost, but cotton, chick-peas, and henequen were no more affected than were industrial installations.

If one examines sectoral and regional details, the picture changes: from 1907 to 1929 the production of maize and haricot beans, the basic foodstuffs of the people, fell by 40 per cent and 31 per cent respectively, whereas the population increased by 9 per cent. The local reality was even harsher. The Centre, which in 1930 contained 45 per cent of the rural population, saw its total agricultural production fall by 31 per cent, and for the peasants the Revolution meant impoverishment. Production per head fell by 18 per cent whereas the disparity among regions was increased. Taking the year 1900 as 100, Table 12 shows regional growth from 1907 to 1929.

TABLE 12 *Regional growth to 1929 (1900 = 100)*

Region	1907	1929
Centre	112	69
South	115	98
North	60	318

Source: Clark W. Reynolds, *The Mexican Economy* (Yale University Press, 1970), tables 3.3, 3.4, 3.5, and 3.6.

If one examines the situation of the agricultural worker, the same trend is evident. Compared with national index of 100, Valisco has a figure of 137 in 1910, then of 96 in 1930.[30] The rural masses that formed the majority in the Centre and the South, which were the battlefields where the Northerners confronted one another, paid the price of the changes, although their own problems were never resolved. This can be measured graphically in terms of harvests and is shown in Table 13.

TABLE 13   *Cereal crops, 1906–36*

Date	Tons per year
1906–10	3,500,000
1920	2,900,000
1925	2,000,000
1933	1,900,000
1936	1,500,000

Source: Confederación Nacional de las Cámaras de Comercio e Industria, *The present depreciation of our currency* (Mexico City, 1938), p. 35.

In Central Mexico, the political crisis which supervened in 1924, after the problem of the succession to the Presidency, and which finally led to religious persecution, was painfully resented as a setback after the comparative upsurge of 1920–3.

An analysis of the structural variables shows that it was not so much a particular social class as the region itself that took part in the movement (the explanation on a class basis has a negative effect, for the rich and the *agraristas* were against the insurrection). The dependent variable is the number of participants, considered in terms of population density. A society variegated like a mosaic became united in certain regions as a consequence of 90 per cent participation; there was an alliance between different groups, so that one finds side by side men like Pedro Quintanar, Juan Carranza, and Simón Cortés, who had fought after 1915 against Villa's old followers, Justo Ávila and Dámaso Barraza, now their allies, who had taken to banditry; Prudencio Mendoza or Anatolio Partida had fought with old soldiers who had marauded under the orders of the terrible Inés Chávez García; and Zapatists from Guerrero and those from Morelos, who had been bitter enemies after 1915 as a consequence of regional antagonism, were now reconciled. Such a union of opposites, a convergence of disparate elements under the influence of circumstances, demonstrated the unanimous character of a movement with its roots in the soil, and the serious nature of a crisis that stirred both the Indian communities most deeply rooted in the past and the more modern peasantries of the Western region. Each sector was influenced by different variables, and might well have conflicting interests, as is shown by the indices of race, admixture of white blood, urbanisation, density, and modernisation. What, then, was the common variable? It was, without doubt, religion, and this subject will be discussed further in the course of study of motivations. The abstention of the North, which constituted a different society, a different culture, where the Catholic Church had not yet become firmly established enough to challenge Freemasonry and the Protestant churches, is an example of a contrary tendency. With regard to Old Mexico, in each case, the combination of circumstances in the region will be explained, in order to resolve the apparent contradictions.

CHAPTER 7

The Cristero Army

Without plans, lacking organisation, with no leaders, the Cristeros rose in rebellion and began operations by disarming the nearest enemies in order to take their rifles. Without uniforms, with no standard equipment, identified first by a black arm band, the sign of mourning, and later by an arm band in red and white, the colours of Christ, they were organised first in bands, then in companies, then in regiments, and finally in brigades. At the end of 1927 they called themselves the Army of National Liberation. When there were divisions composed of several thousand men, the shortage of ammunition was to limit the war to guerrilla operations; the basis still remained the local unit supported by one of the villages which supported the insurrection, where the combatants could return after the battle and the dispersal of their forces, and wait until the next time they mustered for an operation.

The war did not involve only the combatants, and the *Cristeros mansos* (non-combatants) guaranteed a rudimentary but effective logistical organisation. The people of the countryside provided both the soldiers and their civilian allies, whereas those of the towns worked to improve organisation, propaganda, and supplies; town and country were in continuous communication with each other, and the flow of refugees reinforced this continuity.

The army was a reflection of the peasantry from which it was recruited, and, since the rebellion cut across all historical categories, like a fire deep down in the earth crossing various geological strata, and appeared in the most diverse regions, the army was a federation of republics and communities in arms. Sometimes it really was a case of a village republic, or the confederation of an entire region, controlling its territory and providing its government, and sometimes the women and children followed the men into the desert and abandoned the village to the Federal troops. Sometimes only the men went away and, protected by the whole population, moved in safety round the built-up areas that they could visit at night, and that a lucky shipment of ammunition might allow them to attack and capture.

The Cristero Army

Military Organisation

This developed, over the course of time, as follows. In 1929 25,000 men were still organised only into bands of varying sizes, operating autonomously and without any order in their territories; 25,000 others had formed themselves into cavalry regiments under the command of a general-in-chief and into brigades recognising the supreme authority of Gorostieta. His continuous presence in the region made it possible to perfect the organisation of units which proved capable, at Tepatitlán, of defeating the Federal troops in a pitched battle. The Altos, between the Río Lerma and the Río Verde, and the Tapatia region (the former cantons of Guadalajara, Lagos, La Barca, Sayula, Etzatlán, and Zapotlán), which in 1926 contained three-quarters of the population of the state, were the most solidly Cristero regions. There were few villages in the state that did not provide a contingent for the movement.

Jesús Degollado was not able to organise his vast region until 1928. Until then the area had been characterised by complete disorder.

Aguascalientes raised two regiments, under the command of José Velasco. Likewise, in the Sierra Gorda, Guanajuato, the two regiments constituting the *Brigade of the Cross* were led by Manuel Frías. In Michoacán, there were 12,000 Cristeros, of whom scarcely 3,000 were organised into regiments. The first zone, that of Zamora, contained 5 regiments commanded by José María Méndez, Maximiliano Barragán,

TABLE 14   *South Jalisco Division, (9 regiments)*
Commander, General Jesús Degollado

Regiment	Commander	Area of operation
1st Regiment	Carlos Bouquet	South Jalisco
2nd Regiment	José Verduzco	Colima
3rd Regiment	Manuel Michel	South Jalisco
4th Regiment	T. Placencia and Calvario	Tuxpán and Colima
5th Regiment	Vicente Cueva	South-west Jalisco
6th Regiment	Andrés Salazar	Colima
7th Regiment	Luis Ibarra	Western Centre of Jalisco
8th Regiment	J. González Romo	Coalcomán (Michoacán)
9th Regiment	Lorenzo Arreola	Nayarit

In addition, there were 15 units, each composed of 100–200 men.
Total: 7,000 men.

TABLE 15 *Altos Brigade (Jalisco and western Guanajuato)*
General: Fr Aristeo Pedroza; 5,000 cavalry, organised in 7 regiments and
6 half-regiments

Regiment	Commander
Ayo Regiment	Fr Aristeo Pedroza, *later* Lauro Rocha
San Julián Regiment	Miguel Hernández
San Miguel Regiment	Victoriano Ramírez
San Gaspar Regiment	Manuel Ramírez de Olivas
1st Gómez Loza Regiment	Gabino Flores ⎫
2nd Gómez Loza Regiment	Cayetano Álvarez ⎬ Fr Vega
Jalostotitlán Regiment	José María Ramírez

TABLE 16 *Quintanar Brigade*
Commander, General Pedro Quintanar; 5,000 men

Regiment	Commander
Guadalupe Regiment	Justo Ávila
Valparaíso Regiment	Aurelio Acevedo
Castañón Regiment	Trinidad Castañón
Regiment of the Free men of Chalchihuites	
Regiment of the Free Men of Huejuquilla	
Regiment of the Free Men of Jalpa	Chema Gutiérrez

Guerrillas commanded by Porfirio Mayorquín in the mountains of Nayarit
on the coast of Sinaloa

TABLE 17 *Anacleto González Flores Brigade*

Regiment of Felipe Sánchez (Tlaltenango)
Regiment of Pedro Sandoval (Florencia)
Regiment of Teófilo Baldovinos – under-strength

Anatolio Partida, Prudencio Mendoza, and Ramón Aguilar, who worked
in close liaison with General Degollado in the west and with General
Gorostieta in the north.

The second zone, that of Coalcomán, contained the First Western
Division (3,000–5,000 men), in a territory virtually liberated from the
Federal army. Anarchic conditions prevailed there, and this prevented
these very numerous forces from operating outside their region. The
third zone enjoyed a similar autonomy: Ignacio Villanueva and Ladislao
Molina were the principal leaders in this area, which stretched from the

Tarascan lakes to the hot lands. The fourth zone contained several separate regions in juxtaposition.

The thousands of men from Durango operated in bands which recognised as their principal leaders Trini Mora, Valente Acevedo, and Federico Vázquez. In this region, as in Guerrero and the Zapatista zone, there was no question of formal organisation. In the remainder of the Republic there were only bands of from fifty to 400 men, not counting the temporary bands of Coahuila, San Luis Potosí, Chihuahua, Tabasco, the Tuxtlas, and Huatusco (Veracruz).

The army of the Western Centre, which took its orders from Gorostieta, was composed of 25,000 men capable of manoeuvring above regimental level: south Zacatecas, Jalisco, Aguascalientes.

The growth of, and changes in, the troops of the Western Centre was a continuous process: in May 1927 Manuel Michel was commanding forty men; in June this figure rose to ninety-four, in July to 200 and in October to 500, which made it possible for him to organise a complete regiment, divided into four squadrons, subdivided into troops, and commanded by the appropriate officers and non-commissioned officers. He arranged for his men to have military training and inculcated discipline. His 3rd Regiment even learned to engage in combined operations with Andrés Salazar's 6th Regiment, and took part in operations commanded by General Degollado, together with several other units.[1]

Manuel Ramírez, after the disappearance of the first commanding officer of the San Gaspar Regiment, reorganised it, and by May 1929 it was up to strength with well trained and disciplined troops.[2]

The Quintanar Brigade was composed of five regiments of between 400 and 600 men each. At first, the self-defence groups had provided the cadres for the insurrection, but very soon these groups, consisting of about thirty men each, proved insufficient to provide an organisation for 2,500 men and conduct a proper war against a regular army. The arrival of General Gorostieta at the end of 1927 was the signal for proper organisation on the basis of battalions, divided into four squadrons of three sections each, sub-divided into two platoons and three squads. Basing his methods on a military manual captured from the Federal troops, Aurelio Acevedo organised his own regiment and then the five others, which were soon up to strength, properly mounted, and armed with good rifles.[3] Each regiment corresponded to a municipality, and within each squadron this principle of geographical recruitment, based on the need to live off the country, was observed. The last parade, held on 28 June 1929, mustered twenty squadrons of between eighty-four and 120 men; their ages varied from thirteen to sixty-seven. Half of them had joined the insurrection in 1926–7 and the other half in 1928. Forty per cent came from villages and 60 per cent from hamlets; the effective strength varied from the numbers given above to twice that number, maintaining itself between 400 and 500 in the course of 1929; the Valparaíso Regiment lost forty-seven men in three years, and the total losses for the brigade were nearly 500. They were all killed in battle or shot by firing squad.

These units, like nearly all the Cristero units, were composed of cavalrymen; the only infantry soldiers in the Quintanar Brigade were the men of Huazamota, commanded by Florencio Estrada. The volcanic region of Colima was the only locality where the infantry predominated in the Cristero units; elsewhere, their army generally consisted of cavalry regiments, better mounted and with better horsemen than the Federal regiments.[4]

Arms and Equipment

At first, the Cristeros fought on foot or were very badly mounted; they were armed with slings, sticks, machetes and poor quality fire-arms. Their arms always varied in quality and type, although there was a tendency for them to become more uniform and to improve considerably. In 1927, a squadron from the region of Manuel Doblado was armed with twenty-nine Mausers, nine ·30-30 carbines, thirteen 8 mm rifles, four carbines of 8 and 18 mm, and thirty-six pistols of various types (Russian ·44 and also ·38, ·32-20, ·45, ·32 in., short ·32, and ·45 in. regulation parabellum), which made more complicated the problem of ammunition supply.[5]

In 1928, one finds the same variety in the weapons of the 3rd Regiment of Manuel Michel, but here the majority of rifles were Mausers: 7 mm or 20 mm short rifles, 7 mm long rifles, 7 mm and 8 mm carbines, ·30-30 Winchesters, 7 mm Mausers, ·32, ·45, ·38 in., and 9 mm pistols. Out of 250 long weapons (for 400 men), there were 150 Mausers.[6] On 1 Jaunuary 1929, the same unit had sixty-nine ·30-30 Winchesters, twenty-five 44 mm carbines, four ·38, eight ·32-20, 170 Mausers, fifteen 20 mm rifles, and seventy-three ·38, ·44, ·45 m, and ·32-20 in rifles. This made a total of 289 long weapons.

In 1928 the Quintanar Brigade was already very well mounted, having an average of two horses per trooper, complete with saddlery, and its arms were improving. Justo Ávila's men had unearthed their old ·30-30s from the time of the Revolution, which explains the high proportion of this weapon found in the Guadalupe Regiment; the other regiments had

Mausers, ·30-30s (these two types constituted two-thirds of the 1,500 long fire-arms) and various types of rifles, carbines and blunderbusses.[7] In 1929, the Valparaíso Regiment had 400 rifles bearing the serial numbers of the Federal army, whereas it had begun in 1926 with ten ·30-30s and a few ·32-20s. They had some seven to eighteen rifles captured from the 84th Regiment (the list of serial numbers of rifles of a squadron of the 84th, which fell into the hands of the Cristeros, showed them that they had all but four of the rifles), Mausers captured from the 6th, 59th, and 84th Regiments, and horses, saddle-cloths, and trumpets from the 6th and 59th Regiments.[8]

In the same way, the San Gaspar Regiment, commanded by Manuel Ramírez, finished the war with not only the officers but also the sergeants and troopers completely equipped with Mausers and pistols. The officers even had Zeiss binoculars.[9]

In camp, or in the villages of the liberated zones, the craftsmen in the army.worked on the production of cartridges, adaptation of calibres, and the preparation of bombs, and even a few rudimentary cannon. The specialists were those who had made rockets and fireworks in peacetime; grenades were sometimes made of leather pouches filled with buckshot, but more often from old food tins; some of them, which alarmed everybody, consisted of bottles filled with highly unstable mixtures of chemicals. Since the great problem for the Cristeros was the capture of church towers and fortifications, against which their rifles were powerless, they tried to manufacture small cannon, of the calibre of a mortar. The Southern Division (south-Jalisco) and the Cristeros of Coalcomán made some rudimentary pieces of artillery that gave very good service; the Navarro brothers, from near Etzatlán, made one cannon in which the charge had to be held in place by newspaper well rammed home, and which was fired by touching a lighted taper to the hole. It was effective, but it had the disadvantage of occasionally exploding. The Cristeros also used cannon with barrels made of wood bound with iron.[10] Using unexploded aircraft bombs, in Colima and the Altos, these artificers filled hundreds, even thousands, of cartridges, and from one bomb they could make seventy grenades. They also used commercial explosives, and became familiar with electrical detonation.[11]

Whereas their arms were restricted to light weapons, and the lack of ammunition restricted operations, the situation of the combatants as regards clothing and equipment was utterly miserable: 'If you have any coats, send them, and also sandals; we're short of both, and the men are already working barefoot.'[12]

Manuel Michel wrote to his sister: 'I've got a lot of men without clothing, and I need blankets ... there are also some without shoes. I want more cigarettes, salt, five kilos of best quality wool, two dozen batteries for reflectors, 100 aspirin tablets, oxygenated water and salve.'[13] Salt, tobacco, and soap were, in addition to cartridges and horseshoes, the most sorely needed commodities, and there was an acute shortage of them. The Cristeros never had anyone but themselves to rely on for supplies: 'All the arms and ammunition with which we are fighting the Government, we took from the Government itself; and a proof of this is that all the horses which we handed over when we laid down our arms were Government property.'[14] Or, as Acevedo put it: 'Who can deny the fact that I set out on the 26th with twenty men and three weapons, and my commander had but three armed men? And who can deny that on the 29th the two of us had over 2,000 men, all fully armed?'[15] 'Why, we being so little, and insufficiently armed, without military discipline and experience, go and fight with those who were so well prepared for war, with so much equipment just to fight simple *rancheros*, why could such a miracle happen? Because we little ones beat the big ones, like David.'[16]

The Financial Problem

Money was, above all, needed for the purchase of ammunition, rather than of weapons, for the Cristeros usually captured the latter from the Federal troops. Often battle was the only way to fill the ammunition pouches, but surprise dawn attacks like that of 26 December 1926, when Quintanar's men and those of Herminio Sánchez (of the Anacleto González Flores Brigade) found 600 rounds on the corpses of the defeated soldiers of the 59th Regiment, were not frequent. Sometimes, the situation fovoured the combatants: the Federal troops, besieged and starving in Coalcomán, secretly handed over magazines to women who in return brought them food and, since 'it would be the worse for everybody if this arrangement were discovered', everyone kept quiet.[17]

This made it possible to survive from day to day, but not to undertake large-scale operations as Gorostieta wished. He wrote: 'Give me three million rounds and I can control the Bajío.' It was, therefore, necessary to buy from civilian and military arms dealers, and this was expensive – 20 cents per round for ·30-30 ammunition, which was already becoming rare, and 15 cents per round for Mauser ammunition; sometimes, in times of crisis, such as October 1927 and March 1929, the price rose to one peso per round.

They could not count on the help of the rich, and so, besides the taxes which had to be paid by the people, the Cristeros were obliged to requisition the goods of the big landowners and exact ransom for them, although such leaders as Manuel Frías and Dionisio Ochoa refused to do this. Ezequiel Mendoza explained to his soldiers:

We must be as brave as lions in the face of the enemy, but not tyrannical, as they are towards us, we must be honest at all times; we will take, from their goods, what we need to live and fight, but we must not steal other men's goods; all worldly goods come from God and we must not make bad use of them; if we take what is His in order to live and defend what is truly the cause of God, it is not stealing, we have only disposed of our own goods, of those of our Father; I give this explanation so that you will understand, and not describe as good something that in itself is bad, nor call bad something which in itself is good; our ignorance is great because we do not know the truth, we see something as red when it is white and as white when it is red. Our Lord Jesus Christ was walking one day with his followers, and they crossed a cornfield, the Apostles were very hungry and picked the ears of wheat and rubbed them with their fingers and ate the grain, but those guarding the cornfield said, these men are stealing, but our Lord defended his people and said to those who were complaining, have you not read about when King David and his people were hungry, they ate the shrewbread, which was for the priests alone? And thus neither the King nor his people sinned, since all goods are created by the same God and for the good of all, just as the sun shines and the rain falls on the just and the unjust, so we are not stealing from any man.[18]

On the occasion of the ineffectual abduction of the rich men of Autlán, Degollado had been strong enough to refrain from carrying out his threat without losing face, but quite often there were tragic consequences. Padilla Cruz, a rich merchant of Tepatitlán, was executed when his ransom was not paid,[19] and in the course of three years five other hostages met a similar fate.[20] The most surprising feature is that this did not happen more often, because the press reported over seventy cases of kidnapping, of which fifteen were carried out by the urban group in Guadalajara. The biggest sum paid out was 20,000 pesos, which Pedro Martínez claimed as a ransom for E. J. Bumstead.[21] The Cristeros kidnapped big landowners and Americans who were working in the mines; the urban groups abducted for ransom businessmen, well-to-do doctors, and politicians.[22]

Attacks on trains were another method of acquiring money, but the two biggest *coups* of this kind were nullified by the dishonesty of the rich Catholics, to whom were entrusted the 400,000 pesos carried off by Fr Reyes Vega and General Gallegos in early 1927. Subsequently, attacks on trains took place more as a result of strategic considerations than of financial expectations.

The accounts of a regiment [23]

Half the revenue from civil taxes was handed over to the military authorities, but the amounts involved were small: the revenue of the municipality of Huejuquilla was 920 pesos in May 1928 (540 of which represented the basic contribution), 360·98 pesos in August and 510·60 pesos in September. This meagre income was supplemented by the war tax, an exceptional measure, which the rich, as always, refused to pay. In one year the municipality of Mezquitic donated 10,000 pesos derived from this tax, of which only one-third was in cash and the rest was in the form of cattle on the hoof, which were difficult to sell because they could not be taken to Zacatecas, the only possible market.[24] Cristero soldiers who wished to return to civilian life paid a tax of 80 pesos, and the safe-conducts issued to merchants and *agraristas* brought in from 10 to 50 pesos each; the country was poor, and the war tax, ear-marked for the purchase of ammunition, varied from 50 cents to one peso per year for each head of livestock. In this way, the 126 heads of families of the Ameca hacienda contributed 964·14 pesos in 1928.[25]

The slenderness of these resources provoked extraordinary measures: two kidnappings of mine employees in three years, which brought in no money because the mines refused to pay and the Cristeros could not make up their minds to kill their hostages. The young American who was thus forced to spend several months with them taught them the handling and maintenance of the Thompson submachinegun;[26] when the property of haciendas was requisitioned and there were forced 'loans' after the capture of a village, the Cristeros were often ashamed to ask for money and still more ashamed to accept it. Thus, when they captured Fresnillo, they went to raise taxes from the American mining company, and gave it a receipt for 3,000 pesos;[27] later, the cashier told them that 50,000 pesos was waiting for them in the safe, and they could take them; he himself was only waiting for their orders to hand it over, because he was a sympathiser. 'That shows you what fools we were,' concluded Aurelio Acevedo.[28] The total sum of money was small, but 'it was by means of these miserable contributions that we were growing big'.[29]

An examination of the accounts gives an idea of the amounts which passed through their hands and of the care with which the books were kept.[30] In the accounts of the funds of the Valparaíso Regiment, the second ten days of May (the accounts were closed and checked every ten days), show an income of 377·77 pesos. Between 3 May and 10 June 1928, the regimental cashier handled 867·38 pesos and spent 751·72, including the purchase of twenty-five pieces of cloth at 8 pesos each (that is, 200 pesos) to clothe the soldiers who were in rags. Between 4 July and 18 August 1928, a total of 322·65 pesos was spent on the troops (there were 450 soldiers on the permanent strength). In 1928, 'chiefly the voluntary contributions of sympathisers, especially for food and clothing' made it possible to reserve for other purposes the money collected, which was 7,028·93 pesos; the war tax provided 5,127·89 pesos.[31] For the purchase of ammunition 4,200 pesos were sent to the League (this money was lost, because the League never sent a single round), 862 pesos were distributed to the troops, 463 pesos were used to defray general expenses, 227 pesos were used to purchase maize, and 165 pesos to shoe the horses, making a total of 6,704·73 pesos.[32]

The Leaders

Who were the military leaders of the Cristeros? In answer to this question, there are available biographical details of some two hundred of them, representing the majority of the officers, ranging in rank from major to general.[33]

The officers, whatever their rank, were at first acclaimed or elected by their soldiers, before being confirmed in their appointments by the higher authorities; the earliest leaders were, quite simply, men who in their respective region led the insurrection, or those whom a group of rebels had invited to lead it. The election was always carried out democratically, by vote and acclamation;[34] a commander with whom the troops were discontented could not remain in his appointment for long, and had to return to the ranks or leave the unit; the soldier who disagreed with the choice of the majority withdrew from the army, went off to serve under another commander, or resigned himself to obeying the existing one.

The qualities most appreciated in a commander were personal bravery and military experience; of the two hundred officers whose biographies it has been possible to trace, about forty were familiar to some extent with the career of arms, because they had taken part in the movements of Villa, or Zapata, or the self-defence groups, and twelve were former officers of the Federal army (these were old professional officers from Porfirio Díaz's time, or revolutionaries integrated into the new Federal army). Adding the ten or so former military men (soldiers or policemen), one finds that as many as 30 per cent of the officers owed their appointments to their military experience. Among those who had taken part in the movements of Madero and Villa were General Justo Ávila, Colonel

Miguel Hernández, and Colonel Emilio Barrios, and they had been confirmed in their military ranks by Obregón. Don Justo, born in 1860 near Valparaíso, Zacatecas, had taken part in insurrections from 1910 onwards, and his first campaign had been with Pánfilo Nátera; later he had commanded a brigade in Villa's army and taken part in the capture of Zacatecas. After the defeat of Celaya, his brigade had become famous throughout the region for its extortions. He had not laid down his arms until 1920, and of all the commanders who had surrendered he was the only one to escape alive after the massacre of Palmira; in 1926, the General told the Cristeros that he was too old to begin again, and he did not decide to take up his command until the end of 1927. 'Tired of killing innocent people in Villa's revolution, he was always willing to enter into an arrangement with the enemy.'[35]

Emilio Barrios had fought in the same campaigns, and had also fought at the Ebano; taken prisoner and incorporated into Carranza's army to fight Zapata's rising, he deserted and rejoined Zapata.[36]

Miguel Hernández, who followed Villa's movement until 1920, and had then become a supporter of Obregón, had left the army in 1921. In 1927 he went of his own free will to offer his services to the Cristeros of San Julián, Jalisco, who at first distrusted him because of his military background.

There were, in all, twenty-five former followers of Villa, including Dámaso Barraza, the commander-in-chief of Mezquital, Durango; Simón Cortés, an old companion of the bandit Inés Chávez García and of Renteria Luviano, before he became the pacifier of the Sierra Fría in Michoacán; Sabino Salas, leader of the fearsome 'Blacks' of Laguna Grande, Zacatecas; Fernando Pedroza from Lagos; Félix Barajas from Zapotlanejo; Chema Gutiérrez, who fought at the Ebano at the age of fourteen; José Velasco, Pedro Cordero, and Pedro Sandoval, who were just as young, and many others who, like them, had been common soldiers.

There were Zapatista leaders who took up arms again, such as Generals Victorino Bárcenas, Benjamín Mendoza, Manuel Reyes and his brothers, Felipe Barrios, Ángel Jaime, J. Abacuc Román, Maximiliano Vigueras, Federico Fabila, Juvenal Palacios, and the Hernández brothers from Tepoztlán.

Often old Revolutionaries themselves, the leaders of the self-defence groups became useful officers: Prudencio Mendoza, a man of prestige and enjoying absolute authority, had held sway since 1905 in the mountains of western Michoacán. In his zone there was not a single bandit, and during the Revolution he fought indiscriminately against all the factions and the Government to impose a respect for order. Squatting on his haunches and rolling cigarettes in maize-leaves, he received those with complaints or requests. At the age of 60, when he joined the rising, he carried the whole of the mountain region with him as one man. Simón Cortés, Dámaso Barraza, and Juan Carranza in the Sierra Gorda and Pedro Quintanar in Zacatecas played similar roles.

Don Pedro Quintanar, born in 1866, had taken part in all the wars, in order to protect the region from all intruders. In 1914 he took part in the siege of Zacatecas, as did Justo Ávila on the other side. Ávila lost a brother there, and Quintanar a son; after working as a carpenter in Aguascalientes, he returned home two years later to put down the banditry being carried on by Villa's former followers, and he hunted down Justo Ávila. He owned a small herd of cattle and bought or resold stock, and administered the hacienda of the Felguereses in Valparaíso. This independent-minded man, who had spent his infancy in the saddle and hit the bull's eye every time he fired a shot,[37] inevitably had his disagreements with any government, even though he himself was on the side of order; pursued by the *Rurales* before the Revolution, he later quarrelled with the Revolutionaries, who tried to disarm him, and he had his fights with the *agraristas*. The latter invited him to a party to celebrate the reconciliation, and confronted him with a bull calf which he was supposed to bring to the ground: at the very moment when he leaned forward in his saddle to catch the animal's tail, he saw his host, the head of the *agraristas* of San Agustín, take aim at him. Without dismounting, he unsheathed his knife and struck the man down. 'How shameful it was for me to go to bring my family out of the dead man's house!' was the old centaur's comment. Imprisoned for murder, he was liberated by the rebels fighting for De la Huerta, and joined their army. After that, he was troubled no longer, and was working on his ranch near Milpillas when he was surprised by the crisis of 1926. Once again he found himself unexpectedly at war, and his fame brought him followers from the entire region as far as the Pacific Ocean, from Huejuquilla, Jalisco, to Acaponeta, Nayarit.[38]

Andrés Salazar, Ezequiel Mendoza, Federico Vázquez, and Valente Acevedo were the leaders of *defensas* or *acordadas*, and their militias constituted the cadres for the insurrection. The Federal army provided only a few men: Colonels Lorenzo Arreola and Ismael Guzmán, who resigned in 1926; Major Juan Silva, who deserted; and Major Felipe Montoya. General Rodolfo Gallegos, an old revolutionary, the right-hand man of Obregón, had resigned because of his hostility to Calles just before he organised the insurrection in Guanajuato in 1926.

The remaining 70 per cent of the leaders were not professional soldiers, although they were perfectly well able to ride a horse and handle fire-arms. Riding and shooting was part of the peasant's way of life in some regions; this perhaps prepared men for war and provided good recruits, but it did not teach them how to organise a campaign or fight a pitched battle. In professional terms, the officers were hardly distinguishable from their soldiers: 92 per cent of them were country-dwellers, and few of them were rich or well-to-do (there were three 'landowners', three hacienda managers, and ten '*rancheros*'), and more than half of them had worked as agricultural labourers or craftsmen.

Certain activities, perhaps, prepared these peasants for the exercise of command: the muleteer who was always on the roads got to know quite a lot of the world; to have been in a position of authority made it easier for a man to exercise command, and one finds many *caporales* (overseers) among the lieutenants and captains. Some municipal presidents were automatically elected to positions of authority by those whom they had administered in peace, but just as many remained private soldiers.

Education was not a significant criterion: only sixteen of the two hundred officers had completed, or even commenced, secondary education, as shown in Table 18.

TABLE 18 *Education and occupation of officers, from second-lieutenant to general, from a sample of 64 officers*

Education	Total	Percentage
Never attended school	36	52·0
Primary education	23	40·0
Secondary education	5	8·0
	64	100·0
Hacienda manager	2	
'Hacendado'	1	12·5
'Ranchero'	5	
'Landed proprietor'	21	33·0
Agricultural labourer	13	
Muleteer	7	
Craftsman	5	54·5
Others	10	
	64	100·0

TABLE 19   *Education and occupation of the soldiers*

Education		Total	Percentage
Never attended school		185	59·5
Primary education		121	38·0
Secondary education		8	2·5
		314	100·0
'Ranchero'		4	1
'Owner-farmer'		93	30
Agricultural worker	'bracero'	66	
Muleteer		44	
Craftsman		39	64
Others		50	
Agraristas		16	5
		312	100

Source: Questionnaires

Age was not an important factor: that of the officers ranged from eighteen to seventy, from Miguel Anguiano, a young commander-in-chief and successor to Dionisio Ochoa (twenty-six years old), to Pedro Quintanar and Justo Ávila. A third of them were under thirty, a third aged from thirty to fifty, and a third over fifty. The young General Acevedo (born in 1900) gave orders to the veteran Don Justo Ávila, and Miguel Anguiano was the superior of Andrés Salazar, who was twice his age and had twenty-five years' campaigning experience.

In the final reckoning, it was the troops who recognised their officers, and military efficiency is not sufficient to explain some of their choices: Manuel Frías, who had a horror of violence and who was denounced by his subordinates as a coward, remained in unquestioned authority throughout the war, even though he had at his side the renowned Juan Carranza, the leader of all the defensive operations in the Sierra. General Jesús Degollado was the first to draw attention, in his memoirs, to his initial ignorance of military matters, yet he was the recognised leader of 7,000 men in the Southern Division, which stretched from Nayarit to Michoacán. A forty-five-year old sacristan of small stature, Trinidad Mora became the leader of Durango, even though at his side there were formidable warriors such as Valente Acevedo and Federico Vázquez. The strength of these leaders lay in their ability to command obedience and to mobilise for their service the talents of such dangerous military figures as Esteban Caro and Vicente Cueva. To impose their authority on men who could easily have become the leaders of revolutionary bands, in emulation of Pancho Villa, and to do this by moral force, discretion and virtue – that was what finally established the position of the leader. The troops looked up to a man who was independent, incorruptible, and unshakeable, and who knew how to behave towards his friends, his relations, his officers, and his soldiers. This gift (the *don de gente*) was indispensable, for the Cristeros were free men who were unmoved by considerations of pay, advancement, or punishment. Being all volunteers, they had little respect for the classic type of leader, the *macho*, quick to kill, 'drunken, party-loving and wenching', and *machismo* was not a factor in the relationship between officers and soldiers.

Among themselves, the officers readily seized opportunities for conflict, but they were kept in check by their superiors and were watched closely by their soldiers, who usually declined to support them in their quarrels or acts of insubordination.[39] Furthermore, they were united by a common background, like the old comrades of earlier campaigns, by family ties (Perfecto Castañón was related to Quintanar, and Toribio Valdés was godfather to the child of Rodolfo Loza Márquez), and, above all, by their fighting spirit. In the West a secret organisation took over, at the highest level, the old role of the Unión Popular; this was the 'U', founded at Morelia by the future Archbishop of Mexico City, Luis Martínez. It was the 'U' that called on Degollado to join the Cristeros, and that mobilised the most staunch militants of the old UP. Its first leader was Anacleto González Flores, and its second, Luis Ibarra; spreading out into Jalisco, Michoacán, Colima, Aguascalientes, and Nayarit, it recruited the principal leaders as members.[40]

The Civilian Base and Logistic Support

The Federal generals unanimously denounced the civilian support as constituting the principal strength of the insurgents; as a result, the army made no distinction between Cristeros and 'tame' peasants, and struck blindly at the entire rural population. In the towns, the Cristeros had the same support, and their urban base supplied, if not combatants, at least a large quantity of war matériel. The urban networks functioned with redoubled efficiency in the towns of the Western Centre, owing to the influx of refugees. The population of León and Guadalajara doubled in the space of three years, and the police and the army ventured only in force into the suburbs or the working-class central districts. There the Unión Popular still had cells and an organisational structure, and collected money and supplies and distributed propaganda; it looked

after the needs of the emissaries or leaders who came in from the rural **areas.** The Cristeros came and went without difficulty; they even sought refuge in the towns when the pressure in the countryside became too strong. José Velasco, the commander-in-chief of Aguascalientes, and Marcos Torres from Colima, carried their audacity to such lengths that they rode into that town and stole, in broad daylight, one hundred army horses from the railway station.[41]

The urban committees collected the war tax and organised voluntary collections, the direct action groups took part in kidnappings, and the workers re-made cartridges in order to achieve the required calibre or re-used empty cases; they manufactured bombs, grenades, and detonators, which the organisation passed on to the combatants. The miners of Concepción del Oro, Coahuila, Angangueo, Michoacan, and Cinco Minas, Jalisco, stole and collected powder, Bickford cord and dynamite; workmen from La Barca derailed the express train in April 1927; and in June 1928 the army shot three workmen caught trying to sabotage the permanent way near Colima. The craftsmen in the villages furnished modest but essential technical assistance: an example of this was the blacksmiths who, at the risk of their lives, shod the horses of the Cristeros.

In the West, when news arrived of the demise of the League, a Directing Committee was set up to co-ordinate the activities of the numerous cells and Women's Brigades that had been founded in the summer of 1927; the committee was soon afterwards named the Western Military Control. Its organisations is shown in Fig. 3.

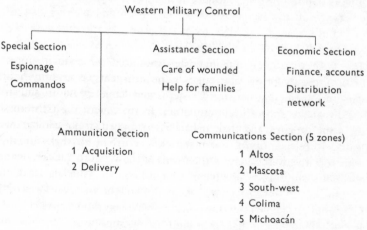

Fig. 3. Organisation of the Western Military Control

The Western Military Control served to co-ordinate the activities of the Unión Popular, the Women's Brigades, and the 'U', that secret organisation which was to become the backbone of the underground movement and which explains its effectiveness in Jalisco, Michoacán, and Colima. In each village there were people responsible for the different activities, from the feeding of the combatants to the burial of the dead, and including intelligence, the billeting of troops passing through, and assistance to the families of the Cristeros. Civilian and military organisation were so neatly dovetailed that each military sector took orders from its civilian administrators: the south-western zone of Guanajuato, incorporated into the Altos, was divided into two military sectors, north and south, corresponding to three civilian centres (Manuel Doblado, Jalpa, and Piedad in Michoacán).[42]

The commissariat hardly posed any problems: 'the people maintained us without our having to worry about it. We concerned ourselves with procuring horses and arms. I never gave a thought to food; there was more than enough, one didn't need to ask for it, the people gave it.'[43]

This food supply was patiently ensured by thousands of *gorderos*, sometimes known as *tlacuileros*, men or women who carried rations for several men in their bags. The same people transmitted messages learnt by heart and letters written on silk paper and slipped beneath the soles of their sandals. Many of them were caught and shot.

The essential problem remained that of ammunition, which was captured from the enemy by laying an ambush for him, or purchased from corrupt officers. In the more urbanised zones the networks were able to function, and get their supplies directly from the national cartridge factory: from the factory this merchandise found its way to the big market of La Merced, hidden among the grain, and there it was picked up by the girls of the Women's Brigades who wore heavy jackets which they filled with cartridges that they then took to the battlefield. Another method consisted of sending boxes by railway, marked as heavy freight: soap, medicines, nails, spare parts. The sender knew nothing about it and the consignee was a 'dummy'.[44] Yet another method was the obtaining of supplies in the United States, but this was almost impossible owing to the attitude of the American authorities: a boat hired and loaded in California was stopped and searched off San Diego, the trafficker having betrayed them to the U.S. guards.[45]

It was, therefore, necessary to get supplies from military arsenals, with the help of numerous acts of complicity[46] and corruption.[47] These collaborators kept the Cristeros informed of troop movements: all correspondence by telephone and telegraph reached General Pedroza, who still keeps in his archive the communications sent by Generals Ávila Camacho, Figueroa, Rodríguez, and Cedillo, to name only the most important, between January and June 1929. With twenty-five telegrams being sent every day, this meant a telegraphic service and a considerable courier organisation. In Encarnación de Díaz the telegraphist, Valeriano Flores, kept Colonel Manuel Ramírez informed; Aurelio Limón did the same at Ayo, Ponciano Rosas at Aguascalientes, and so on. Fr Pedroza even obliged the telegraph company to transmit Cristero communications instead of reserving a monopoly for the army; it was because he obtained satisfactory service that the lines were not cut.

The Women's Brigades

History[48]

The origin of this organisation, predominantly female as far as its troops and officers were concerned, can be traced to two men, Luis Flores González and Joaquín Camacho, a woman, María Goyaz, and a trade union, the Catholic Employees' Union of Guadalajara (UCE), affiliated to the Unión Popular. The Women's Brigades achieved in an exemplary manner the synthesis of all the logistical problems and ensured the essential co-operation of the civilians. This was a society to promote morality, the members of which included shop girls, office workers and seamstresses; it recruited from the middle class and among the people, and organised adult education courses. From 1922 onwards, Luis Flores González spoke of the day when women would have to take up arms, for the slaughter in front of the church of San Francisco led him to comment 'be prepared, very difficult times are coming'. The young María Goyaz had a source of support, as the daughter of Francisco Goyaz, the manager of the combative newspaper *El Cruzado*, edited by Agustín Yáñez.[49] Anacleto González Flores, the 'Maestro', the head of the Unión Popular, had mobilised the women after 1925 in his civic campaign, and they had been the staunchest supporters of the boycott; for them this period had been exciting and joyful, but after the fight in the Sanctuary in August 1926, the boycott was relegated to second place, and some people began to prepare for war. At the beginning of 1927, Anacleto González chose some members of the UCE to organise support for the Cristeros, and after his death, Luis Flores put this idea into practice.

On 21 June 1927, the first Women's Brigade was founded at Zapopan. It consisted of sixteen young women: Cesarea García, Narcisa Delgado, Elodia Delgado, María Bernal, Lola Bernal, María Saldaña, Trinidad Hernández, Enriqueta Landázuri, Nacha Elizondo, Filomena Castellón, Rita Quirarte, Joaquina Vázquez, Sara Flores Arias, Juana González, Josefina Arana, and Carmen Sandoval. There was also one man, Refugio Ramírez. A few days later the Brigade had 135 members, all from the UCE, and according to the records the seventeen founders soon grew to 17,000. As a military organisation for the purpose of collecting money, supplying the combatants, providing them with ammunition, intelligence, and channels of communication, the Women's Brigades, a clandestine organisation, imposed on their members an oath of obedience and secrecy.[50]

At the same time Joaquín Camacho, the director of a Catholic school, founded a similar society, the members of which were teachers; here too, secrecy and organisation in cells was the rule; the two groups soon amalgamated, recognising the authority of Don Luis Flores and later, after his death, of María Goyaz (alias Celia Gómez, alias, Celia Ortiz). The efficiency of the organisation was so remarkable that the Government did not get wind of its existence until the spring of 1929. During this period the organisation spread throughout the country: on 7 January 1928 the first brigade in the Federal District was founded by María Goyaz. This caused discontent among the women of Guadalajara, who resented seeing their general establish herself in Mexico City, although it was, nevertheless, easier to acquire ammunition. In March 1928, the Women's Brigades had 10,000 militant members. The only real problem faced by the Women's Brigades was the hostility of the League.[51] Its representative, Antonio Ruiz y Rueda, could not resist the temptation to try to bring them under his control, as they were acquiring money and ammunition. The enemies of the Brigades were the same people who had clashed with Anacleto González Flores and later with Gorostieta: Frs Leobardo Fernández, Ramón Martínez Silva, and Iglesias (all three Jesuits), and Frs P. J. Mendoza and J. Hipólito Alba in Guadalajara. These priests kept the dossier on the Brigades which prompted Rome's decision on the matter and obliged Mgr Orozco to rescind the oath of secrecy on 7 December 1928. However, Antonio Ruiz y Rueda[52] soon attracted the hostility of the Cristeros of the Western zone and was forced to retreat, but Fr Leobardo Fernández, SJ, continued his work.

In this affair, the League finally discredited itself in the eyes of the Cristeros and of Gorostieta, who had nothing but praise for the services of General 'Julia Ortiz' (Carmen Macías); he exclaimed angrily: 'These were the sources of supply which I have organised for each regiment to acquire its ammunition, and we were all going under in the course of the last battle which you have had with the Women's Brigades.'[53] And General Manuel Michel wrote in consternation: 'I repeat that the Devil has us cornered in this matter and it is there that he is best able to win ... politics troubles people, and this can only disturb matters and slow up the work.'[54]

Obliged to abolish the oath of secrecy, the Women's Brigades went through the most difficult period of their existence. The commander-in-chief invited all the militants 'to take up their duties again in accordance with standing orders, but taking no notice henceforth of the oath sworn. Therefore, the General Staff leaves to each of the sisters the responsibility for observing the discretion required by their business and their commitments.'[55]

Secrecy was so well preserved within the organisation that the rank-and-file members and even those higher up knew nothing of the difficulties with the League; fortunately they had the consolation of support from a Dominican, Fr Mariano Navarro, who explained to them that the pronouncement 'it is not fitting' by Rome was not equivalent to a condemnation;[56] this consolation was eminently necessary at a moment when the police, for the first time, were beginning to discover the channels by which the ammunition was delivered from Mexico City to Guadalajara. Among the 25,000 members of the Women's Brigades, there was not a single recorded defection, and, despite the crisis, the Government did not make the first mass arrests until the end of March 1929.[57]

The first police raid was on 12 March, at Guadalajara railway station, and for the first time the police discovered the system of using vests to transport ammunition; two days later the other end of the conduit was discovered in Mexico City, and on the 16 March arrests were made at Acaponeta and Tepic, Nayarit. On 22 March a second network was discovered at Guadalajara, and on 1 April a third network at Sayula; the police followed the trial to Mexico City, where twelve women were arrested. On 3 April a cell in Guadalajara was discovered, on 11 April the secret police broke up an organisation in Tacubaya, Federal District, and on the thirteenth another one in Mexico City; on 18 April at Coyoacán, Federal District, and on 8 May at Yurécuaro and La Piedad arrests were made; the wife of the Cristero General Degollado was arrested on the thirteenth at Guadalajara. Whereas between 1 January and 3 April the police[58] had arrested only twenty-seven girls, between 4 April and 15 May they arrested 129; on 9 June the Government scored a success by capturing María de la Luz Laraza de Uribe, whose *nom de guerre* was Tesia Richaud, the General of the Guadalajara Division, the only senior officer to be captured during the three years of the war.[59] These pinpricks never endangered the organisation as a whole, which continued until the end to provide effective assistance to the Cristeros.[60]

The Organisation of the Brigades

The organisation of a brigade, which in theory consisted of 650 women, was military: at the head of each brigade there was a colonel, assisted by a lieutenant-colonel and five majors, each having under her command captains, lieutenants, and sergeants. The organisational structure, designed by Luis Flores, is shown in Fig. 4.[61]

Each detachment (*destacamento*) of thirty women, commanded by a lieutenant, was divided into five sections, responsible for war, liaison, finance, intelligence, and welfare. (Welfare was in practice confined to nursing work and the organisation of small field hospitals, for the food supply of the Cristeros and their families was organised by the Unión Popular).

Two divisions, the Western Division (Guadalajara) and the Centre Division (Mexico City), were composed of eighteen and eight complete brigades respectively. The generals, all of whom came from Jalisco, were María Goyaz, who commanded first the Western and later the Centre Division; Sara Flores Arias, who succeeded her at Guadalajara and died as a result of the bomb explosion;[62] Carmen Macías, who was replaced for reasons of health by Francisca Chávez; and finally María de la Luz Laraza de Uribe.[63]

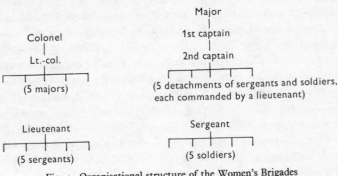

Fig. 4. Organisational structure of the Women's Brigades

To complete the organisation, there were medical brigades, under the command of Dr Rigoberto Rincón Fregoso, and Direct Action groups commanded by Andrés Nuño and Josefina de Alba. Carmen Macías and C. Pérez were responsible for propaganda and organisation, Amalia Camacho for ammunition, Josefina de Alba for military operations, while Fr Ayala ('Don Wences'), the parish priest of Puerto Vallarta, in addition to carrying out dangerous tasks concerned with espionage and ammunition supply, was responsible for maintaining contacts with the Unión Popular.

In addition to the twenty-six complete brigades, there were thirty others composed of between 100 and 250 women, which gives a total of 25,000 militants; there were five complete brigades in the one city of Guadalajara, and these organised the brigades in Jalisco, Colima, Aguascalientes, south Michoacán, Zacatecas, Sinaloa, Durango, Nayarit, and San Luis Potosí. In Jalisco, there were complete brigades in Zapotlán, Atotonilco, Tepatitlán, Ameca, Ocotlán, Tonala, and Arandas; in addition, the organisation controlled fifty-four villages, which each submitted a monthly report, besides all the hamlets. Each Cristero regiment was made the responsibility, as regards supply, of one leader of the Women's Brigades: Lola Castillo supplied Degollado; Josefina de Alba, Arreola; Elodia Delgado, Lauro Rocha; Filomena Ortiz, Esteban Caro; Elpidia Rubio, Luis Ibarra; and so on. In all the villages and hamlets there was a detachment or a company; the Guadalajara to Mexico City road was covered as far as San Juan del Río by a continuous network. In Colima, the Women's Brigades organised from Guadalajara extended their activities to San Jerónimo (Cuauhtémoc, Comalá, Tecomán, and Manzanillo), under the command of Francisca Quintero, Petra Rodríguez, and María Ortega.[64] Amalia Castel, Viviana Aguilar, and Salomé Galindo managed the hospital in the volcanic region of Colima. The Women's Brigades were strong principally in the West, in Mexico City, and along the road between Guadalajara and Mexico City, but they also established themselves in Michoacán, at Cotija, Sahuayo, Morelia, and Angangueo,[65] and in Guanajuato, Zacatecas, and Oaxaca in 1929.

Who were these young women who, in such great numbers, worked under the nose of the army and the police, with such notable efficiency and dedication? Young and unmarried for the most part, aged between fifteen and twenty-five, and led by generals none of whom was over thirty, they organised auxiliary groups[66] which included older women, married women, and even children.[67]

They were recruited from all social classes, though the great majority came from the proletariat: girls from the working-class districts of the cities, and peasant girls from the rural areas. Although originally the leaders were drawn from the lower middle class (the UCE in Guadalajara) and from girls from the Catholic schools,[68] which was not necessarily an indication of social origin, appointment to officer rank was swiftly achieved by the daughters of the people; the proportion (90 per cent) accurately reflected the background of the troops. Even in the case of the generals, the social and occupational background was humble: they were typists, like María de la Luz Laraza de Uribe or junior employees like María Goyaz.[69]

Activities of the Women's Brigades

The women's brigades were able to benefit from a certain amount of complicity in Government circles: a woman of Calles's family lent her house to serve as an entrepôt for ammunition in Mexico City, and the story has been told of the Federal officer who used his cloak to hide the cartridges that had fallen from a suitcase which was too old and too heavily loaded.[70] However, their activities were so essential to the Cristeros and so prejudicial to the Government that it is impossible to believe that the police and military apparatus was generally indulgent. It was nothing more nor less than an organisation which for two years mobilised thousands of women day and night to run the shuttle service between the cities and the battlefields, for, from the state capitals, the Women's Brigades conveyed the ammunition right to the Cristeros: they went out of the towns, hiding the ammunition in coal, cement, or maize lorries. Then, when the Cristeros could not get into the village concerned, it was necessary to go out to meet them, with pack animals, baskets, or the famous vests. Towards the end of the war, the brigades were working on a big scale, sending cases of ammunition from Mexico City by train, with the complicity of certain of the railway employees, disguising the shipments as heavy freight. In 1929 Carmen Macías was sent to the United States, following a route of the organisation by way of Mazatlán and Nogales as far as San Francisco; she collected $7,000 among the Mexicans living in California for the purchase of ammunition, but she cancelled her order on hearing the news of the suspension of hostilities.

Besides conveying material, the girls of the brigades also conveyed the Cristeros themselves: they ensured the safety and the movements of the senior officers obliged to come into the towns or to travel; it was they who made it possible for Degollado to come to Guadalajara in 1929, and they organised his meeting with Gorostieta. In addition, some of them who possessed considerably more scientific knowledge than the peasants worked as artificers and instructors, teaching the Cristeros to manufacture explosives, blow up trains, and handle batteries and detonators.[71]

The brigades took their military mission extremely seriously, and did not hesitate to have recourse to violence, kidnapping, and executions in order to obtain ransoms, protect the combatants, and deal with spies. Using every means at their disposal, they even organised dances in the villages so as to win the confidence of the officers, allay their suspicions, and obtain information.[72] These latter-day Judiths led by Josefina de Alba organised, with the help of Andrés Nuño, the Direct Action group of the Women's Brigades, and distinguished themselves by killing with a knife a schismatic priest, Felipe Pérez, who was a Government spy.

The care of the wounded hidden in the villages or towns was the responsibility of the brigades, working under the direction, in this sphere, of Dr Rigoberto Rincón Fregoso,[73] and they also managed the rudimentary field hospitals in the Altos, Colima and south Jalisco, and the undergound hospital in Guadalajara.[74]

The brigades also concerned themselves with the food supplies of the Cristeros, but in this sphere they were merely assisting, and at times coordinating, the efforts of all the peasants who were relatives and friends of the Cristeros, who supplied the food directly, without the intervention of the brigades. Together with the UP they published propaganda and ran the underground press set up near Zapopán, and later near Tlaquepaque;[75] also with the UP they partially ensured the political and military courier system of the Cristeros,[76] and assisted with their intelligence network.

A woman was never left for long working in the same place and the same branch of activity, once she achieved a certain degree of responsibility; the senior officers continually changed their identity and residence. The ammunition carriers made at least one trip every three weeks, and the record of Sebastiana Acuña, the widow of Vázques, is typical: in November 1927 she placed herself under the command of Lauro Rocha and Miguel Gómez Loza; from November 1927 to April 1928 she made three trips to Mexico City, one to Guadalajara, and numerous trips to the villages; she worked mainly as an ammunition purveyor but also as a nurse.[77] All the women were filled with passionate fervour for the cause: 'I was overcome with joy. That willingness with which everybody worked! That silence that they all kept!'[78]

CHAPTER 8

Cristero Government

Cristero Democracy

The mass uprising of January 1927, a resort to arms that was more symbolic than real, was a manifestation of an archaic conception of democracy, because it asserted a belief in popular suffrage and the immediate virtues of the unanimous presence of the people: it was not necessary to be armed; it was a question of demanding one's rights by the mere assertion of the multitude. This insurrection, accepted as a necessary evil by Anacleto González Flores, even though he resented it as a relapse for which the Government was responsible, was carried out in an atmosphere of primitive social rebellion, the League being either absent or ineffectual, and all 'reasonable' people (*gente de razón*) being certain of the victory of the state, renouncing the fight and leaving the peasants to fend for themselves.

What were the people, as a disorganised crowd and unarmed, trying to do? The abolition of the municipal councils and their replacement by authorities elected on the spot, by acclamation, was a proclamation of the downfall of the Government: in April 1927 Coalcomán informed the Federal Government that the canton no longer recognised its authority and was proclaiming its independence, since the Federal pact had been broken unilaterally.

From the first day, the insurgents made clear their desire to give themselves a just government; this aspiration to self-government, to village democracy, was strengthened by military necessity and took the form, wherever possible, of a parallel government, and sometimes of a unique government, organised in autonomous republics from which the Federal army had been expelled. The case of Zacatecas will be studied in detail because, in addition to being exemplary, it also has the advantage of benefitting from a historical accident: the civilian and military archives of the Cristeros have been preserved almost intact by one of the first Cristeros, Aurelio Acevedo, commanding officer of the Valparaíso Regiment, and later a general and acting Governor of Zacatecas.[1] 'We were not just going to take part in a brawl, we were going to fight in defence of our liberty, it was the opposite of a revolution, the opposite of the chaos of Carranza's movement. We had to organise ourselves properly,' said Acevedo. It was necessary to raise taxes legally so as not to have to live at the expense of the inhabitants, and for this purpose the Cristeros had to constitute a government and assume responsibility for protection, justice, and even education. Thus, as soon as the Cristeros of this region, and of the Western Centre in general, controlled a village, they organised it efficiently.

Almost at once the five regiments of the Quintanar Brigade found themselves in control of a vast region extending over nine municipalities: Chalchihuites, Fresnillo, Monte Escobedo, Susticacán, Tepetongo, and Valparaíso, Zacatecas; there were 100,000 inhabitants, spread over an area equivalent to that of the states of Colima, Aguascalientes, Morelos, and Tlaxcala combined. In this 'liberated' territory the capital was established at Huejuquilla, a township of 6,000 inhabitants, well-situated strategically, at the entrance to the mountain region and close to the ravines. The Federal army was never able to maintain a garrison there, so that save for a few days the place remained in the hands of the Cristeros for three years. Their control was so complete that Acevedo was able to travel alone from Laguna Grande to Huejuquilla and the Cristeros could live in the villages, moving out only at night to avoid ambushes. After the raids of the Federal army, the entire population went into hiding in the ravines of San Juan.

Pedro Quintanar was the man whose prestige and authority made possible the success of the organisation, which was the work of Vicente Viramontes and Aurelio Acevedo, after the visit of Gorostieta in the winter of 1927. Acevedo organised what was really a constituent congress at Mezquitic in May 1928:[2] this was attended by the mayors, the judges, their secretaries, and the military commanders (two generals and five colonels); the ten priests who were living in the zone under the protection of the Cristeros were invited as observers.

The tone was set by a speech of Acevedo's that attacked the military commanders: in order to avoid the repetition of what had happened only too often, it was necessary to remove the villages immediately from the control of the Cristero military commanders and establish democratically elected civilian authorities, chosen for their competence and honesty. Finally, Acevedo appealed to the members of this constituent assembly to give the civilian authorities the means to ensure that their orders were obeyed, even by the military men. The mayor of Monte Escobedo then demanded that the administrative authorities should have control over the local militias, to use them for law enforcement and the administration of justice, so that soldiers who committed crimes should not go unpunished. A committee was appointed, consisting of five members elected by secret ballot (a priest, a civilian, a judge, a mayor, and a military commander), and it drew up a General Ordinance, which contained seven chapters and fifty-four articles.[3] The military were to be subject to civilian justice, the administrative authorities were to be autonomous, but without there being a separation of powers, which would have been dangerous in time of war. The regional militias, organised on a military basis, were given a dual function (Article 37): they had military responsibilities during a campaign, and acted as police at other times, taking their orders from the military commanders in the first case and from the mayors in the second. It is apparent from the deliberations at the Congress of Mezquitic that the Cristeros considered themselves to be free and sovereign, and, with a remarkable confidence in the future, were laying the foundations of a reconstruction of the nation in which they were sure that they would play a part.

Justice

This was administered by the *Juez menor* and the justices of the peace appointed in each municipality, and by the military commander, with the right of appeal to the *Juez de letras* in Huejuquilla. The judges succeeded in countering the pressure exerted by the military commanders, who wanted to protect their men, and their archives, which were extremely well kept, containing details of a great number of civil and criminal proceedings: the most frequent crimes were the theft of cattle and maize,[4] rape,[5] and deliberate or accidental homicide.[6] There was one case of adultery.[6]

Since it was not really possible to imprison those found guilty, they were subject to fines, which in the case of murderers were accompanied by floggings. Jesús de la Torre, condemned for murder, was obliged to pay 500 pesos to the mother of the victim; this represented a quarter of his capital. Military justice was extremely severe: one soldier who had killed a comrade-in-arms was tried, condemned, and executed.[7] Desertion and treason, which were rare, were punished with death, as were real rapes, as opposed to traditional abductions with the consent of the victim.[8]

On 27 October 1927 and 7 March 1928, two Government supporters, Jesús Franco and José Nava, were shot for 'defaming the Fathers'. 'Murmurers' such as these were at first punished by a series of fines; instead of being executed, at the fourth repetition of the offence they were given a certain time to seek refuge abroad.[9]

Pedro Quintanar was both the secular arm and the military judge. The colonels exercised the same dual function in their regiments, and were able to take measures outside the strictly military sphere. Thus Aurelio Acevedo obliged the *hacendados* of San Juan Capistrán to deliver up their manager, who was accused of rape, ill-treatment of the workers, and dishonesty: he had attributed to the Cristeros imaginary acts of requisition, which had allowed him to make lucrative profits.[10]

Civil Government

The municipal authorities, with the support of the militias, fulfilled their functions without trouble. The register of births, marriages, and deaths, the collection of taxes, the postal service, the education of children, the administration of property left untenanted or confiscated from the enemy, were their responsibility, in addition to the campaign against gambling, prostitution, concubinage, adultery, public entertainments, and sale of alcohol (the two latter activities were discouraged for political and military reasons).

These authorities collected ordinary municipal taxes, state taxes, Federal taxes and the profits from the management of confiscated property. Fifty per cent of the revenues were ear-marked for the army, 25 per cent for regional defence, and 25 per cent for the municipality.[11] The municipalities were responsible for the functioning of the schools, which they maintained even in the small hamlets – for example, at Tanques de Santa Teresita, where fifteen families had sixty children of school age; there the school consisted of two women teachers who wrote on a blackboard set up under the trees. Parents who did not send their children to school received a warning, and, if they still failed to send them, they were punished.[12]

In March 1928 Acevedo had appointed an official responsible for establishing schools. He was also the inspector-general of all the schools financed by heads of families, who took up a collection to pay the teachers. The chief obstacle was not the inertia of the parents, who were swiftly convinced by the passion for education that inspired these men, who had often taught themselves to read and regretted that they had not been

141

able to go to school; the principal opposition came from the managers of the haciendas.[13]

At the end of 1927, the municipality of Valparaíso alone had nineteen schools containing 600 children of both sexes, and two years later these numbers had doubled; in June 1929 the municipality of Huejuquilla had thirty-six schools, dispersed in the most remote *ranchos*; Tenzompa, Llanos, Soledad, Puesta de Lagos, Paisanos, San Nicolás, Sauces, Rancho de Abajo, Adoves, Tecolotes, Salitres, Mesa de Piedra, Muralla, and others.

'The spirit of the movement of Liberation being thoroughly moral, which essentially distinguishes it from previous movements', military and civilian authorities both strove zealously to establish peace and morality. For both military and moral reasons, 'we did not allow scandals involving women. A man who was not properly married either had to get married according to the law, or separate, receiving guarantees, or he was sent to prison [in the Bolaños ravine].'[14] As a result of the religious fervour which reigned in this period, the habitual prostitutes were the first to refuse to sell their charms, and they gave considerably less trouble to the authorities than the traffickers in alcohol or the owners of cabarets.[15] Drink and gambling, which were the origin of much of the violence in peacetime, and an inadmissible cause of social disintegration at all times, were severely repressed during the war. Fiestas were themselves forbidden, after the period of mourning commenced in August 1926; the Cristeros had nothing against music, far from it, but, in addition to the symbolic silence, one had to remember that 'where there was music, there was wine, and the enemy might surprise us when we were drunk'.[16] The alcohol which Acevedo was sent to fetch, as a muleteer, as far as Tequila, he confiscated from the shops where he knew it was to be found and poured it out on the ground.

During this period of crisis and economic, social, and religious disarray, the Cristeros were struggling against the degradation of social mores which had taken place since 1910 – against wine, gambling, and 'scandals involving women', because they always meant conflict, violence, and the death of someone within a camp that should be united against the real enemy, for these were the traditional scourges of the rural world, and their eradication meant a step towards perfection, the preparation of the Kingdom. When Acevedo protested against the adjective 'revolutionary' being applied to him, and asserted that the movement was the exact 'opposite of a revolution', he was expressing that desire for the reconstruction of a society which would be better than the previous one and incomparably superior to the prevailing chaos. The difficulties of day-to-day existence, which had multiplied since 1910, the unleashing of official and private violence, the disappearance of peace and of that minimum of justice which made the age of Porfirio Díaz seem, in retrospect, like a Golden Age, the decay of certain institutions, banditry, insecurity, and the economic crisis – all these factors had given the peasants a very definite experience of social disintegration; and in consequence the Cristeros were trying to re-establish the relations of neighbourliness, and to restore to their honoured place the ancient social values. It is in this light that one must interpret the obligation to marry, the struggle against adultery, and the condemnation of concubinage. It was not a reaction against social change, for at that time there was no such change – it was purely negative, a process of disintegration and aggravation. The system of government adopted by the Cristeros was dictated, on the one hand, by the fact that theirs was a popular army living at union with the people, and still less capable of ill-treating it because it was building the Kingdom of Christ, and, on the other hand, it was a reaction against the social lawlessness which was becoming the rule. It was neither conservatism nor revolution but reform, at a time when the ancient traditional models of behaviour were in crisis, without others having arisen to take their place.[17] The Cristero solution consisted in solidly re-establishing the rural world on its family and religious bases, profiting from the mood of mystic exaltation which makes possible a new morality and a new perfection; it restored, among the peasants, the hope of a brilliant future for the country.

Economic Organisation

All matters concerning the economy, supplies, finance, and taxes might just as well be studied in the chapter on the Cristero army, because one cannot draw a sharp distinction between the civilian and the military spheres, between peace and war, between combatants and non-combatants. These two spheres have been separated merely for convenience of analysis: it has already been observed that the municipalities raised the taxes and remitted 50 per cent of the proceeds to the regiments and ear-marked 25 per cent for regional defence. The economic burden of the war was very heavy, and it was this that influenced all the economic decisions of the government.[18]

It is obvious from a study of the archives that it was the municipal administration that obtained the meagre resources which made it possible to finance, albeit inadequately, the war: taxes (on rural and urban properties, the shoeing of horses, slaughterhouses, markets), the revenue from fines, ransoms, and the Federal contribution, the extraordinary contribution (referred to as the 'war tax'), loans, the revenue from the (carefully recorded) use of maize taken from the haciendas and the enemy, bail payments for safe-conduct, and the special fine payable by a soldier who left the army and returned to civilian life. Military finances are discussed elsewhere in this work, but it is worth bearing in mind that resources were very limited (between 300 and 600 pesos per year, which came from municipal taxes, half of which went to the army), and this provoked serious problems for the Cristero commanders, who sometimes came into conflict over this matter.

The authorities were responsible above all, for, directing the economic life of the region, to ensure the supply of both combatants and civilians, organise stocks to offset the effects of the *reconcentración*, plan agricultural tasks, supervise commerce to avoid squandering and speculation, and resist the scorched-earth policy put into practice by the army. It was necessary to improvise in order to remedy the crisis in the supply of essentials, punish economic crimes, control commerce and prices, adapt the system to the autarchy imposed by the war, remedy the destitution of the people, and supply the needs of the Cristeros. The easiest measures to take were those against squandering: 'There exists in the hacienda of San Juan this serious evil for the Movement of Liberation: the wastage of the few goods that remain in the hacienda ... The followers of Martínez alone killed two hundred head of cattle. Remember that most of the meat, hides, etc., are wasted by the defenders.'[19]

As late as June 1929, General Quintanar severely reprimanded Florencio Estrada and his men for taking horses from the hacienda, because they were farm animals and quite useless for war, and they were obliged to abandon them two or three days later in a piteous condition. He ordered them to bring the horses back, as well as those which they had managed to commandeer elsewhere, and he forbade the slaughter of cattle except when it had been captured from the enemy, 'because you are constantly rounding it up to sell it'. Finally, he too denounced the squandering of meat and hides.[20]

It was difficult to put an end to this confused situation, because the excessive consumption denounced by Fr Arroyo was caused by a psychological reaction: it was difficult to resist the temptation to carouse when the opportunity presented itself, because tomorrow the enemy might appear and burn what had been carefully saved.

Hunger, which was always present, was a bad counsellor, and there was above all an element of revenge in people's behaviour: squandering affected primarily the possessions of the haciendas – for example, of those fourteen vast properties which covered almost the total area of the municipal district of Valparaíso. There was an element of revenge, too, in that over-consumption of meat which was denounced in all the documents. It was the act of people who had eaten very little meat in their lives, at a time when there seemed to be an abundance of cattle because the hacienda managers did not dare to say anything to peasants who were armed and who were also masters of the local government. The cattle remained where they were, because the Cristeros forbade them to be driven away (so that the Federal troops could not have them), while the Federals were carrying out an economic blockade of the products of the region. Finally, cattle were captured in military operations.

The basic problem was that of maize: 'Since two years' harvests have been lost, and one assumes that the third year's will also be lost, I take the liberty of requesting your headquarters . . . to order that the important help we have in the region – the water from the hacienda dams – is not lost.'[21] Water was requisitioned, as was the fallow land of the big landowners.[22] The military commanders also requisitioned the lands which the *agraristas* had abandoned and those of the Cristeros' wealthy enemies, the proprietors and merchants of Mezquitic, who had taken refuge in Jérez.[23]

Ploughing, sowing, and harvesting were carried out by a mobilisation of the entire labour force, both civilian and military:

In view of the fact that in most of our territory there is a shortage of workmen to do the sowing, our only source of wealth and of the essentials of life, we have thought it prudent and necessary to order that for the present agricultural year, all males above the age of 12 are to help with the sowing . . . and anyone of this age who does not work at the sowing during the next rainy season is to pay a fine of 100 pesos.

This decree was strictly enforced.[24] The military organisation was used for agricultural activities, and the regiments were transformed into gangs of ploughmen, sowers, reapers, and muleteers; reaping had to be done quickly, to beat the Federal troops, who were anxious to lift the maize crop or, when they did not succeed in doing that, to burn the crop where it stood.

The harvested maize was distributed under the supervision of the authorities among the soldiers, their families, the agricultural workers, and the refugees. Such a policy, although it was extremely pleasing to Acevedo and the men of the Catholic trade union who in 1923–4 had dreamed of carrying out an agrarian reform in their own way, was very unpopular with the haciendas, which were seriously affected by this system of mobilisation.

It was necessary to prevent speculation in maize, beginning with the production of the small and medium-size proprietors, which was immediately absorbed by the money-lenders. The municipal authorities supervised the markets, and the military authorities controlled all the transport and transactions in the hamlets and on the farms; furthermore, the grain corresponding to the ecclesiastical tithe was used as a reserve to help the most needy and to lower the price.[25]

From June 1928 onwards, the Cristero government exercised a strict control over the trade in maize,[26] reinforced by sanctions. To the rich, such a policy was scandalous, and after the war they were the first to persecute those whom they never imagined would set aside their traditional respect for the social hierarchy and their resignation to their material lot and question the right of the rich to engage in their dealings and to speak as masters. What had happened was that war, a rough teacher, had given the Cristeros a lesson in political sociology: not only was it the poor alone who died for Christ the King, and not only did the rich not help them with their money, but they even increased their fortunes, actually eating up the people. 'Those who are making money are our enemies, the maize dealers, and that is not what we want, it is not the time to be making money and sucking the blood of the people who are sacrificing themselves for the Cause of God.'[27]

In Jalisco a similar system of government existed in the regions where the Cristeros were in full military control; it was organised in the Altos by the Civil Governor, Miguel Gómez Loza, and later, after his death, was put under the overall supervision of General Gorostieta, and in the rest of the state by Generals Degollado and Manuel Michel. In Colima, government was supervised by Dionisio Ochoa, Miguel Anguiano, and Andrés Salazar. In the Coalcomán region, Michoacán, and the Sierra Gorda, it was under the supervision of Manuel Frías, who was more competent in peaceful than in warlike activities; everywhere, there existed municipal governments, a system of justice and tax collection, schools, and the necessary control of the economy.[28]

The territory of Coalcomán, resembled a real autonomous republic; it had proclaimed its secession in April 1927, officially informing the Government that it had ceased to recognise it. Although Coalcomán was 'liberated' territory, carrying on a war along a static frontier marked by strong-points, and had effectively thrown back major attempts at re-conquest, yet here life continued somewhat as normal, because only the authorities had been changed and the people in arms followed their occupations in accordance with the agricultural calendar. The rich departed and did not return until peace was concluded, and there was no economic problem in this region, where for so long the inhabitants had been accustomed to living on local resources. Only once or twice a year, on the occasion of the fair at Peribán, there would go out from Coalcomán droves of mules laden with cheeses or hides for sale. Government presented absolutely no problems: policing was carried out and justice administered by the same people who had been in office before 1927, and in some instances since 1910, such as that of Ezequiel Mendoza Barragán, leader of a band at the age of eighteen, in the time of Porfirio Díaz.[29] Above all these authorities, there stood as arbiter the tutelary figure of the priest, Fr José María Martínez, who had been the real governor of the entire region since before the war.

In the neighbouring state of Colima, which was in close communication with Coalcomán and south Jalisco, there was also a priest in the role of counsellor, and he was a real *éminence grise* behind the military commanders: Fr Enrique de Jesús Ochoa, brother of the first head of the state, Dionisio Ochoa. Because of the nature of the war, it was not possible to establish a real civil government; both the civil and the military organisations were fully occupied with the extremely harsh war that was, for three years, the fate of the people of Colima. As at Coalcomán or in Zacatecas, the Cristeros were with their families, but instead of being able to stay with them in their villages, they had to take them with them up into the volcanic region. Four regiments, divided into squadrons, lived thus in the country with their families; the military camps, fortified with trenches and barbed wire, were on lower ground, while the families lived further up. Divided into small groups (of between twenty-five and seventy men), the Cristeros were able to live by picking wild fruit, hunting birds and animals, and by animal husbandry and a nomadic agriculture. For such people, there was no life other than the war and no government save that of the colonels and the general. Elsewhere in the state, an organisation similar to that of Zacatecas could be established, notably in the municipal district of Minatitlán, where the Cristero municipal authorities functioned normally.[30]

In the other states there did not exist, as in the volcanic region of Colima, an entire society living in the *maquis*, with its bishops, its priests, and its families. One finds either the liberated territory, the autonomous republic (as in Zacatecas or Michoacán), which for the three months of the spring of 1929 extended to the whole of the Western Centre, or an insurrectionary government parallel to the organisation of the state.

In south Jalisco, at the foot of the volcanoes of Colima, General Manuel Michel was the embodiment of both military and civilian authority, because he commanded a regiment and at the same time administered a sector.[31] His archives[22] reflect his responsibilities, which included everything from spiritual problems (finding a priest to act as chaplain to the soldiers) to arbitration in cases of concubinage or inheritance, in addition to all the administrative, economic, and military tasks. The experience of Aurelio Acevedo was similar, though on a smaller scale.

Manuel Michel was well known and highly esteemed in the region of Zapotitlán, where he had rented a big *rancho* which he worked with the help of twenty-five agricultural labourers. He had no difficulty in raising a regiment of 500 men and then organising the entire region. In this poverty-stricken area the General arranged for continual activities for everybody: when the soldiers were not campaigning, they received military and civic instruction during their leisure hours, and the rest of the time they helped the civilians in labour in the fields and themselves grew maize, haricot beans, and vegetables on lands cleared for that purpose or on the fallow lands of the haciendas distributed by Manuel Michel in the same way as in Zacatecas. The General imposed this system even on the *agrarista* communities, protecting them from the Government and from other Cristero groups.[33] 'All the inhabitants hereby apply in writing to you and your respectable person to complain of the abuses committed by A. Contreras and F. Cobián [former *agrarista* leaders who had become Cristeros] and to beg you to take action against them.'[24]

Having installed the judicial authorities, and having appointed the mayors and ratified the traditional authorities of the Indian communities, which were numerous in the region and which supported the Cristeros, Michel received the complaints of the people as supreme justiciar and took swift and severe action against wrong-doers.[35] This severity, which contributed to his popularity, extended to social behaviour and economic matters: he did not tolerate drinking, gambling, or prostitution, and insisted on his troops saying the Rosary every day.[36] It was unnecessary to insist on the Rosary, which was so dear to those soldiers, but it was more difficult to put a stop to the habit of drinking.

Manuel Michel displayed the same energy and efficiency in the agricultural sphere, and he soon brought the entire zone under exploitation, as though it were one vast hacienda. He insisted on an absolute respect for private property, and preferred 'to die or hunger rather than not pay' for what he needed,[37] but it did not take him long to realise that the rich were more guilty than men driven by necessity. Having in vain requested the rich to give their full co-operation, and having sent them a warning, he took action, requisitioning a percentage of the harvests of the haciendas, deemed to be the equivalent of the sums he claimed, and brought the fallow lands under cultivation.[38] All the small and middle-sized proprietors had, either willingly or forcibly, to deliver part of their harvest to the Cristero authorities, and the mayors were responsible for deciding the amounts of these contributions in kind and then for delivering the cereals and haricot beans to the military authorities.[39] This was done out of necessity, to compensate for the losses that the civilians had suffered as a result of the resettlement measures, since the proprietors had been spared by the Federal troops. At harvest-time, Michel mobilised all his followers so as to get it done quickly: 'with your men go and get maize from the *ranchos* of Platanar, El Guallavo and San Miguel, and get beans too. Make the civilians load and drive the donkeys, and you protect them with all your men.'[40]

With his knowledge of agriculture and experience as a farmer, Michel was able to give free rein to his talents, co-ordinating the production of the haciendas of several municipal districts, and encouraging the cultivation of maize and stockraising everywhere else:

I have sent workers to the land which you are managing [he wrote to one farm-manager], so that they can work there after the next rainy season, and I am informing you of this so that you do not put any obstacle in their way, and as regards payment, if we are left in peace to harvest your products, we will without fail pay you what we owe.[41]

This enforced agricultural activity was prompted by the desire to 'work on the largest possible scale in the zone controlled by the Movement of Liberation, in order to improve the situation of the poorer class'. Michel sent his representatives as far as Minatitlán, Camotlán, and Cedros to hire a sufficient number of animals for ploughing, always with the order that they should 'protect the interest of the contracting parties'. The relevant circular ended with a threat: 'I do not think that the owners will be guilty of obstinacy and selfishness.'[42]

Michel, in order to diversify these economic activities and obtain money by the scale of the products, encouraged an increase in the production of coffee, pimento, and sugar-cane, supervising the refining of sugar and the distillation of alcohol, making sure that the hides of slaughtered cattle were properly tanned, establishing workshops to process leather, fibres, iron, and wood, planting tobacco so that his troops would have something to smoke, and keeping accurate accounts of all the cereals harvested in Zapotitlán, Tolimán, and Tuxcacuesco.

The Cristero detachments, transformed into gangs of soldier-labourers, lived dispersed with their families, working the land under the orders of their officers, mustering to set off on a campaign or to beat off the attacks of the Federal army. The Federal troops, however, were never able to conquer this sanctuary in Cerro Grande, an area crowded with the families that had taken refuge from other areas and where the general established nine schools for more than five hundred children. The lower slopes of the volcanic region of Colima was the zone subjected to his system of agricultural *dirigisme*, but his overall administrative authority extended as far as Ciudad Guzmán, San Gabriel, Atoyac, and Sayula, where the authorities, although appointed by the Government, secretly collaborated with him.[43]

The Region Covered by the Unión Popular: Jalisco and Western Guanajuato[44]

Throughout this vast area, the Cristeros did not have any respite during the three years of war, except for the months of March and April 1929, during which they were in unchallenged control of the region. Moreover, the principal task of the clandestine government was to support the war effort by organising the population to provide logistic support and intelligence; at the same time, it transformed the Unión Popular into a network responsible for the military and administrative partitioning of the area. Anacleto González Flores, who fell at the beginning of 1927, was replaced by two men: Andrés Nuño, a trade union leader aged fifty, responsible for the UP; and Miguel Gómez Loza, appointed Civil Governor of Jalisco (he was thirty-five years old, a lawyer, had been imprisoned fifty-eight times before 1927, was a trade union leader, and died in March 1928). Andrés Nuño remained in office until the end of the war (although he disappeared in June 1929). Gómez Loza's successor was Rafael Martínez Camarena, from March until June 1928, and later Agustín Sánchez and J. Montes, men closely controlled by Gorostieta; however, owing to the strict supervision exercised by the General, they did not have the importance of the early civilian leaders. It may be said that until the summer of 1928 the civil government acted as an autonomous institution, although there was continuous collaboration with the military authorities, and subsequently Gorostieta imposed his authority in every sphere, while preserving intact the organisation that had been set up.

The Altos region[45] was under complete Cristero control, within a polygon formed by Guadalajara, Poncitlán, Ocotlán, La Barca, Yurécuaro, Jalpa, San Diego, Lagos, Jalostotitlán, and Cañadas; it was divided into nine sectors, each under a responsible leader. A tenth sector, Western Guanajuato, was under the direct authority of Miguel Gómez Loza, for it was part of the geographical region under his command, and it worked in close military collaboration with Frs Reyes Vega and Aristeo Pedroza.[46] These sectors were themselves divided into sub-sectors (that of South-western Guanajuato was divided into three civilian commands), municipal districts, hamlets, and *ranchos*. The highest authority, the governor, set up his base near Arandas and established a clandestine printing press in the caves. Travelling up hill and down dale, he constantly organised and inspected the subordinate authorities, which supplied him with weekly reports through the proper channels. Education, justice, the police, and finance were the principal functions for which the administrators were responsible.

In September 1927 the administrative apparatus had already been established, and the government created a special zone for the city of Guadalajara; General Degollado was approached with the request that he set up civilian commands in the south and west of the state. The government was divided into six principal committees: finance, war, propaganda, welfare, and information (espionage and the courier service) and justice. In December, there were twenty-five Cristero municipal councils in the Altos, fifteen in the northern part of the state, five in the west, and twelve in the south. The organisation continued to extend itself until 1929; by that time, there were ninety-two Cristero municipal councils in Jalisco and eleven in the south-west of Guanajuato – that is to say, 90 per cent of all the municipal councils of the region. In each village, there were committees functioning on behalf of the war department. A network of spies and couriers, working in collaboration with the Women's Brigades, covered the entire zone, and was operated principally by the leaders of the smallest administrative units, the *ranchos*. Schools, financed by the parents, ran in a semi-clandestine fashion. Assistance to families, widows, orphans, and the wounded was the responsibility of local committees which worked in collaboration with the Women's Brigades. The propaganda department, which operated the clandestine printing press in the Cerro de la Culebra, published the newspaper *Gladium* and tracts which were distributed throughout the state. Commissions of justice sat in all the villages, and popular juries were established in all but three municipal districts.[47]

In 1928–9 General Gorostieta merely extended the system of government established by Miguel Gómez Loza, and instituted three administrative levels: at the base was the post; then came the section controlling several posts; and finally the sector controlling several sections. The sector head was responsible only to the civil governor of the state, and he worked in close collaboration with the commander of the corresponding military sector. To achieve harmonisation and collaboration between the civilian and military sectors, Gorostieta gave them the same regions to control.

The civil governor made his subordinates fill in a monthly questionnaire, which served as a report, to keep up to date the annotated list of active and passive enemies, the list of tax-payers, and that of 'Catholics killed by tyranny'. Of fundamental importance for the prosecution of the war, the only outcome of which appeared to be victory and the establishment of a Cristero government, were financial matters, and these occupied a large part of the energies of the administrators.

Decree No. 1, issued in September 1927 by Gómez Loza, imposed a tax of 2 per cent every six months on the real value of all capital held. In each municipal district a committee was responsible for assessing the amounts of capital. Sometimes one could use the municipal records for this, but more often one had to start from scratch: thus, in order to establish the real value of the haciendas, the Cristero authorities discreetly carried out a classification of the land, a superficial survey, and an assessment of the livestock and investments, with the assistance of the peons who were made responsible for this task.[48] Only capital sums of over 250 pesos were taxed, and those who were serving in the Army of National Liberation were exempted; capital goods which had been requisitioned were discounted from the tax payable; those who were up to date in their tax payments escaped the requisitions; those who paid taxes 'to the Calles faction voluntarily' would be regarded as collaborators (Article 7); the 'tax-collectors of the usurping and criminal regime who use force will be judged as accomplices of the Tyranny'.[49] As a result of the work of the committees, which completed their labours in November 1927, Miguel Gómez Loza was able to carry out a cadastral survey and fix the amount of the tax at 300,000 pesos for the Altos region. Then came the great resettlement programme of the winter of 1927–8, and to alleviate the effects of this and of the ill will of the rich, Miguel Gómez Loza reduced the tax to 1 per cent every six months, exempted all capital amounts lower than 2,000 pesos, and entrusted the collection to the military authorities.[50] Delays in payment were sanctioned by doubling the tax due, and after this the military had recourse to requisitioning or sequestration of goods. The civilians retained their control over ordinary accounting, and even defended themselves against the interference of the military: 'No commander of the Army of National Liberation may impose any loan without the previous authorisation of the civil authorities and of the commander of the Altos Brigade. No loan of any kind may be exacted from individuals who have paid their taxes.'[51] The civilian authorities alone were responsible for collecting fines and taking punitive action against the rich; these items accounted for 70 per cent of the Cristero revenues.

This money collected with so much difficulty was scrupulously accounted for, and then shared between the civil and the military authorities. The civil government always reserved for itself the larger part, for the acquisition of ammunition: thus, in January 1928, Miguel Gómez Loza sent 25,000 pesos to a correspondent of the League in San Antonio,[52] and noted bitterly that the integrity of the Cristeros was not displayed by everybody, because

here we have received nothing, and this money is from this region and earmarked for the purchase of ammunition for us and for no other purpose. I need to know whether we can expect anything, because if not, this will have the very worst consequences for us, because all the taxpayers will see that their efforts have been of no avail, and they will call us swindlers. This worries us, because it means that we lose the hopes that inspired their labours. They have done nothing to help us. Everything that has been done has been due to the efforts of us here.[53]

After this disastrous experience, the Cristeros of Jalisco never again entrusted money to the League, but worked themselves, in collaboration with the Women's Brigades, to ensure their supply of ammunition. Their accounting improved after the Government had suspended resettlement because, as a permanent system, all measures were taken so that future re-groupings of the population should not affect the Government. The organisation controlled the resettlement itself, and the resettled people were properly mobilised.

In May 1929, the government of the Altos alone had more than 2,000 civilian leaders and 300 schools.[54] In its competence were the supervision and taxing of commerce,[55] the setting up of workshops for the manufacture of powder and bombs, uniforms, shoes, newspapers, and pamphlets, and the organisation of supplies to the combatants (in the Altos each soldier who was the father of a family received a ration of maize) and to families in need.[56]

Concerned for its public image, and mindful of the prospect of coming to power, the Cristero government emphasised justice and morality. The health and habits of the people were watched over, and there was an offensive against drinking, gambling, and prostitution; the soldiers were subjected to extremely severe discipline, and there was condign punishment for anyone who committed abuses against the civilian population. Taverns, gambling-dens, and brothels were closed, and marriage encouraged; theft and rape committed by a Cristero soldier were punished by death.[57]

The severity of the military authorities and the unconditional support they gave to the sentences of the judges provoked complaints: 'We [the inhabitants of Lagos] refuse to put up with Fernández any longer: he goes round with women, causing a scandal, and lets off shots when he is drunk.'[58] Victoriano Ramírez, after holding an inquiry, ordered a soldier accused of having stolen maize from two peasants to be shot. Colonel Pedroza punished certain of his soldiers whom the civil authorities of La Gloria had caught collecting a toll from the muleteers on the road from Arandas to Atotonilco.[59] Judicial proceedings were held against Cristero soldiers who had assaulted civilians in Lavaderos, and against members of Calles's faction who were not protected by this system of justice: the Federal Captain Barbarito Serrano, for theft, rape, and the murder of a priest; the former mayor of Atotonilco, Rafael Fonseca.[60]

It must be remembered that this civil government, established in zones where the Cristero troops were most numerous and controlled either a 'liberated' territory, or an overwhelmingly sympathetic population, was indeed a war administration, the essential function of which was to organise the people so that it was one with the Army of National Liberation. Besides this, however, this government contrasted its own legitimacy with the usurpation practised by 'the Tyranny', and, owing to the course of events, was led to envisage its own accession to power. From then on it functioned against a perspective of national reconstruction which can be described as revolutionary, because it desired a complete break with what had taken place in Mexico since Independence. Without having any more precise ideology than a hope for the advent of justice and its sequel of Christian virtues, the Cristero government was the natural outcome of the insurrection itself. It is a remarkable fact that the League played no part in this,[61] and that the rural inhabitants, for the only time in the history of Mexico,[62] were left to themselves to organise the Mexico envisaged by Morelos – a federation of natural geographical regions, formed by theocratic village republics. The archaic (or futuristic?) demand for equality, democracy, and justice was accompanied by the need for effectiveness and speed.

1. Cristeros with the Virgin of Guadalupe, Altos, 1927

2. Cristeros of the Sierra de Michis, Durango, belonging to Federico Vázquez's group

3. Soldiers of the Valparaíso Regiment, under the command of Aurelio Acevedo, and their families; Zacatecas, 1927

4. Fr E. Cabral celebrating Mass as required by Sabino Salas and his men before entering battle, 6 November 1927, at Adjuntas del Refugio, Zacatecas

5. Cristeros of the Altos de Jalisco, commanded by Fr General Aristeo Pedroza

6. Federal officers, San Julian, Altos de Jalisco, 1929: rear, civil governor of San Luis Potosí State; front, left to right, General S. Cedillo (hatless), General Beltrán, Miguel Aranda Díaz

7. Federal officers (in uniform) and Cristero prisoners, 1929; Cristero chief Jesús Macías, of the Altos de Jalisco, between the two officers

CHAPTER 9

The War

The War of the Federal Army

The Federal army was known among the people by the more familiar name of 'the Federation', an abbreviation of the full title 'Armed Forces of the Federation'. The term employed well expressed the real situation: the army was one and the same as the government of which it formed a part, and in the religious conflict it was openly partisan. As an active agent of anticlericalism and the antireligious struggle, it carried on its own war of religion. General Eulogio Ortiz sentenced to death a soldier who wore a scapular, and some officers fell in their troops to the cry of 'Long live Satan!'. Colonel 'Blackhand', responsible for the massacre of Cocula, died shouting 'Long live the Great Devil!'. What was this army entrusted in January 1927 with the task of subduing a rebel people?

The Budget

The army and the military factories cost 79 million pesos in 1926 (out of a national budget of 320 millions), and 96 million pesos in 1929 (out of a national budget of 270). In fact, the budget covered only current operations, and in 1929, for example, Escobar's rebellion cost an extra 100 million, of which 30 million went in additional payments to the army.[1]

This army, which took the lion's share of the national resources, was always short of money and men. The officers were sometimes paid two months in arrears,[2] and this encouraged their habit of living off the country. The accounts should have included the ravages of war; the policy of scorched earth and resettlement of the population ruined the regions devoted to food crops: in Durango production fell by half in 1929.[3] In an unfavourable national and international context, the war, a 'severe drain on government financial resources', aggravated the economic depression from which the country had not recovered since 1926.[4]

Strength

It is not easy to calculate this exactly, because the figures on paper often do not reflect the reality: the official report of the Ministry of War gives a figure of 71,000 men for November 1926, but on 18 January 1927 the American Military Attaché calculated the real strength to be 40,000. As a result of cross-checking, the author prefers the lower estimate, for the first half of 1927 was devoted to filling the fifty-one battalions and eighty regiments with soldiers of flesh and blood, as opposed to a purely 'paper' strength which made it possible for the officers to pocket the pay, supplies, and rations of phantom soldiers and imaginary horses.

TABLE 20.   *Strength of the federal army, 1927–9*[5]

June 1927	79,759 men	
February 1928	76,243	
June 1928	72,441	plus 15,000 auxiliaries
June 1929	70,367	plus 30,000 auxiliaries
December 1929	59,596	

The figures shown in Table 20 conceal a continual instability, both of units and of men, who disappeared as a result of rebellions, desertions, or death in battle. As a consequence of these factors, the reorganisation of units and the enlistment of soldiers took place continually, so that, for example, within a few weeks, different figures are obtained for the 76th Cavalry Regiment. By June 1929, some units were reduced to only half their strength.

Besides the Federal soldiers, there were the auxiliary corps, the state militias, the Gendarmerie of the Federal District, and, above all, the *agraristas*. In 1929 the Government called to arms the soldier-colonists of General Cedillo, who formed the Centre Division of 8,000 men, and it also raised regional battalions, composed of peasants, workers, convicts, and the unemployed.[6]

Each arm did its own recruiting, and enlistment was, in principle, voluntary; in practice, use was made of the traditional *leva*, and anybody was taken: convicts, the unemployed, the peasants, and sometimes, when things got very bad, miners from Pachuca and elsewhere, who deserted in the first battle. The army was principally composed of the 'flower of the rural sub-proletariat' and the Indians. The Yaquis, after they were crushed in 1926, were incorporated into five line battalions, in addition to the irregulars encamped in Sonora. Juchiteques and Tehuanes from the state of Oaxaca made up eight units, the Indians of the Sierra de Iguala (Guerrero) formed three units, and the Tarascans four. These infantrymen were renowned for their endurance and courage.

Apart from the 36th, 61st, and 63rd Cavalry Regiments, recruited in the North, the remainder of the troops were of mediocre quality; the poor peasants forcibly enlisted into the 28th Battalion deserted, as did the peasants of the 50th Battalion, raised in Hidalgo. The 15th Battalion and the 34th Regiment, raised in the Federal District, were 'very bad, degenerate, vicious, cowards and deserters'; the 45th Battalion (Puebla), the 60th Regiment (Morelos), and the 71st Regiment (Tlaxcala) were recruited from the unemployed, workmen, and city-dwellers who did not know how to ride a horse.[7]

Although he displayed endurance, often of superhuman quality, the Indian infantryman's 'chief weakness was his indulgence in alcohol and marijuana'. Murderous, addicted to looting, lacking a proper supply service, and undisciplined, he gave no thought to politics and merely followed his leader, who was virtually the proprietor of the unit. Except for the men from the North, he was a bad horseman and ill-treated his mount, which he had no idea how to look after. The soldier was paid every ten days, when things were going well and the treasurer had not run off with the funds, at a rate of 40 centavos per day.

Badly paid, badly fed, recruited against his will to fight in a war that was not his concern, the Federal soldier was a potential deserter. Desertion (see Table 21), which was common enough in peacetime, became massive in wartime, even though Amaro employed fearsome brutality in his efforts to discipline his army.

TABLE 21   *Desertion in the Federal army, 1926–32*

Date	Deserters
1926	9,421
1927	Not Known
1928	28,000
1929	21,214 between January and June[a]
1930	9,000
1931	7,784
1932	10,958

[a]They took with them material to the value of 144,252 pesos.

An American observer found the phenomenon difficult to explain, because the soldier's pay was higher than that of a worker, and his material conditions of life improved continuously from 1924 onwards. 'It is probable that the campaigns against the Cristeros ... may have caused a large number of desertions.'[8]

With regard to the desertions, the testimony of the Cristeros, the consular agents, the American military attachés, and old soldiers are in agreement: the soldiers led a dog's life. People smoked marijuana at that time when they were in the depths of despair, and there were two categories constituting the principal consumers of this product: convicts and soldiers. If it was a dog's life in peacetime, it became sheer hell in wartime. Apart from *coups d'état*, which were often accompanied by little bloodshed among the common soldiers, the Cristero War was much more fearful and it dragged on forever. That was why Amaro was not able to muster more than 70,000 men, although he spent his whole time recruiting fresh soldiers: there were 20,000 desertions per year out of 70,000! It must be remembered, however, that many deserters found themselves obliged to avoid capture by enlisting in the army again under a different name. One escaped from the army by returning to it.[9]

Officers

Officers were very numerous, for in 1927 there were 14,000 of them, of whom one-third were classed as field officers. Amaro reduced the strength of this swollen category, and tried to improve recruitment. In the early stages, the immense majority came from the army formed by Carranza's followers; there were some former followers of Villa, such as Generals Ortiz and A. López, and, on rare occasions, former followers of Zapata, such as Genovevo de la O (who was suspected of harbouring Cristero sympathies), Abundio Gomez, and Adrián Castrejón (who had been one of Zapata's murderers).[10]

The most important generals died in 1923–4, and the secondary figures – Escobar, Manzo, Aguirre, Topete, and Caraveo – could not be compared with Hill, Maycotte, and Estrada. Amaro, supported by Cedillo, Almazán, and Cárdenas, found it easier to work.

A captain was paid 6·50 pesos a day, a colonel 12 pesos, a general from 18 to 54 pesos, but the latter derived an income from several sources: the soldiers' pay, rations, dealings in military equipment which even included sales to the rebels, and looting of the country.

The American expert expressed himself harshly when he commented:

'Open drunkenness and vicious conduct and entire lack of responsibilities as to money matters appear to be exceedingly common. The type and conduct of a considerable proportion of the newer Mexican officers, from the grade of general down, are about those corresponding to a tough New York truck driver.'[11] Those acquainted with these characters did not find this judgement too harsh. Northerners almost without exception and mostly former Carranza followers or men who had joined Obregón in 1920, these generals and the other officers, who had risen from the ranks and had little education (except for A. Guerrero, who had been a lieutenant in the old Federal army) were not all capable of supporting Amaro in his efforts to create a Prussian-style army.

Although there was no equipment problem, thanks to the American arsenals[12] and almost unlimited credits, Amaro had plenty of work to do in organising his army. A man of steel, a notable horseman like all the men of Zacatecas, implacable and bloodthirsty, he used his sharp intelligence to compensate for his lack of education. 'The Indian Amaro', he wore a pearl ear-ring, was civilised by his wife, a woman of good family, and learned the ways of the world, playing polo and writing verses in French. Violently anticlerical, extremely nationalistic, anti-American but carefully concealing his animosity towards the indispensable ally, he was to swing to the right and then the extreme right around 1940, and became converted to Catholicism.

Methods and results

Fifty battalions of 500 men each, eighty-one regiments of nearly the same strength, fifty-seven aircraft, seventy-two 75 mm guns – such an army was obviously fit only for the maintenance of order, as a deterrent against putsches, and as the arm of the Government in a civil war. Strategy was simple: to succeed, a revolution in Mexico had to have American support and use the northern frontier as a firm base or make use of a big port which would allow the massive importation of arms. One could then be content to hold the towns and the railways, crossing, ravaging, and terrorising the rural areas where the rebels were invincible. In the event, tactics were rudimentary, and there was not, in practice, any need to manoeuvre above unit level. Pitched battles were avoided whenever possible; this explains why there were few losses in the wars fought between the military men. Losses became heavy only when the Federal army fought the Cristeros; the latter also avoided battle when they were short of ammunition, but harassed the army closely and effectively, and set ambushes and exploited them properly. In an ordinary battle the Federals would open fire at between 1,000 and 1,500 metres and then withdraw. The infantry, which was no use against the excellent Cristero cavalry, was stationed to guard the railways, as was the artillery.

Drawing his inspiration from the system invented by Weyler in Cuba and applied by the British in South Africa, and following the advice of the American Military Attaché to use the methods employed by the Americans in the Philippines,[13] Amaro specialised in the technique known as 'reconcentration'. This consisted of clearing the civilian population completely out of a given area, before ravaging that area systematically. In Jalisco, Michoacán, Colima, Durango, and parts of Guanajuato, Querétaro, Zacatecas, and Guerrero, reconcentration caused indescribable suffering to the population concerned (nearly one million people). It also produced the opposite effect to that which was sought; it spread the rebellion.

Though incapable of winning victory and hard-pressed by the insurgents, who were always better armed and organised, the Federal army, drawing its strength from American support, allowed the Government to remain in the saddle for long enough to secure an advantageous peace. This was done at the cost of a war which lasted three years and in which the Federal troops became infamous for their exactions. This phenomenon, which derived from the logic of war, did more to encourage the rebellion than all the propaganda. This exaggerated degree of violence can be explained by the fact that a war of religion took the form of a conflict, within a context of revolution, between a regular army and an insurgent people. One might call it a colonial war, both from the technical point of view (aviation, artillery, railways) and from the ideological point of view (the Government's ignorance of and contempt for the rebels).

The atrocities that characterise all revolutionary wars are the expression of passions and of a logic that find their outlet in horror and sadism. Terror was supposed to be a deterrent: this was the reason for the mass executions, the public hangings, the exposure of corpses, torture, and, at the strategic level, the policy of scorched earth. The desires of the leaders, who were often fighting an ideological war, were reflected in the behaviour of the soldiers, who were naturally inclined to indulge in the exactions to which every army is prone. Guerrilla warfare contributed more than anything else to the demoralisation of the soldiers, and impelled them towards cruelty, cowardice, and despair. The acts of sacrilege that stemmed from the firmly held convictions of certain leaders unleashed, among the soldiers, a neurotic and murderous delirium born of feelings of guilt.

There is no need to quote specific examples: the evidence is overwhelming and ubiquitous; the veterans of both sides, the press of the time, the diplomatic reports, and debates in Congress, all retail the same litany of horrors, perpetuated in the photographs taken by the Federal army. No prisoners were taken; civilians taken as hostages were murdered. Torture was systematic, and was used not only to obtain information but also to prolong suffering, and to oblige Catholics to renounce their faith, since death was not sufficient to persuade them to do this. To be forced to walk on the flayed soles of the feet, to be flayed, burned, have their bones broken, to be quartered alive, hung up by their thumbs, garrotted, electrocuted, scorched by blowlamps, racked, subjected to the torture of the boot and the water-torment, stretched out, dragged behind a horse — such was the fate of those who fell into the hands of the Federals.

The despoliation of the zones subject to reconcentration was organised methodically, and the livestock was shipped by rail to Mexico City or the United States; the houses and simple possessions of the villagers were abandoned to the soldiery. The acts of sacrilege were surrounded by an atmosphere of horror, which was consciously assumed and shared by the participants and the spectators. The course of events itself was often banal enough: churches were desecrated by officers who rode into them on horseback, trampled the Host under the hoofs of their chargers, used the altars as dining-tables and turned the building into a stable. Statues of saints were used for target practice, and those of the Virgin were undressed and the soldiers danced with them. The soldiers dressed up in the ecclesiastical vestments, and ate the consecrated Hosts and drank *café au lait* from the chalice. Among the Federals there were some who did not share this passion for sacrilege: Anacleto López, who was superstitious, said: 'I don't get mixed up with the priests. Goni killed two priests, and the same week they killed him.'

As for the people, although they were certainly astounded, as the Federal generals intended them to be, they reacted in the opposite way to that which was expected: 'But what did General Domínguez achieve with all this? What happened was that those who had not gone against him now did so, and made every effort to help us, as much as they could.'[14]

The Cristeros at War: Defects, Problems, Limitations[15]

The defects of the Cristero army were derived from its very nature: it was an army of peasants, of volunteers, and it benefited from the qualities and suffered from the defects of the society of which it was the armed projection. At first, exaggerated democracy led to anarchy, everyone doing as he pleased, each officer and each soldier fighting his own war; it was difficult in an atmosphere of absolute egalitarianism to admit that the commanding officer had a right to the horse and the binoculars, when there were not enough of them for everybody. Everyone expressed his opinion openly and criticised freely, emphasising minor details and personal defects, and this murmuring sometimes led to disasters. Extreme individualism led to quarrelling and fighting; the group as a whole displayed the same partisan spirit; and this sometimes led to two bands fighting each other. Finally, the characteristic of guerrilla warfare encouraged the trasition to banditry and excesses of all kinds: anarchy and indiscipline were often accompanied by sudden outbursts of severity, with the execution of offenders. The Cristeros were conscious of this problem, and they made every effort to diminish the danger, although they were not able to eliminate it entirely.

'The first group of Cristero soldiers made a very bad impression on me. Badly dressed, dirty ... they looked to me like peasants on a pilgrimage who had been accidentally armed with carbines,'[16] wrote a young student who joined their army.

Often, the strength of a unit fluctuated: despite the vigilance of the officers, soldiers would take leave for a variety of family reasons – to get news from home, to plough, or to earn a little money to help their families. Sometimes an entire squadron or even a regiment would go off to do the ploughing because the rains had come, or quite simply because the soldiers were homesick and wanted to see their villages once more, where their wives could delouse them and change their linen.[17] Sometimes, the men went home in rotation: 'I knew families where one time the father would come home, and at another time one of the sons, and at another time another son.'[18]

This mobility, which nobody was able to prevent, was the cause of many deaths; the Cristeros could easily go back into the villages, because there was nothing to distinguish them from the civilians, and sometimes the visit was fatal. To remedy this, some units, like the Valparaíso Regiment, organised themselves so that each squadron was encamped near the soldiers' families, so that every week a corporal could go on leave with his six soldiers: 'Thus there was more protection, more vigilance, more cleanliness and, in addition, more tranquillity for everybody. But the experiment was costly, for the losses were heavy.'[19]

Another problem from the military point of view (though it did have certain advantages) was that the combatants did not like moving too far away from their home territory, and refused to follow commanders who invited them to do so.

The insurrection, a rural phenomenon, lacked leaders, and these had to be formed in battle; among the senior officers themselves there were divisions, exacerbated by the universal poverty. Major Refugio Lucatero and his men abandoned their posts guarding a strong-point because 'the Colonel said that either we should withdraw or he would, because we were engaging in outright robbery, because we killed two cows, and he had already washed his hands of us because we had gone for two days without anything to eat'.[20]

There were innumerable occasions of conflict among the lower ranks: the delimitation of zones of recruitment, requisitioning, the collection of the war tax, the sharing of booty, and co-operation in battle.

Pedro Sandoval, abandoned in the middle of an attack on El Teul by Felipe Sánchez and Chema Gutiérrez paid them back with the same treatment a year later.

I would reiterate my complaint [wrote Acevedo] and request that an inquiry be held to delimit responsibilities. I say responsibilities because Major Anguiano has withdrawn without having received the order to do so; when he deserted, he took with him, in addition to his own men, another 200 men who were not under his command ... It is true that he was in the advance guard, towards Santa María, and therefore he had all the less reason to withdraw, since he had not fired a single round, nor had his horses suffered, nor were his men tired from battle. The desertion of Anguiano in the Colotlán campaign made it necessary for our forces to withdraw, leaving the others in danger, and having to suspend the operations which would have given the most resounding victory to our movement, despite our agreement with Generals Sánchez, Arnáiz and others.[21]

Ammunition

This remained the fundamental and insoluble problem. Gorostieta noted that 200,000 rounds were needed for an operation which mobilised 2,500 soldiers for less than four days; and this was distributing the minimum, because the individual allocation of a Federal soldier was at least 250 rounds a day. At the outbreak of the war, the lack of ammunition regularly obliged the Cristeros to break off the fight after fifteen minutes, and for three years the capture of church towers to which the Federal troops fell back when they were surprised remained the principal problem, for the lack of artillery which would have reduced them in five minutes allowed the besieged to hold out until the arrival of reinforcements. Thus the attack on San Juan de los Lagos, a large-scale and successful manoeuvre consisting of a surprise attack by 2,500 cavalry on the town, did not achieve complete victory, and the Cristeros left the place as victors, it is true, but without the ammunition with which the capture of the barracks would have provided them. Each church tower was the scene of a heroic deed; sappers and grenade-throwers, covered by picked marksmen, tried to come to close quarters with the enemy sheltering in those buildings of hewn stone, armed with jam-tins filled with powder and stones, which made more noise than damage. Finally, the asphyxiation of the enemy by the smoke of armfuls of pimento branches proved extremely effective. It was not until the spring of 1929, as a result of the retreat of the Federals during Escobar's revolt, that the Cristeros, who now controlled the whole of the Western Centre, were able to fill their ammunition-pouches and accumulate small stocks of ammunition.

The valour of the peasants (*valor ranchera*) at first conflicted with military effectiveness, for the Cristeros could hardly resist the temptation to fire on every enemy who came into their sights. In November 1927 the senior officers Arreola and Caro, overjoyed at having captured Ameca and somewhat drunk, telephoned the Federal headquarters to invite them to evacuate the place. Santiago Bayacora's men did the same thing at Mezquital, and were obliged to make a hasty withdrawal, firing off their last cartridges. 'The duties of the defenders of religious freedom', said a priest hostile to the Cristeros, consisted, in 90 per cent of the cases, in running away, because they did not have enough ammunition to face the enemy; they therefore had to inflict the greatest possible damage while suffering the minimum losses, and all this using as few cartridges as possible.[22]

Morality

Representing the two extremes are two priests, both of them generals. Fr Aristeo Pedroza, was 'the pure man', who imposed on his troops, and later on the Altos Brigade, an iron discipline that Gorostieta admired. Fr José Reyes Vega, the commander of the two Gómez Loza Regiments, the 'Pancho Villa in a cassock', ought to have embraced a military career; he let himself be carried away by his passions and made no boast of setting a good example to his parishioners. He was particularly criticised for his affairs with women and for his habit of ordering Federal prisoners to be shot. Gorostieta, though impressed by the faith of the Cristeros, once explained that he felt it impossible, on human grounds, to accept the idea of Confession because of such priests. There were few others quite like him. Federico Vázquez and Valente Acevedo both had a weakness for women, but this characteristic did not involve the use of force. The old followers of Pancho Villa saw in this war an opportunity to efface the sins of the preceding one, and, as Acevedo said, referring to the old Justo Ávila and the fearsome Sabino Salas, 'the tigers had changed their skins'. As for the bandits, they had to choose between conversion and death: among them Nemesio López was disarmed and then set free by Quintanar in December 1926; J. Rosario Guillén was shot by General José Gutiérrez; Esteban Caro, guilty of rapes in Atenguillo and Soyatlán, was demoted by General Degollado and mended his ways.

The struggle against alcohol was a military necessity, as is shown by the history of Fr Ramón Pérez the chaplain to the Southern Division, who upbraided the Cristero officers who were celebrating victory at an inn in Cuautla. He walked in and broke the bottles and the guitar, to the great anger of the drinkers,

but they respected him as a friend and as a father, after the first moment of rebellion had passed. All drunken men are rebels. They held themselves in check, which is praiseworthy, because with arms in one's hands, and power, and everything, it is not so easy to hold oneself in check. When one is lost, then one asks forgiveness, but when one has all the power, one does not usually ask forgiveness.[23]

The vigour with which discipline, morality, and order were imposed[24] explains how

the Cristero forces ceased to be a rabble and became transformed into a disciplined and moral army which, though it was poor, obliged Calles to order Portes Gil, 'We have finished with Escobar, but we will not finish with the Cristeros, so find a way to come to an arrangement with the priests and put an end to this war which is annihilating us'.[25]

The Theory and Practice of Popular War: Gorostieta

When Gorostieta intervened at the end of 1927, from a solid insurrectionary base, he established an organisation which was nominally similar to that of the Federal army: he confirmed the senior officers in their appointments, recognised the soldiers' right to vote, but he reduced the ranks of most officers, getting rid of nearly all the generals and recognising as colonels only those who commanded complete regiments. His severity, his extreme strictness, and his lucidity of mind were displayed in his Circular No. 4 of July 1928.[26]

In February 1928 he estimated that the stage of guerrilla warfare had been superseded, but that, owing to lack of ammunition, it was impossible to capture swiftly the important localities, which was necessary in order to feed a column of over 1,000 soldiers. Strategy continued to be affected by these material limitations, and the Cristeros rejected the temptation to engage in operations beyond their means.

It is worth reproducing this paragraph of the very precise instructions given to commanders of units:

(i) In battle, you should bear in mind that the object of the same is to break the will power of the enemy and impose one's own will, an end which is achieved only when success is complete and the enemy are pursued after the victory; thus, battle should only be joined when there is evidence of superiority in numbers or position or when the enemy are taken by surprise. . . . To put this another way: you will only fight where it suits you to do so and never where it suits the enemy. You must never tire of manoeuvring until you tire the enemy and oblige him to fight a battle in conditions unfavourable to him.

In his instructions (which clearly show that skill in guerrilla warfare is not innate among the peasants, who did not know the purpose of scouts or sentries), Gorostieta was working in a dual perspective, the military one and the political one, in taking steps to educate and organise what had been a horde, then a multitude of independent bands, and establishing a political government so that this army should not degenerate into a crowd of bandits.

The War

General Gómez López has told the story of how he was invited, with his brother, to join the insurrection in January 1927, by Miguel Gómez Loza, and he did this with seven companions, who grew to forty in March, and were obliged to disperse in April owing to lack of ammunition. They mustered again in July and were transformed from a flying column into an organised unit. In October 1927 Carlos Blanco organised the Gómez Loza Regiment in four squadrons, made up of 660 men. The squadron remained the basic operational unit.[27]

This story was typical of the movement in general. Insurrections took place continually from August 1926 to May 1929, and the strength of units rose constantly from July 1927 onwards, after the mass mobilisation of January and the immediate dispersal. Although the combatants of the unorganised bands displayed until the very end their habit of returning home after each operation and indulged in a freedom bordering on anarchy, there were no more deserters from their ranks than from the Cristeros of the properly organised regiments. There were few real deserters – it was more a question of men who withdrew from the fight for a while and then re-enlisted – and still fewer went over to the Government side.[28]

At first the Cristeros, the majority of whom had no military experience, were 'real pigeons',[29] and their indiscipline and attacks of panic were the despair of General Degollado. In August 1927, his expeditionary column, consisting of recruits with a few weeks' service, broke and fled at the battle of Perico, and then at the battle of Las Peñas, in Michoacán, in the most distressing way. When General Beltrán advanced to meet them, only thirty-four men of the 600 remained with Degollado, and later 150 cowards were brought back into the battle by Bouquet and Flores. More than 400 did not come back until the battle was over; despite the valour of certain individuals, it was sheer unreliability, the immediate transition from the charge to headlong flight, that characterised the early months of the war. At first, the Cristeros did not know how to be sparing with their scarce ammunition, and this explains their frequent panic. 'There was a mistaken belief that the revolutionary was obliged to fire at the government troops at all times, whatever their numbers, and even if this led to the worst catastrophes through failure to withdraw in time.' Indeed, audacity was the other initial failing of the Cristeros, and pride, which ignored all criticisms, led to the death of more than one imprudent soldier. 'Things changed, and I led my men to fairly easy victories, which gave them confidence in me and in themselves, until I had a picked force of 600 men who could beat the enemy anywhere, even when he was superior in numbers and in open country.'[30]

The Cristeros soon learned to make war, because their hearts were in it; this does not mean that they necessarily had a taste for violence: Perfecto Castañón, who had fought for Villa when he was fifteen, no longer had any love for war, and followed Quintanar because he did not want to 'go back on his word', crying all night long before he left his family;[31] Aurelio Acevedo and many others recorded the consternation they felt when for the first time they heard their enemies speaking Spanish: 'When I took up arms, through the fault of Calles, I was astonished, in the third battle, to hear them speaking Spanish, because I had expected them to speak English, and that is why I had never learned English, in order not to understand my enemy and thus be able to kill him.'[32] But they knew why they were fighting and against whom they were fighting, and they were fighting on their own territory; and men do not fight well except for causes which they fashion themselves and with which they identify passionately. And they made this war out of love, even while they were cursing it, just as they instinctively loved any task that required their skill and their patience. This war was their war without their having wished it, without their having rushed to the front, from the moment when they had taken their decision. 'I have an obligation to the Blessed Virgin,' said Quintanar to his wife. Castañón did not want to go back on his word as a Christian. The mother of Epitacio Hernández, after his death, sent her twelve-year-old son to the war. The father who had already lost two sons waited for the death of the third son before joining the insurrection.[33] This behaviour stood in sharp contrast to what the orators and the newspapers, the bishops and the politicians were saying, namely, that 'constancy was not a Mexican quality'.[34] Nothing was more normal than suffering and death, since they were accompanied by happiness and salvation. Obedience to the will of God would be more total, zeal would bear its fruits more quickly – the victory of the faith in this world and salvation in the next. Although the victory of Christ the King, and his coming, were connected with the vague promise of a new profane world, they emphasised above all the idea of a contract between the Mexican people and God, who had twice conferred special favours on Mexico, who had twice made Mexico His Kingdom, by sending to it the Virgin of Guadalupe and by proclaiming there the Kingship of His Son. In the context of this collective contract, the ills of Mexico, in its special position *vis-à-vis* the United States (which threatened to swallow it whole), derived from the faults of the Mexicans; and the recognition of this failing, which had developed in the people since the century before, was related to a very ancient tradition. To speak of the lack of obedience to the covenant concluded with God was to emphasise human responsibility for historical events; it was a reassertion of the idea of the Franciscans in the sixteenth century, according to which the New World might succeed, New Spain might succeed, where the Old World had failed. Like Mendieta in the sixteenth century, the Cristeros were conscious of being the Christian nation, the Kingdom of Christ, for which they were shedding their blood.

This explains their enthusiasm, a quality which impressed the Federal army, who described them as 'fanatics, drug-addicts, drunkards', and feared most of all that hand-to-hand fighting which was sought eagerly by the Cristeros, who liked to save their scarce ammunition and were experts with the machete and the dagger.[35] E. J. Bumstead, an American kidnapped by Pedro Martínez, testified to their enthusiasm, the strength of their convictions, their sworn promises to die for the cause, the devout attention with which they listened to the daily harangues of their leaders, and, besides all this, their abundant gaiety.[36] When they had won a victory, their attitude towards their prisoners varied greatly, but it was always considerably less bloodthirsty than that of the Federals.

The death of Gabino Álvarez was a fine example of this courage:

He asked them for a glass of water, and they gave it to him hot; he threw it in the face of a Federal soldier, and the Federal soldier said, you are only hastening your death, and he answered him, it has been delayed too long already, and he turned to José Flores and said to him, 'Don't be downhearted for we were born to die.' Finally he asked them not to shoot him in the forehead, and they did not.[37]

Discipline, which was quickly learned ('if he who commands is mistaken, he who obeys is not'[38]), was another asset that made it possible for them to fight only when they were prepared, for it was difficult to force them to fight. Moreover, the country was fighting on their side, as they dug in behind the *cercas*, the stone walls which divided up the Altos into enclosures (*potreros*), and constituted really impregnable fortresses, or they lay in ambush in the ravines or near fords. Ramón Aguilar had carefully prepared the annihilation of the 2nd Regiment: he had cut the grass in order to ensure a good field of fire and posted his men behind the stone walls.[39]

The prudence of such commanders as Trinidad Mora, who fought only when they were certain to win, explains the terrible losses suffered by the Federal troops, which were much heavier than those that they inflicted on the Cristeros. 'We admit it quite frankly, we have fled on a number of occasions; in other words, we were winning the war by decamping, making use of cavalry charges, or *jupias* as they called them in South Jalisco.'[40]

These men were for the most part excellent marksmen, and necessity obliged them to be sparing with their ammunition, and then to hit the bull with each shot,[41] with the ammunition which the Federals, much against their will, had come to deliver to them, and which they fired off regardless.[42] Dispersed in small units, the Cristeros gathered together to go off on operations and scattered just as quickly, without giving the enemy they had attacked time to reply. These hit-and-run methods contributed more than anything else to the demoralisation of the Federal troops.

There were different styles of war, and each region had a war that was peculiarly its own, a local product like the black haricot bean and the pimento. In Durango, a state where the inhabitants are said to be as terrible as scorpions, the Cristeros moved about in the mountains with their entire families, in more or less temporary encampments and living from a nomadic agriculture; the extremely mountainous country made it possible for this infantry to lay murderous ambushes for the Federals, who could not operate for more than a few days in a sierra where supply was impossible; their baggage-train and, in particular, their supply columns were the favourite prey of the men of Mora, Vázquez, and Acevedo. In Zacatecas and Jalisco, the cavalry, indispensable in that region of broad plateaux, reigned supreme. In the volcanic region of Colima the combatants and their families lived in fortified camps and fought infantry warfare, with trenches, barbed wire, and mines. In the terrible mountains of the district of Coalcomán, the Cristeros never fought a pitched battle against the big Federal columns, but harassed them day and night, the groups in each region taking their turn as the advance of the enemy progressed. On another occasion, they allowed the Federals to enter Coalcomán without striking a blow, and then contented themselves with surrounding them there and starving them out; on another, they indulged in their favourite occupation, to *colear* the retreating enemy — that is to say, to place riflemen all along a defile and open fire when the last soldier of the column had entered it, in order to trap the whole column literally by the tail, as one does to a steer in a rodeo.

In these battles, stones played an important part: the Cristeros rolled them down on the enemy who were advancing up a slope:

The Federal cavalry spurred their horses on, but each time they were driven back, not only by our fire, but also by the stones; and the Federals shouted, 'You Cristero down-and-outs, you're fighting with Our Fathers and Hail Marys,' and the Cristeros answered, 'Yes, here comes a Hail Mary,' and it was a great rock that sent them tumbling back down the hill; another would say to them, 'Here comes an Our Father,' another said, 'Here comes a bull, try and fight it,' so great was the number of stones raining down on them that they could not escape.[43]

A hail of stones, hand-to-hand fighting, insults: the morale of the soldiers was related to the vigour of his exclamations, and insults were accompanied, as in Homer, by blows: 'If you don't surrender, we will bring our women to bugger you good and proper'; 'If you let them, that

means you are not men, and long live Christ the King, son of a whore!';
'Death to Christ and to his mother the great whore, long live Satan, long
live the great Devil!'[44]

Challenges were exchanged, and sometimes there was single combat
between two champions, such as Reginaldo Arellano, the Cristero, and
Andrés Carrillo Guzmán.[45] Sometimes, as in the Middle Ages, two units
would decide to meet and fight a pitched battle, as when the regiment of
General U. Garza was challenged and subsequently annihilated at
Troneras, near Tototlán, by Nicho Hernández. The challenges sent out
by the tipsy Cristeros, Arreola and Caro, led to disaster, when they called
the Federals by telephone and then, having forgotten about it, returned
to their daily tasks.

Sieges were marked by fierce fighting and big battles sometimes lasted
several days. In June 1928, the *agraristas* of Valparaíso defended the
town house by house. Dislodged with grenades (made by filling leather
pouches), they fell back to the church tower, and then came down to
fight with the energy born of desperation in the church, from which they
were smoked out by burning branches of pimento wood.[46]

The use of the *agraristas* by the Federal forces led to 'a terrible confusion, because they were easily confused with the Cristeros on account of
their dress'. The confusion was prejudicial to others than the Cristeros,
for 'the *agraristas* were killing each other and, after the withdrawal of our
men, the Federals attacked them so fiercely that this battle was a disaster
for the Government'.[47] Before the battle, the Cristeros chose a distinctive
emblem – they rolled their left sleeves up to the elbow, went bare-headed,
and wore an arm band – but the *agraristas* were not recognisable as such
from a distance.

The Federal General Cristóbal Rodríguez, who served in the garrison
at Querétaro in 1927, and later at Aguascalientes under the orders of
Genovevo de la O, testified to the popular character of the insurrection:
fields and standing harvest were abandoned before the advance of the
Federal troops, 'farms and entire villages were emptied of their inhabitants', while the men went off to join the Cristeros, who were 'always
retreating, hiding in holes in the mountains like cavemen, hungry, sleep-
ing out in the rain and cold, leading a real dog's life.'[48] It was these dogs

who beat us yesterday between Temasquián and Salitre, that is to say, at Villa
Guerrero (Jal.)... With regard to your intention of coming here in person, I
would advise you to do it with a good number of troops ... There is no one
prepared to give us information, not even the mayors. The attackers made
every effort to encircle us, for there is no doubt that they were led by some one
with a knowledge of military tactics.[49]

It was these men who did not allow the Federal troops a moment's respite.[50]

For a long time the Mexican Government failed to realise the extent of the war, and contented itself with speaking of the 'imbecile fanaticism of the peasants' and the conspiracy of the clergy. When it was necessary to admit a military reverse, the Government attributed it to treachery and cowardice; the fact was that the army, despite all the efforts of General Amaro, was not properly trained or prepared for this war, and, when the soldiers did not desert, they had an alarming tendency to disperse, especially the infantry, who were no match for the magnificent Cristero cavalry.[51] Gorostieta could justifiably assert, in May 1929, that Mexico had never had, nor would ever again have, so many soldiers of such quality.

Without bringing in the question of motivation, one can hazard a sociological explanation of the superiority of the Cristero army over the Federal army: the former benefited from a very high degree of cohesion because it was a social group and not merely an organisation of armed men. Its effectiveness in battle and its superior morale were related to the organisation of the primary group which served it: the family, the clan, and the parish. It was fighting on its own territory, and the combatants fought shoulder to shoulder, among their relations and their neighbours from the same village, under the eyes of their own people. They were defending both their village church and *the* Church, their property, their family, and their honour. Spatial proximity operated in their favour. In these circumstances, one can understand the ineffectiveness of the Government's propaganda, which was, nevertheless, both abundant and imaginative: pamphlets dropped from aircraft, lectures, plays, newspapers, rewards for each weapon surrendered, repeated offers of amnesty, and the distribution of blank safe-conduct forms. In comparison, the Federal army, consisting of men recruited from all parts of the country, nomads without roots, was vulnerable, after the first military disintegration, to the more modest propaganda of the Cristeros, notably in their conversations with civilians, especially women. It was then that their instinct for self-preservation came to the fore, and they would be told how to save their lives and be helped to desert.

Military Summary

The small state of Colima, a zone limited in extent and isolated, offered all the conditions whereby a regular army, supported by mountain and

marine artillery and aviation, should have been able to crush a peasant insurrection. After a series of large-scale offensives, launched
every year by the best generals, and directed in person by General
Amaro, the Cristeros remained unconquered, controlling a vast 'liberated'
zone and frequently carrying out incursions into the state capital.

As a proof of their ability to progress from tactical superiority to
seizing the strategic initiative, General Degollado was able to capture
the port of Manzanillo, as a result of a large-scale operation prepared
several months in advance.[52] From 1927 to 1929 the violence, number,
and scale of the battles increased continuously, and in 1929 the sabotage
of railways began to create serious logistic problems for the Federals.
As the American Military Attaché wrote: 'The bandits attacked as often
as the Federals. The Federal reports on the bandit losses are so unreliable
that they are not mentioned.'[53] For the Cristeros, the first year of the
war was spent in escaping from the army; as for the Federals, they led
their columns through the country areas, always hearing the trumpet of
the rebels, attacking a group which withdrew, finding it again twelve
hours later, always to the sound of the blowing horn of the rancheros.
After three years of war, the Federals again found themselves shut up
in their garrisons, on the main axes of circulation, striking blows into
the void – a void where the rebel government was installed. In the spring
of 1929, a series of big battles fought by Gorostieta paved the way for
the capture of Guadalajara, Aguascalientes, and Tepic. Durango fell.
After the big battles of Ocotlán, in Puente Grande, against Cárdenas's
division, which was advancing from Sonora, this plan was abandoned,
because of lack of ammunition and also to keep clear of towns which were
'worse for us than Capua was for Hannibal', and escape the fate of
Hidalgo at the bridge of Calderón. This disorderly retreat was reserved
for the Federals under the command of Cedillo, who were crushed at
Tepattlán after a fine battle.

In short, the Cristero War, which was interminable because victory
could not be won and inevitably lingered on because no one could win
the decisive battle, could last for as long as the Government possessed a
firepower one hundred times superior to that of its adversaries. With
money and equipment one could build and rebuild a mediocre army, even
if one could not crush the insurrectionary movement, which controlled
the social, if not the political, base. In order to break out of this vicious
circle, Gorostieta tried to carry the Cristiada into the political sphere,
but here too he came up against the United States, which was supporting
the Mexican army to the full. The 'arrangements', which were the work

of Morrow, led to the defeat of Vasconcelos and the definitive establishment of the regime, by virtue of the harsh logic of the proverb 'Poor Mexico! So far from God and so near to the United States!'

Statistical Summary

Despite the great difficulties involved, it is possible to make a tentative estimate of 100,000 combatants killed during the three years of war. The losses suffered by the Cristeros occurred daily and were usually small, on account of the tactics they pursued; there were, however, some big massacres. Examples were the annihilation of the group under Domingo Anaya in March 1928 near San Francisco del Rincón: in the battle, 116 were killed, and 47 were shot afterwards. At San Pedro Apulco, 200 were killed when a group was ambushed at 3 a.m. by General Maximino Ávila Camacho. However, with losses mounting up day after day, the totals were eventually impressive: there were 200 confirmed deaths in the municipal district of Juchitlán, Jalisco, which had 5,000 inhabitants in 1930. Nevertheless, the Cristeros considered that they were suffering only light losses, which was certainly true in comparison with the Federal losses, which were two or three times as heavy.

The technical facilities at the disposal of the army still did not make it possible for it to alter the balance of losses in its favour. Compared with 60,000 Federals killed (including 12 generals, 70 colonels, and 1,800 other officers), the Cristeros lost 40,000. A regiment which fell into an ambush was usually annihilated. General A. López said that the army had lost five regiments in this way in the mountains of Durango; General Mendoza lost 1,000 men in 1927, and Juan Domínguez the same number in 1928 during his march on Coalcomán; 3,000 Federals were killed in three years in the small state of Colima.

It remains to estimate the losses of the civilian population, but that is impossible in the light of the effects of reconcentration, famine, and epidemics: in three years, for example, the population of Colima fell from 85,000 to 60,000.

The cost in demographic terms was high, and the economic cost, which is similarly difficult to estimate accurately, was also heavy. The war, which affected the agricultural heartland of Old Mexico, precipitated a crisis in yields (see Table 22) and made its influence felt even in the national accounts.

Between 1924 and 1930, the area sown with maize in the whole country fell by 8.34 per cent, while the yield per hectare fell by 27.75 per

TABLE 22   *Harvests in the state of Colima (tons)*

Crop	1926	1927	1928
Rice	3,736	1,733	1,760
Coffee	176	160	150
Sugar-cane	40,520	33,000	15,000
Haricot beans	1,279	725	619
Maize	15,000	8,926	7,791

Source: Banco Nacional de Crédito Agrícola.

cent – that is, the amount of the harvest fell by 33·85 per cent.[54] These figures are confirmed by the 1930 census, which recorded a decrease in the area sown and in the value of the harvest: 1926, 6 million hectares and 475 million pesos; 1929, 5 million hectares and 400 million pesos. The production of maize fell from 2 million to 1·4 million tons, and that of haricot beans from 188,000 to 95,000 tons.

The Cristero regions were very seriously affected, and in Zacatecas the 1929 harvest was the worst of the century except for that of 1907, production being only one-quarter of normal production. In the Bajío, the loss was 35 per cent, and in the Altos, 60 per cent.

Emigration to the big cities or to the United States (500,000 persons) was the only remedy left open to the peasants when they were dispossessed of everything. For the first time this exodus, which traditionally had affected only the hamlets, struck the villages and small towns. This period sees the first gross increase in the population of the provincial capitals like Guadalajara and León, where the refugees from the countryside established themselves. The exodus to the interior of the country affected 500,000 people; a similar number crossed the American border, and established on a definitive basis the big Mexican colonies in Detroit, Chicago, and Los Angeles, and accentuated the Mexicanisation of California, where one finds, occupying entire streets in Mexicali and Tijuana, the old refugees from San Gabriel Tolimán, Tuxcacuesco, and other places in southern Jalisco, surrounded by their numerous progeny.

The misery and exodus of the people was accompanied by the ruin and bankruptcy of the big farmers: in January 1929 the National Chamber of Jalisco requested the banks to authorise the suspension of the payment of debts. Not only were they unable to do the sowing and harvesting, but they could not find a market for the small amounts of products that they could collect. Paralysis, destruction, and requisitioning finally brought about the ruin of the haciendas; this destruction, precipitated by the war, adding its effects to those of the world crisis, obliged Calles and Cárdenas to reorganise the agriculture of the nation on a new basis, and allowed them to carry out the agrarian reform at less cost, without having to destroy flourishing agricultural enterprises. The haciendas, which had managed to survive between 1910 and 1920, never recovered in those regions of the Bajío and the West which were ravaged by the Cristero War.

Finally, the war caused a modification of the rural areas and of the distribution of the population; the great rupture of 1926–9, with its sequel of resettlement, pillage, and burnings, which were prolonged as a result of the atmosphere of insecurity until 1940, left indelible traces. The network of villages, on the whole, survived, but that of the hamlets was destroyed. Those *rancherías* that had suffered so much from revolutionary banditry, wrecked and burned once again, could not be rebuilt and were simply wiped off the map. The death of the hamlets and the growth of the villages could be seen within each municipal district. The villages themselves had often been close to death, and some of them had been left totally deserted. In the places where the proprietors and the tradesmen had lost everything and had left, economic life never recovered. The Corcueras, the Negretes, and the López Portillos went to live in Guadalajara or Mexico City. San Gabriel, in 1930, was but a shadow of its former self; and Ejutla, with its impressive number of churches, convents, and schools, stood empty.

CHAPTER 10

Culture and Religion, Faith and Ideology

The peasants did not share the culture of the elites; or, to put it more precisely, their culture remained rooted in a base which was once common to all and which the elites in the Western world had abandoned at least as early as the eighteenth century. According to the answers to the questionnaires, 60 per cent of the Cristeros had never been to school, which did not mean that they were complete strangers to the written word; the author knows of many who learned to read by themselves, and devoured devotional books, legal textbooks, and works on astronomy. The archives of the combatants reveal the problem only too clearly; in illustration, a letter is reproduced below:

. O fi Sio nume ro Cators
Me deri jo a esade lega Sion de esta jefa tura a mi Cargo digo Lo Ciyi ente C erre Sebi Sus Sin seros rrecaudo en mis manos Ente rado de ellos Con elmismo C a riño des ien pre di jo auted que ento do es to y a lerta No mas es perando La ora y en Se jida el por ta dor les dira lo Siguiente L o que l o deseo y es Perando Ce ara el ul timo Sa crifisio Para lo gra r esa o portu nidad y C edo en es Pera de mi ju en deseo

[Signature][1]

This pathetic attempt to make himself understood in writing is from the pen of General Federico Vázquez, one of the great warriors of Durango. Although in studying the Cristero rebellion the written word certainly facilitates the work of the historian, he must be mindful of the fact that he is involved with a popular culture whose lively traditions derived from the Middle Ages and the sixteenth century. Manuscripts and interviews bear abundant witness to refuting any supposition that illiteracy confirms idiocy in rural life: on the contrary, they show that these people were remarkably capable of expressing themselves on matters close to their hearts. Accounts of travels, reports of battles, personal adventures, and often the most arduous metaphysical questions – for example, the comparative merits of different religions or the mystery of the Trinity, provided exercise for these rustic brains. This culture was basically oral, even in the written supports that it employed: a book would be passed from hand to hand, and read standing up by someone who could do so, before a circle of women working or men on guard. It was a truly oral culture, from the catechism of Fr Ripalda to the secular and sacred plays that were acted in the porches of the churches.[2]

Everything passed by way of the eyes, the ears, and the mouth, and a prodigious vocabulary was possessed by these men commonly regarded as inarticulate, who amused themselves with 'sayings, witticisms, proverbs, verbal games, jokes and subtle and ingenious tricks which provoked astonishment and admiration'.[3] Their educated contemporaries from the city did not understand one word in three of their beautiful Castilian speech of the fifteenth and sixteenth centuries, the delight of linguists. It was the language of a life deeply rooted in popular culture, based on the Bible, the apocryphal Gospels, the Golden Legend, the romances of chivalry, the courtly lyric – in short, the culture of the Christian West up to and including the Spanish translation of La Fontaine's fables in the eighteenth century. Listen to Ezequiel Mendoza:

> Un pavo un espejo halló,
> y por ver su gallardía,
> acercóse a una bujía
> y la cola se quemó.
> Cierto mono que escuchó
> sus lamentos de amargura,
> viendo su triste figura,
> le dijo con mucho gusto:
> Siempre halla castigo justo
> la vanidosa locura.

And:

> Cierto goloso ladrón
> del venenoso aguijón
> tuvo que sufrir la pena;
> ahora dice la miel es nuy buena
> es un bocado exquisito
> pero por el aguijón maldito
> no volveré al colmenar
> porque esto sí que es encontrar
> la pena tras el delito.[4]

It is merely intended here to emphasise that the peasant did not lack vocabulary or concepts, and that his cultural inferiority is not, at that moment in history, evident. Did he have an inferiority complex *vis-à-vis* the townsman? Doubtless he did, but to counter-balance this Aurelio Acevedo asserts: 'I feel proud of being a *ranchero* because that means being free from the politicking, trickery and ignoble behaviour of the townsman. The *ranchero*'s way of life is alien to the hypocrisy and double-dealing of the politics of the cities.' Their historical testimony was action, action over a long period, actual events.

Religious Life

The language of the Cristeros was that of the old Spain of St John of the Cross and of Cervantes; their religion was the same. Neither the imprisonment nor the exile of the clergy prevented the conduct of worship, at least in a simplified form. In places controlled by the Government, priests were hidden near the bedsides of the dying, most often assisted by 'holy women'; Mass was celebrated in secret; and, there were especially solemn and well-attended demonstrations of religious fervour. For three years the sanctuary of Guadalupe, in Mexico City, and the churches throughout the country, were not left empty for a moment.[5] Daily life was full of small manifestations of religious feeling, which were severely punished.[6] A military pass was necessary in order to wear mourning, which had become a symbol of resistance.

Often there were no longer any priests, and a layman undertook the direction of liturgical life, as did Cecilio E. Valtierra at Jalpa de Cánovas; every morning he read the Church's office in the presence of the faithful; these 'white Masses' were accompanied by other innovations, under the pressure of circumstances. Valtierra was authorised to baptise and even to celebrate marriages, and he received the consecrated Host in custody to give to the sick or those in danger of death.[7]

The Mass was the essential event, and it was all the more desired for being infrequent; it was lived with a new intensity:

What prayers and pleas were heard there, addressed to God and to the most pure Virgin, to all the saints of Heaven! What thanks were given to them for favours already received! And what requests for new favours for us poor and miserable sinners! How brightly lit was the altar, the special palace of the King of Kings, Jesus present in the Sacrament for our temporal and eternal good ... The sermon which the Father preached made us cry for sheer joy. He thanked us and gave us his blessing, and crossing ourselves many times we went out into the square feeling very happy. Among the people, who had been deeply moved by the festival, all was joy and happiness.[8]

Singing hymns and saying the Rosary were an accompaniment to daily life on the march and in camp; the Cristeros prayed and sang far into the night, saying the Rosary together on their knees, singing praises to God between each decade. The combatants asked for blessing before going off to fight, and their commanders urged them to make a true act of contrition before the battle, and they charged the enemy singing psalms and crying out, 'Long live Christ the King! Long live the Virgin of Guadalupe!' It could not be otherwise with these men, who had sworn before God to conquer or die. The nickname Cristos-Reyes or Cristeros, applied to them by the Government, which has come down to posterity, emphasises the most essential element of all – Christ, living in the Trinity, and accessible through the Sacraments.

Ideology and Motivations

The theme of the Kingship of Christ, considered in its eschatological sense (*Thy Kingdom come*) is situated at the crossroads of ideologies, faith, and mental processes; it reminds us that we are living in an environment poor in popular history, because everything happens at the level of élites, and in Christian education. It has no other monuments except churches, convents, and bishops' palaces, which provide a negative demonstration on account of their transformation into barracks, libraries, and governors' palaces. Toponymy is almost entirely religious, and the peasants might well say that 'Mexico was the son of a priest'.[9] In a difficult life the Cross has always appeared as a mystery based on reason, honoured and revered for the very reason that it is the sign of the Kingship of Christ. This Kingship is remembered in the Third Sorrowful Mystery: the crowning with thorns. This crown marks the promise of God; for them, this Kingdom of which the peasants speak, without it being possible for us to see in this a manifestation of chiliasm, because they do not confuse the two kingdoms, that of this world which has been delivered for a time to the Prince of Evil, and the heavenly Jerusalem, the promise of salvation. The politicians knew nothing of this great expectation, the clergy distrusted it, but the Cristeros *lived* it.

Recognising the legitimacy of established powers, because all authority came from God, and without the will of God 'not a leaf stirred', the Cristero was prepared to render unto Caesar the things that were his, as long as he did not make war on God. From the day when Caesar became Herod, threatening the salvation of men, he deprived himself of legitimacy, and, like Antiochus, he had to be fought by the new Maccabees. In the words of Ezequiel Mendoza:

All those impious men who, from Cain to those who desolate the universe now, who appear to be great and powerful, who make a great noise and demand that men worship them, are only princes of error; they are nothing but beasts come up out of the abyss, but God has always sent truly great men to fight them, ever since the Archangel Michael in Heaven, all history is the history of this war. Woe to the tyrants who persecute Christ the King! They are the beasts in human shape of whom the Apocalypse speaks! ... Now the Calleses are pressing us, they say it is because we are bad, because we are stubborn in wanting to defend the honour and glory of Him who died naked on the highest Cross between two thieves, because He was the worst of all humans because he did not wish to submit to the supreme lord of the earth.

In other words, government was a human affair, the sovereign was a sinful man like the rest of them, put there by God. As long as it does not conflict with one's moral conscience and the honour of God, he is to be obeyed, for revolution will only bring to the top new masters as sinful and as mad as he. The state is nothing more than a human institution, without any charisma. This conviction, which may operate in a conservative sense, now operated in a revolutionary direction because Caesar had become evil, he had been struck by the folly of the great, he was the bad politician *par excellence*. The Cristeros said that 'Pharaoh had hardened his heart'; and Ezequiel Mendoza exclaimed; 'Poor bats! They think they're birds, and they're mice.'

Calles, regarded as the *Rex iniquus*, the tyrant spoken of by Daniel, St Paul, St John, and the prophets of Israel, simply had to be fought, 'because I think it is better to die fighting for Christ the King and the Virgin of Guadalupe and all Their family, and not take a single step against the one true God, even if the Devil is angered.'[10]

The war was, therefore, just, and the Cristeros were 'fighting the best of fights, in this deceitful world, some with arms, and the others helping in a thousand ways the defenders who, leaving everything, were venturing themselves for only three loves: their God, their country, their home'.

Besides being a religious movement, the Cristiada was a patriotic one; the affair of the flags was a symbolic manifestation of this, and was all the more important because symbolism counts for so much in men. The Cristeros had been shocked by the scarcity of national flags among the Federal troops, not to mention the *agraristas*, whose red flags reminded them of butchers' emblems. They reported with indignation the treachery of an army which had abandoned the tricolour flag in favour of red, black, or red-and-black flags, or flags which were immediately given various interpretations: a hoisted flag to signify that no quarter would be given, crossbones and a broom on an earth-coloured background, which symbolised the desire to sweep religion from Mexico. The Cristeros, however, flew the oldest national standard, the tricolour flag of Independence, and charged with the Virgin of Guadalupe on one side and the eagle devouring the serpent on the other. The Virgin had been represented on the banners of Morelos, who had defended Mexico and the faith against the foreign (Franco-Spanish) heretic. To the Cristeros, who considered themselves the heirs of Father Morelos, the 'Turk' Calles, the hireling of international Freemasonry, represented the Yankee and Protestant foreigner, desirous of concluding the enterprise begun in Texas. The subhuman situation of the immigrants had not been forgotten by the Mexicans who had worked temporarily in the United States from 1910. The Virgin of Guadalupe and her servant Morelos symbolised the peculiar motivations and values of the combatant group. They did not adopt any national heroes after the time of Morelos and Iturbide, certainly not those proposed by the Liberals or the followers of Carranza; among men, apart from the fathers of the Independence movement, they recognised only certain bishops noted for their energetic conduct or their sanctity. Even then, they chose regional rather than national heroes. They called themselves, or were called by the people, the 'Popular forces', 'the Liberators', 'the National Guards'.

Azuela was right to assert: 'honour ... together with patriotism and religion made up the personality of the Mexican ... those who know the *ranchero* of the Altos zone of Jalisco or of the Bajío will understand what I mean'.[11] Peasants, workers, and family men, they had no love for war:

What a tragedy! What treacheries, what misunderstanding, what envy and usurpation of the just rights of others! What injustice on the part of the bad government and also on our part! There is no respect for the rights of God nor the rights of one's neighbour, and with good reason God is punishing us with war, hunger and pestilence, the greatest plagues of the earth. Oh God, have mercy on us and forgive us, Holy Mary, pray to God for us.

And they pitied their enemies: 'Poor devils, they did not know what they were doing, everything went off at half-cock; this is what happens to those who believe themselves to belong to Satan, through those that serve him to ruin souls.' Their concept of the just war was not lacking in complexity, because the death of the enemy was not pleasing to God; only the blood of the martyrs could wipe out sin and conquer Satan, and the Cristeros did not want to become like their enemies. In this context, suffering and death were part of normal obedience to the Divine will.

The former Governor of Durango, Pastor Rouaix, who had been a member of the Constituent Assembly, was understandably surprised by the insurrection and by the passionate fervour, for example, of Santiago Bayacora, an Indian village renowned for its peaceable and resigned nature. The universal astonishment that was felt at the extent of the movement led those who felt it to reassure themselves by attributing the Cristero rising to the fanaticism and ignorance of peasants who were the victims of the criminal hypocrisy of a politically minded and rapacious clergy. The priest given to intrigue, the stupefied peasants, a political error (the Calles Law) – this was the scheme of causation which made it possible for the observer to eliminate the Cristeros as a factor in their own war. Of course, the presence of the priest could serve to strengthen the decision of the insurgent group, but this priest, when he approved the Cristeros' doings, was merely reflecting the rural milieu from which he had sprung. At the same time, it is true that, although the priest was not responsible for the rising, he was at the same time the cause and the pretext, and this allowed the Government to cast him as the guilty party, falling into the error of *post hoc, ergo propter hoc*.[16]

As a cause and a pretext, in sociological terms as well as on the ideological and eschatological plane, the priest was indeed in two senses the centre of the life of the Christian peasants: the church, as has been observed, was the centre of local life because it guaranteed entertainment, information, and education, and the priest was the head, the counsellor,[13] the 'natural' leader, at the crossroads of the scarce networks of co-operation existing in the rural world. The Government's antagonistic attitude towards him was an attack on the keystone of rural society. It is difficult to under-estimate his role, which spread far outside the religious context, as President Lázaro Cárdenas (1934–40) well understood. The priest had originated in the peasantry, and he was the symbol and pride of that peasantry, while those who drove him out *manu militari* came, precisely, from outside, from Mexico City, from Guadalajara, supported by the group which had benefited from the Revolution, called in by the local anticlericals, threatening the position of the priest within the community, and indeed the community itself.

The priest was also the one who dispensed the Sacraments; he was at the centre of spiritual and sacramental life, and his disappearance brought with it the death of the soul, which was much more to be feared than that of the body. That was why the peasants took up arms – because the Revolution was trying to take the priest away from them; the measures against the priests affected the whole of the people at the same time, and represented a radical rupture in individual lives and in the history of the community as a whole, which was unacceptable and was, indeed, not accepted. The religious fervour of the future Cristeros is sufficient to explain their attitude, and the clergy had no need to become involved in manifestations of that fervour in which some have supposed the presence or the instigation of the priests.[14] The pilgrimages, which were mystical forms of protest, the acts of public penance in 1926, practices which had normally taken place in times of trial,[15] where the participants were the people living in their faith and in its manifestations, were considered as acts of provocation by administrators and the police, who understood nothing of this mentality.[16] In fact, they served as a prelude to the insurrection; they were both training for it, and a last warning to the Government.

The universal motivation of the masses (though this motivation did not exclude others) was religious.

We did not want to abandon the Church in the hands of the military men. What would we do without it, without its festivals, without its images which patiently listened to our lamentations? What were they condemning us to? To pine away among the stones and work the dry ground? To die like street curs, without any complaint, after leading a life of misery? It was better to die fighting! There is no evil that lasts for a hundred years, and he who spits at heaven, his spit falls to the ground again.

As Jerónimo Gutiérrez put it: 'There was more than enough reason to fight,' and in those words 'more than enough' there was room for all particular and general grievances, and all combinations of local circumstances — the execution of a priest, of a relative, general repression.

This explains why peace-loving people felt able to give their blessing to their sons and send them into battle:

The government is taking everything from us, our maize, our pastures, our little animals and, as if that were not enough, they want us to live like animals, without religion and without God, but this last they will never live to see, for every time it is offered to us we will cry, Long live Christ the King! Long live the Virgin of Guadalupe! Long live the Unión Popular! Down with the Government![17]

It was, therefore, a reaction of self-defence, and a very natural one. The peasant knew only one thing: they were closing the churches and persecuting the priests. He saw only one thing: the soldiers arrived, closed the church, arrested the priest, shot those who protested, hanged their prisoner, set fire to the church, and raped the women of the dissident village. These outraged peasants, who loved their village, their church, and their priest, quite naturally rose in rebellion. It mattered little that other interests and other grievances were mingled with the primary motivation. At a moment when religious feeling was dominant, spiritual structures, to which one cannot deny at least a sociological reality, were a powerful force, acting at the same time as and under the influence of other events. They might have many grievances against the Government (this has been observed earlier in this work), but above all they could not tolerate the attempt to eradicate religion. Inseparable from culture, religion pervaded their daily lives at every level, and the aggression profoundly disturbed the psychological, affective, and existential equilibrium of the population. To extirpate Catholicism (which Narciso Bassols was to try to do in the 1930s by means of socialist education), was to impose a process of deculturation (or, according to the Positivist hypothesis, of acculturation) that inevitably led to violent conflict. The people, both through the Church and to a wider extent than the Church, underwent an experience that provoked anguish, obsession, and neurosis. Deprived of their priests, their spiritual leaders, tormented by feelings of guilt because they had been submissive up to that moment,[18] the people, until then so patient, rose in arms, to the astonishment of everybody – and in the first place, of their bishops.[19] To the stupefaction of the narrowly rationalistic authorities, which had not foreseen the consequences of their acts and did not even realise the entire scope of them, there began an insurrection very different from the traditional agrarian risings or political rebellions. One thing was certain – the fierce determination of the people to defend their rights, after the crucial moment when they realised that the initial step had been taken, that they had broken irremediably with the world which they had known and accepted all their lives. That was why the volunteers said goodbye to their families: 'We will never see each other again.' A new and terrifying truth became manifest as they carried out acts such as banding together in conspiracy, or capturing the town council offices after which there could be no return: by these acts, they were participating in a new order, in another world.

The two sides in conflict had no commonly shared values; the Government could not, therefore, give any consideration to the point of view of its adversary. The historian cannot confine himself to a study of the decisions taken, because violent action and war arose out of the clash of two alien ideological systems. The war reflected the social and cultural orientations of the opposing sides, and their particular interests, and, even though it was in fact unpredictable (neither the Government nor the Church had foreseen it), it did not for that reason have any less of a basis in logic. From then on, war and sociology became confused, because society became an expression of pure violence – all the more so because the adversaries were of unequal strength and the Government, being the stronger of the two, wanted to make its law obeyed. It is thus that one must interpret the well-known obstinacy displayed by Calles, that will to power which some have tried to interpret as being characteristic of the man, and which was a fact of power, the result of direct and untramelled pressure.

The classic interpretation,[20] which was essentially the working hypothesis of the Government, was that the real Catholics were to be found only among the lower classes and the women, who were by definition incapable of rebellion and were respectfully submissive to the authorities supported by the army. This would explain how the state could, with impunity, persecute the religion of the majority of its citizens. This thesis, which is correct both as regards the social base of recruitment of the Catholics and the persecution of the majority by the minority, has been demonstrated to be erroneous in its assertion of the passivity of the Mexicans. And this refutation of a thesis which is so reasonable and so often confirmed, was to take an unreasonable form, which was too often to be attributed to collective hysteria or to bloodthirsty fanaticism and the desire for martyrdom.

Martyrdom

Men and wars are not open books to be read clearly, and the spilling of blood is not a proof of deep conviction; it does not automatically transform the hero into a martyr. 'There have been martyrdoms suffered in solitude, amid tortures and tempting offers; other men have died in the collective exaltation experienced by a group, without any depressing preamble to their death nor any offer of tempting alternatives. There are some martyrdoms that are proud acts of defiance, and others that are offered up for the salvation of the executioners.'[21]

One must consider it as a manifestation of the desire for Heaven when one learns that after the rising on Sunday, 27 November 1926, at Totatiche, the oldest people who were unarmed, joined the crowd, saying: 'We are going, we old ones who are good for nothing, to give our lives to God.'[22] Remarks such as these were common: 'We must win Heaven now that it is cheap,' and 'How our grandfathers would have loved to win glory like this! And now God is giving it to us! I'm off.'[23] Claudio Becerra, spared because of his extreme youth, the only survivor of the twenty-seven shot at Sahuayo (21 March 1927), later wept before the crypt where his companions were buried, and said: 'I drink, Father, because I am sorry that God did not want me as a martyr.'[24] The desire for martyrdrdom, thought of as a grace and as the means to advance the salvation of Mexico and of the world, was quite evident. 'It was a great adventure, so great and so noble, we were so happy at that time,' said the witnesses, who remarked of the victims: 'Our Lord has been pleased to confer on him the martyr's crown'.[25]

You and I deplore from the bottom of our hearts the death of these men who offered in good faith their lives, their families and their worldly interests, who shed their blood for God and our beloved country, as true Christian martyrs do; their blood, united with that of Our Lord and with that of all the martyrs of the Holy Ghost, will obtain for us from God the Father the blessings that we hope for on Earth and in Heaven; blessed are those who die for the love of God who made Heaven and Earth and is in all things by his essence, potentiality and presence, not like the false gods of Plutarco Elías Calles and other madmen seduced by Satan, who offers them the oxen and the ox-cart in this life and afterwards makes them into stew in the Hell of torments.[26]

The young Honorio Lamas, executed together with his father Manuel Lamas, said to his mother in consolation: 'How easy Heaven is now, mother!'[27] And Josefina Arellano spoke in these terms of the death of her very young brother-in-law:

Silverio, who was younger than my husband, pulled back the blanket that covered the doorway and greeted the Government by saying softly, 'Long live Christ the King!' and when the echo of his voice died away he was already on his way to receive the martyr's palm and crown, for he had always said that he was a Catholic and had no other interest than the love of Christ. A few moments later, I drew back the blanket to go out, leaving the little ones in the arms of Domingo, to go out to die, treading on the dead bodies, I stopped in the doorway, my God, what did I see? Above the stone wall many rifles were pointing at me, my eyes clouded over, my body trembled, but I remembered that this moment was for me, I imagined the crown and I almost touched the palm.[28]

Cosme Herrera Valencia, a civilian shot at Degollado by General J. Carrillo for having refused to serve in the army, said before he died: 'I want the life of the soul, not that of the body.'[29] Carlos Vargas announced the death of his brother: 'On the one hand I am mortified, but at least the poor man died on a good day; he died on Good Friday and they tell me he had a beautiful death, how lucky he was.'[30] 'May God receive them into his Holy Glory; the Kingdom of Heaven is for the humble,' exclaimed Doña Petra Cabral, passing by the bodies of the men hanged by General J. B. Vargas.[31]

The calm confrontation of death by the Cristeros who were taken prisoner always made an impression on the Federals: one might say that this was a characteristic of Mexican wars, that the combatants should give proof of their courage, or their contempt for death. Literature, songs, and the cinema have popularised this image of the virile Mexican, indifferent to life and death, and of his murderers, weeping out of admiration for him. Although the death of the Cristeros might be considered as resembling this model, its content and significance were entirely different, for it was an experience of communion with God and not a posture before men. One might then say of the Cristero movement that, rather than a Crusade, it was a collective 'imitation of Christ', the sacrifice of the Cristeros rather than the pursuit of the death of the persecutors.

The tranquillity with which these peasants went to their deaths, when their greatest preoccupation in peacetime had been to avoid dying a sudden death, to avoid dying without having the time to prepare for the 'transit', above all, to avoid dying in one's sleep and without the Sacraments – this new-found tranquillity is a proof of the great break with the past that 1926 signified, and also a proof that this epoch was that of the 'great mystical adventure, holy and noble'. Poor, insignificant creatures became martyrs and said so quite calmly, and ceased to obey the powers which only the day before they had acknowledged respectfully.

Norberto López, shot in 1928 at Encarnación de Díaz, refused the pardon that was offered him if he enlisted in the army, and said: 'Ever since I took up arms I have had the intention of giving my life for Christ, and I'm not going to break the fast at a quarter to twelve.'[32]

Filled with fervour for the 'good death', for which they had asked in their prayers since their childhood, they expressed themselves like Thomas of Canterbury: 'The victims are many, the number of martyrs grows every day. If only I could have that good fortune!' This was the attitude of the woman of Huejuquilla who wept, and said that she had been abandoned by God because her family had been spared; later her only son fell fighting, and the mother's tears did not efface the joy of the believer.[33]

It is easy to laugh at that ignorant priest, who had had great difficulty in becoming ordained because of his rustic ignorance, and who distributed safe-conducts for Heaven to those who died bravely.[34] In fact, he was saying, as the Fathers of the Church had done, that the blood of the martyrs is the seed of Christians, that the Devil knows that sins are remitted for acts of martyrdom and it is he who tries to 'make us renounce the purple'. What a great sorrow it was, not to deserve to be persecuted for Christ nor to die for the name of the Son of God? The Cristeros said to one another that the persecution unleashed against the Mexican Church was a great favour, a proof of the predilection for that country of the Virgin of Guadalupe and Christ the King.

Aspects of Religious Sociology

The data available make it possible to advance the hypothesis of a Christianity solidly structured as regards religious knowledge and firmly rooted in the practice of Sunday worship and the frequenting of the Sacraments; it is notable that frequent communion was very widespread in 1926, particularly in the form of attendance at Mass on the first Friday of the month. Religious instruction was given to all through the catechism (between the ages of two and six), and later in the confraternities for men and women,[35] the trade unions, liturgical life, and the practice of the Rosary.

It has already been observed that everyday life was pervaded by religion. It was true in the countryside, where churches and crosses were to be seen everywhere; the microcosm of the municipal district covered the entire topography of the nation, which was divided into two spheres, between which the bond of communication was St Isidore the Ploughman: the Church and agriculture. In the recently established villages, the toponymy was almost exclusively religious; elsewhere, the priests often renamed the places with religious names, so that geography was indeed Biblical and celestial, as is apparent in the novels of Yáñez, Rulfo, and Arreola. This religion was functional; it answered the needs of the rural family, the village, and the peasant; it was the projection of their experience of life; it answered their questions, appeased their anguish, and guided their existence; the presence of God, the need to communicate with Him and the most intense religious experience were palpable realities for the rural Mexicans, who formed 70 per cent of the population of the country (90 per cent if one includes the lower classes of the provincial towns).

The values of this society were religious, even though in everyday life there was some discrepancy between values and attitudes; this hiatus, which so shocked the people to whom religion is a system of morality at the service of society, was called sin, and confession and the sacraments were available to efface it. Not all the Christians were saints, but neither were they all drunkards, debauchees, fanatical murderers draped in scapulars and plunged in dark supersitition, as they were depicted in the official literature, that of the Government and of the 'enlightened' Christians. Faith is not the same as morality, and the system had its own logic, for the principle on which it rested was God. In the towns, even in Puebla, with its ecclesiastical atmosphere – and this extreme example is conclusive – values were no longer religious, but merely clerical. Secularisation had taken place slowly, ever since the eighteenth century; in 1926, it was already a *fait accompli* and irreversible, even though Puebla, Querétaro, and Morelia were populated by 'devout' people (*beatos*). The *beato* was a townsman, not a countryman; he lived in a mental universe divided into two parts, and there was no continuity between religion and life, whereas the peasant, a great drinker and eater (when he had the opportunity), a dissolute rascal, passionate and violent, a man of strong emotions, lived in a religious universe which was all of one piece.

In Mexico, before the nineteenth century, the towns were Christian and the rural areas considerably less so. The theme, dear to preachers, of the good and eternally religious peasant, contrasted with the city of perdition, is a mere myth when it is extended beyond its historical limits; the relationships were reversed in Mexico after 1860, and the second process of evangelisation (which was perhaps the first) was still in full force in 1925. To give one example of this: the religious reconquest of Colima took place between 1884 and 1900; six parishes had been founded in the sixteenth century, two in the seventeenth, four in 1803, one in 1814, and one in 1832 – a total of fourteen. Between 1832 and 1884 there was not a single new foundation. Between 1884 and 1900, nine new parishes were founded. Originally evangelised by the Franciscans, Colima had to wait until the end of the nineteenth century to find a numerous clergy, recruited locally, looking after a large number of small and recently founded parishes; small Colima had numerous chapels and churches. The scattered populated areas of this zone were given such names as Capillitas, Monasterio, San Pedro, Merced, Sangre de Cristo, La Pasión, El Beaterio. Everywhere, there were flourishing confraternities and trade unions.[36]

In Jalisco, Zacatecas, Nayarit, and Michoacán, on the basis of superficial surveys,[37] one can observe the same phenomenon. Was this true of the rest of the country? Local monographs and occasional pieces of more detailed research[38] would seem to confirm this hypothesis, which would coincide with the great activity of the bishops between 1860 and 1925, particularly Mgr Munguía and Mgr Orozco.

It is in this context of missionary renovation that one must consider the undertaking of Fr Magallanes of Totatiche, who renewed contact (for virtually the first time since the eighteenth century) with the Huicholes, establishing a catechists' centre at Azqueltán, headed by Fr Lorenzo Placencia, and thereafter making efforts to evangelise the sierra itself.[39]

This symbolic revival of the Jesuit missions of the Great Nayar shows the extent of the second religious conquest of Mexico. In 1925, it can be said that the statements which cast doubt on the Christian character of the faith of the people are as superficial as those apparently more scientific interpretations which saw nothing but syncretism and everywhere denounced 'the idols behind the altars'. In trying to determine the geographical extent of Mexican Christianity, it can be asserted that many Indians of Oaxaca, Guerrero, Michoacán, and Durango were real Catholics; the Indians of Yucatán and the Chiapas, which were different worlds, isolated from traditional Mexico are not under consideration here. Other Indians (Huicholes, Yaquis, and the peoples of the northern sierra of Puebla, among them) were deeply influenced by Christianity; there was a juxtaposition of different religious systems, rather than true syncretism. Finally, there were few pagans.

Reactions to the religious persecution differed according to the region, taking the form of resistance, a lesser degree of resistance, or acquiescence. One might try to explain this in terms of historical factors – the existence of a process of evangelisation in the sixteenth century or during the Colonial period; the nature of this evangelisation; and the occurrence of a second process of evangelisation in the nineteenth and twentieth centuries. Likewise, explanation might be made in terms of the population – depending on whether the region concerned was predominantly Indian, *mestizo*, or white – or in terms of the nature of religious faith. The racial explanation is not very helpful (the Colimote Indians were as passionately Christian and Cristero as the Creoles of the Altos de Jalisco region); one must, therefore, have recourse to other explanations, and analyse the varying forms of religious expression.

The religion of the Cristeros was, with a few exceptions, the traditional Roman Catholic religion, strongly rooted in the Hispanic Middle Ages. The catechism of Fr Ripalda, which was known by heart, and the practice of the Rosary, a system of prayer which taught people to meditate daily on all the mysteries of religion and therefore afforded a comprehensive knowledge of it, provided these people with a basic theological knowledge which was surprisingly soundly based.[40] Christ, known in His human life and in His sufferings, and with whom the believer could often identify himself, loved in His human surroundings the Virgin, the patriarch Joseph, the patron of the good death, and all the saints who occupied an important, and completely orthodox, place in everyday life – this Christ was adored in the mystery of the Trinity; this form of religion, which was so close to the believer, was described as superstition by the American missionaries (both Catholic and Protestant), and this view was shared by European Catholics. In all its aberrations, in all its strange efflorescences, this religion was fundamentally Christian, profoundly personal, and earnestly lived.

The Bible and the liturgy, and spiritual authors whose names and even whose existence were unknown, peopled the spirit and the collective memory of these people, who in their meditations and their actions interpreted this teaching figuratively. There are numerous examples of symbolic thought, of reasoning by analogy, and of explicit references; far more frequent are implicit references and quotations.

The practice of the Rosary, so important, would find a place at the heart of any demonstration of the unquestioned Catholicity of Mexican religious faith. One might study the history and geography of its propagation; here it can only be asserted that the Cristeros recited it from Santiago Bayacora to Miahuatlán. In fact, the Rosary continually called to mind the mission of Christ, basing its teaching on the unique mission of the Virgin in the work of salvation, reminding Christians of the grandeur and the solemn obligations implicit in their baptism that shaped them in the image of Christ and from thenceforth enlisted them in the service of His Kingdom. Leading the mind as it did towards Christ the King and the Virgin, the Rosary differed from the stupid and arithmetical repetition of a magical prayer as much as the cult of the Virgin of Guadalupe differed from Mariolatry. All the partial analyses are correct: woman, maternity, and virginity are present (as they are in Mariology everywhere), but so are Eve, Mary, and the Church. The cult of the Virgin of Guadalupe was in no way different from the cult of the Virgin in Russia (where there are eight hundred places of Marian pilgrimage), in Poland, or in France. The Protestants had rightly observed the close links which united Mary with the Catholic Church, and the Virgin of Guadalupe, far from separating Mexico from Catholicity as Calles and the schismatics hoped, preserved the mystic vision of the Church, which was at the heart of the Cristero movement. Mary was indeed the 'Flower of Mankind', and she was also the co-redemptrix, the co-saviour, and inseparable from the entirety of Catholic theology. It is, moreover, striking that when she appeared in dreams, or in broad daylight, to the Cristeros, the *agraristas*, or the soldiers, she did so in accordance with the modes of the entire Christian tradition.

We are speaking here only of the faith of the majority; there was also the Virgin-Tonantzín revered by some groups, and in this case the pre-Columbian element predominated over the Christian element. Among the overwhelming majority, it was the black Virgin of Guadalupe who took first place, not the idol behind the altar.

Within the vast bloc of the Catholic population, regional characteristics obviously introduced variations. In the Sierra of Durango, which was well towards the north, one found the most simple and primitive Catholics, whom Octavio Paz has described as Catholics along the lines of Peter the Hermit, 'Catholics of the four principles': these Christians, isolated and without priests, were nevertheless baptised, confirmed, and married (after the woman had been 'abducted' according to the traditional ritual), despite their distance from the nearest parish church. Far to the south, in the hot lands of Michoacán, and to the west, on the coast of Jalisco and Nayarit, there lived their brothers in violence.[41] There was violence in their lives, in their emotions, and in their faith. The Catholics of the Altos de Jalisco or the north-west of Michoacán, despite a similar susceptibility to emotion, had benefited from organisation by the clergy from 1860 onwards, and were devout puritans in comparison with the groups mentioned above.

What is remarkable is that the presence or the absence of a priest provoked only superficial variations, which were in no way essential. There is no point, therefore, in looking for differences of behaviour as a result of the ecclesiastical situation in 1925, and it is not true to say that the religious manifestations of the Cristeros are those of a community guided by its priests, as opposed to those of a Christianity without priests.

Would it be right to say that the Cristero movement was rooted in that essential characteristic of the faith – sacramental life?[42] Can one distinguish two zones in which Christianity was practised, one rooted in sacramental life, the other without it? There was a zone characterised by a Christianity that was hardly sacramental at all, where the priest was absent (as in Yucatán), or present but not really known in his capacity as a priest, being regarded as an official in the service of the traditional organisation, deprived of his sacramental functions (as was the case in certain parts of Puebla, Hidalgo, and Guerrero); here priests were persecuted, in the sense that the Sacraments, and above all the Eucharist, were denied, in a region or a village where non-eucharistic Christianity held sway. Nevertheless, the insurrection took place to the cry of 'Long live Christ the King!' and this expression has no sense outside the mystery of the Eucharist. This form of Christianity was to be found in the Indian regions, but the Mixtecs and the peoples of the Sierra Tarasca, in Colima, and the Sierra de Durango were just as Indian, and belonged to the second category.

A Christianity based on the Sacraments, on the Eucharist, when there was suspension of worship and the disappearance of the priest, who might be several days' march away, but to whom one went, led to spiritual death, from which one escaped by means of the insurrection. There is no other explanation for the fact that Durango, an Indian territory, without priests, and the hot lands of the West, which were Indian, *mestizo*, or Creole, and also without priests, display this form of Christianity. On the other hand, in the region of Puebla, where there were always numerous parish clergy, the first form appears to have predominated. The architectural wealth of Puebla and its surroundings, and the absence of religious buildings (apart from a few small churches built by the Colonial missions) in the other regions mentioned, might lead one to think that Puebla was Catholic while Durango was not. Might an explanation be found as a result of historical research, going back in time to the earliest processes of evangelisation?

The Government made a splendid gesture in calling the rebels 'Cristeros', thus placing Christ in the centre of the insurrection, and giving it its sense and its significance. The persecution of the priest, a revered figure, loved as the dispenser of the Sacraments, who brought about the coming of Christ under the semblance of bread and wine, was resented as a diabolical war against Christ Himself; the persecutor was, therefore, the Devil himself. The Government's interpretation hit the nail on the head and gave the real dimensions of the problem; it went a long way to proving that Mexican Christianity, far from being deformed or superficial, was solidly and correctly based on Christ, showing devotion to the Virgin Mary because of Christ, and in consequence was sacramental and orientated towards salvation, eternal life, and the Kingdom. During the war, it was remarkable how the saints were relegated to their proper place, while the ardent desire for Heaven became openly manifest. The priest faded into the background when the great event of the insurrection took place, and the sacrament of blood took the place of all the others.

This religious system covered almost everything: the people on the other side and the persecutors were part of the system when they cried 'Long live the Great Devil!' Calles, as the mirror-image of the Cristero, testified to an entire religious structure.

Without considering themselves to be the true Church, the Cristeros had the opportunity to meditate on the sacred texts; one of their favourite ones was that of the widow's mite: 'Verily I say unto you, That this poor widow hath cast more in, than all they which have cast into the treasury: for all they did cast in of their abundance; but she of her want did cast in all that she had, even all her living.' (Mark 12. 43–4). They referred constantly to St James against the rich men, to Daniel against the tyrant, and to the sayings in the Gospels against the scribes and Pharisees, whom they identified with the rich Catholics.

The passages which inspired them were those proclaiming the great eschatological events: the announcement of the ruin of Jerusalem, the tribulation, the abomination of desolation, the announcement of the Last Judgement, the prophecies of persecution, and, finally, the Beatitudes. Certain that 'the gates of Hell shall not prevail against it', they had the conviction of their own necessity, of their indispensable part in God's plan, so that the recruitment of new saints, the growth of the Body of Christ, should hasten the coming of the Time of Christ, of the Kingdom. To die as a martyr was to work for the advancement of the Kingdom. Ezequiel Mendoza quoted from the Apocalypse: 'it was said unto them, that they should rest yet for a little season, until their fellowservants also and their brethren, that should be killed as they were, should be fulfilled' (Revelation 6. 11).

One can imagine the distance that separated the well-to-do classes (considered as a whole) from these peasants who had remained firmly rooted in the tradition, more or less obscured, of ancient Christianity. The latter group understood nothing of the societies for moralisation, the pious clubs, and the co-operatives for devotion organised by the former; they were quite capable of going to Mass on Sunday, still suffering from the effects of their drunken debauch the night before, and leaving before the end of the service to relieve themselves against the wall of the church;[43] private morality, which the rich man admitted did not apply to politics or business, and which he reproached the common people for not possessing, was alien to the peasants, who were capable only of living a great adventure which was both spiritual and temporal, a vast popular pilgrimage towards the Kingdom of the Beatitudes of the Gospels. At that time, there were cases of real intoxication among the faithful as a result of the contemplation of those ceremonies which were forbidden and were now celebrated with a new depth. When peace returned, it was in an atmosphere of delirium, of ecstasy, that they celebrated their deeply venerated ceremonies in the churches, which had been closed for too long.

'If I am going to die for Christ I have no need to make my confession,' answered Aurelio Acevedo to Fr Correa, who was giving him advice on the matter. 'The majority of us thought the same. This was the baptism of blood which, they say, is better than ordinary baptism.' The people, cut off from their sources of the Sacraments, were administering to themselves the collective Sacrament, that of the bloody sacrifice. Humbly laying down their arms when the priests ordered them to,[44] and having gained no temporal advantage, the Cristero people were perhaps the only people that has been able to distinguish between what is God's and what is Caesar's.

On 31 July 1926, certain men drove Our Lord God out of the temples, from off the altars and out of the homes of Catholics; but other men took action so that He would return; these men did not see that the Government had innumerable soldiers, and arms and money beyond counting. They did not see this. What they saw was the defence of their God, of their Religion, of their Mother the Holy Church, that is what they saw. It did not matter to these men to leave their families, their children, their wives and all that they possessed; they went off to the battlefields, to seek Our Lord God; the torrents, the mountains, the forests and the hills bore witness that these men were speaking to Our Lord God when they cried out the holy names 'Long live Christ the King, long live the Most Holy Virgin of Guadalupe, long live Mexico!'; the same places bear witness that these men soaked the ground with their blood and that, not content with that, they gave their very lives so that Our Lord God should return, and Our Lord God, seeing that these men were truly seeking Him, was good enough to return to his churches, to his altars, and to the homes of Catholics, where we can see Him today.[45]

Part III   After the Peace

CHAPTER 11

Ten Years Later

The last Cristeros laid down their arms at the end of September 1929, 'and have quietly returned to their homes without bothering with the formality of a surrender ... to work on the farms from which they originally came'.[1] 'It was expected that after the religious warfare was ended a number of the Cristeros would turn bandit. This has not resulted.'[2]

For the Cristeros, who were received as victors in their villages, the festivities of the summer of 1929 had a taste of ashes, despite the renewal of public worship, despite the good relations between Church and state. Although the mass of the people rejoiced without a second thought in what they sensed as a victory, the Cristeros felt that the Church had robbed them of a victory which they thought they were about to achieve with their rifles, and refused to believe in the good faith of the Government.

because it is proud, avaricious, envious and voracious, and wishes to assume possession even of things which do not belong to it according to distributive justice or legal honesty. President Portes Gil, the henchman or representative of the Caesar Calles, promised to conclude peace and to return all that they stole from the Church, and as for the dead, there was nothing to be said, amen! But since the agreement was not in writing, for that reason the donkey went on eating the wheat of my co-godfather.[3]

The day after peace was concluded, there began the systematic and premeditated murder of all the Cristero leaders, to prevent any possible revival of the movement; the army embarked on a policy of road-building, and placed detachments in all the villages. The first victim fell ten days after the 'arrangements'. Fr Pedroza was shot on 3 July 1929, and before the year was out all the leaders in Guanajuato and Zacatecas, except for the old fox Ávila and Aurelio Acevedo, were dead. This selective butchery went on for several years, and all the most important leaders were killed: Cueva, Arreola, Gutiérrez, Álvarez, Barajas, Hernández, Bouquet, and Salazar. Between 1929 and 1935 the

201

manhunt claimed 5,000 victims, of whom 500 were officers, ranging in rank from lieutenant to general. There was no escape for the Cristeros except flight into the desert, to the United States, or to the big cities. More than one owed his life to a Federal general appalled by so much treachery, and the state of San Luis Potosí, under the command of Cedillo, provided a haven for many.

The Cristeros felt considerable bitterness, and were filled with hatred against the bishops who had been responsible for the 'arrangements'; there was even a schism, albeit an extremely local one, which was symptomatic of the crisis. In the region of Coalcomán, Michoacán, after the assassination of Fr Epifanio Madrigal, a group of old Cristeros, led by one whom they recognised as their Moses, formed the community of the 'Wooden Cross'; they refused to acknowledge the Church, which had been guilty of apostasy and was corrupted by the Antichrist. They now formed a community which used as its rule of life and faith the Sermon on the Mount, and expressed their faith in a community without any hierarchy, entirely free of the influence of the world and of the priestly caste. Appointing their own ministers, and leading an exemplary life based on non-violence, they chose to flee from a world which rejected them, both as a state and as a Church, and to take refuge in solitude. Exposed to the hostility of the two powers, and excommunicated in 1936 by the Bishop of Tacámbaro, they lived as a pacifist Anabaptist community under the leadership of their prophet Moses, awaiting the imminent Second Coming of Chirst, and then going off to cross the ocean, without wetting their feet, to reach the Promised Land. Moses, dressed in white, struck the waters with his rod and, followed by a great number of people, stepped out onto the waves. Some say that he was drowned, others that he survived, and others that the setback was due to the sins of the people or to the impurity of Moses, who is said to have made advances to a virgin the night before the Exodus.[4]

To leave Babylon in order to lead the holy people out of the land of impurity was a reaction limited to certain geographical areas. When the Government again began to harass the Church and to persecute Christians, after 1931, sporadic warfare broke out once more, accompanied by isolated acts of violence against schoolteachers, *agraristas*, and all the representatives of the Government, despite the prohibitions of Rome and excommunications by the bishops. Rather than let themselves be slaughtered like sheep, men like Estrada, Vázques, and Acevedo took to the *maquis* again, and constituted a dangerous source of dissent in a country that was still pacified, though ill-treated and stubbornly resistant.

'Socialist education' provoked further popular support for several thousands of uncompromising men who would not or could not submit.

The Church of Silence and the Silence of the Church

Between 1929 and 1935, as the power behind the Presidents who were in office for the time, the strong man was Calles, now called 'The Supreme Head of the Revolution'. It was a time of economic difficulties and of factional struggles at the top, a time when the dissatisfaction of the people with its leaders reached its greatest extent, and the scandals became most intolerable. The religious problem was smouldering under the embers, and the Government revived it when it thought fit to do so: Calles's army was in power, and the anticlerical pressure group was at the zenith of its influence and quite prepared to break the truce. Between 1929 and 1931 it was possible to believe in the reality of the *modus vivendi*, but Calles's followers openly sabotaged the programme of President Ortiz Rubio in several states, notably in Veracruz, and in Tabasco, where Garrido Canabal was Governor. The Church remained silent, refusing to confuse the governors with the Government, despite the crisis of the winter of 1931.

On the occasion of the magnificent celebration of the fourth centenary of the apparition of the Virgin of Guadalupe, General Calles called on the President to abandon his policy of conciliation. The Archbishop of Mexico City, taken unawares by the sudden limitations placed on the number of priests, wanted to suspend public worship in his archdiocese, but Rome ordered him to abandon any idea of resistance, and dismissed two bishops who had been so bold as to suggest that the Vatican was ill informed. The reason why Rome took this emphatic stance and forbade any recourse to arms was that it was banking on Ortiz Rubio and wanted to help him in his resistance to Calles. Ortiz Rubio fell in September 1932, and at the end of that month the Pope denounced the violation of the 'arrangements' in the encyclical *Acerba animi*, and again ordered the faithful to submit.

In 1934 President A. Rodríguez was obliged to confront Calles over the Church question: Bassols, his Minister of the Interior and a faithful instrument of Calles, told him that he must renew the struggle, and encourage the Governors to proceed with 'socialist education'. When the President refused, Bassols resigned, and Calles published the famous 'Cry of Guadalajara': 'we must now proceed to this new stage, which I may call the psychological revolution; we must penetrate into, and take possession of, the consciences of the children and the young people, because they belong and should belong to the revolution . . . to the collectivity.' In a memorandum to Cárdenas, he emphasised that 'the state has a perfect right to decide the orientation of education, in accordance with the doctrine and principles which it upholds, . . . and this is what is being done at present in Russia, Germany and Italy'.[5]

Article 3 of the Constitution was interpreted to mean that 'the education given by the state is to be socialist and, not content with excluding all religious teaching, it must combat fanaticism and prejudices'. This programme, which was of totalitarian inspiration and was accompanied by the sex education sponsored by Bassols, provoked insurrections in 1935 and sparked off such hostility among the middle classes that the Government was forced to retreat. This rationalist school, inspired by Ferrer, was the cause of the sterile conflicts which for a long time destroyed the confidence of the people in the public schools. The battle over the schools, which continued until 1937 and ended in defeat, was a trap for those who provoked it. It has been suggested, with some measure of plausibility, that Calles encouraged his successor Cárdenas in that battle in order to compromise him and weaken his position; this was true, but the movement had its own internal logic, because since 1929 Portes Gil had sent out 'rural missionaries' to combat 'fanaticism and alcoholism' in Jalisco. The Cristiada had dismayed, terrified, and inflamed the Jacobins; their response was this 'socialist' education, with its secular, pantheistic, and archaeological liturgies. In the battle over the schools, the Government came into conflict with the Church, which behaved decisively and calmly in the affair, refusing to play Calles's game in the struggle between him and Cárdenas. On this occasion the Church had behind it the urban social sectors, the university, the majority of the people, and American and, finally, world opinion. Graham Greene arrived to inquire into the question of religious freedom in Mexico, and Senator Borah presided over a commission of inquiry into the persecution.

The slaughter of the disarmed Cristeros and the renewal of religious persecution decided the survivors, who were now fighting once more, to ignore the prohibitions of the Church and throw themselves into a hopeless struggle, which they referred to as the 'Second',[6] without daring to add the word 'Cristiada', a struggle of which they still refuse to speak, because their principal enemy was the Church.

Whereas the first stage (1926–9) had been a war of the poor, the second one was a war of the utterly wretched, against a Church that had excommunicated them[7] and a more effective army, which concentrated half of its strength in one region and combed it for a whole year. The appearance of an efficient air force and of radio communications gave excellent results, and these operations were made possible because the insurrection, even at its zenith, never mobilised more than 7,500 combatants, isolated in six great regions. This trial lasted until 1940, when the last unsubdued groups laid down their arms.

These rebels operated in the mountains, often in the most backward sierras (Nayarit, the Sierra Gorda, Oaxaca, and the Sierra de Puebla), and no longer appeared in strength in the Western Centre. The army took quite a long time to reduce this desperate movement of men who embodied a protest against the almighty state, in a country where protest was no longer possible.

This terrorist guerrilla warfare (in three years one hundred school-teachers were assassinated, and two hundred wounded and mutilated) finally had the effect of persuading the Government. In 1935, while Cárdenas and Calles were quarrelling violently over power, an unbridled anticlericalism held full sway: only 305 authorised priests remained in the entire country. When Cárdenas finally triumphed over Calles in June 1935, the Apostolic Delegate, Mgr Ruiz y Flores, who was in exile in the United States, took advantage of the occasion to condemn the Catholic insurgents yet again, and he called on all Mexicans to pray for religious liberty, saying, 'The time for tranquillity has come.'[8]

When Garrido Canabal was dismissed from the Ministry of Agriculture in June 1935, he was replaced by General Cedillo, who protected religion because the people of his province were believers, although he himself did not believe in anything. The promotion of this general, whose troops had made it possible to get rid of Calles, again raised the hopes of the Catholics. In February 1936 the President began a series of speeches in which he denounced the errors of those who emphasised 'the religious problem above all the problems of the national programme ... anti-religious campaigns will only provoke a prolonged resistance, and will definitely retard economic growth'.[9]

Within the next few days, the governors of seven states issued decrees permitting the reopening of the churches. The massacre in March 1936 of a 'cultural brigade' by the exasperated populace of San Felipe Torres Mochas seems to have precipitated this decision. In April, churches were opened in Mexico City and Veracruz, in May the United States Embassy persuaded the authorities to allow a public funeral for Mgr Díaz, and in the course of the summer churches were opened in Nayarit and Jalisco.

In February 1937 the death of a young girl provoked the mobilisation of the population first of Orizaba and then of the state of Veracruz: people hurried to open the churches, and the Government made no attempt to oppose the measure; the same thing happened in Chiapas and in Tabasco: at Villahermosa they found someone to give the order to fire. In 1938 the churches were open and the priests free throughout the country. In 1940 General Ávila Camacho made his famous speech including the words, 'I am a believer.'

How was it that General Cárdenas, the most sincere of the anticlericals and the most convinced of the rationalists of his generation, came to adopt this position? It is certain that his sincere feelings were offended by the more odious aspects of the anti-religious campaigns and that he was hostile to the vulgar crusade of the priest-baiters. Being close to the people, he knew how to handle 'sincere fanaticism', and, tiring of closing the churches only to have them opened again and filled to overflowing, he returned them to the people. The sacristan-president, Cárdenas, who was friendly with the rural parish priests, did not hesitate to oppose the most faithful of the defanaticisers (he was one of their number), as soon as the campaign of defanaticisation hindered the objectives of his government. Personal factors were influential, but what was chiefly decisive was the evolution of national and international politics.

Cárdenas, after having shaken off the tutelage of Calles, who had provoked the crisis of 1934, wanted to remove the detrimental religious problem. At this juncture, for the first time for years, the national question had reappeared in the foreground, with the petroleum crisis, when simultaneously the threat of Fascism was increasing and right-wing groups were pullulating in Mexico. At a time like this, the state did not want to have in opposition to it that Catholic world whose complexity and strength it had so under-estimated, and, since Rome was calling for reconciliation after so many years, an understanding was swiftly reached.

CHAPTER 12

General Perspective

The State

The period studied in this work comes at the end of a phenomenon of long duration, the last stage of the growth and definitive establishment of the modern state, the state that would create the nation, through a centralised system of control and repression intolerant of any alternative – the 'nation-state'. The contemporary political system was established, complete with its institutions and ideology, and provided a solution to the problem of power in Mexican society, made up as it was of superimposed and juxtaposed groups.

If this was the character of the movement in the long term, the short-term crisis, the tragic moment, was that of the struggle of factions within the group that was master of the state and was building the state. Obregón had dreamed, like a new Porfirio Díaz, of having Calles as his devoted González, in order to return subsequently to the Presidency; the function made the man, Calles became a politician and, utilising the traitor Morones (he was a traitor in the eyes of Obregón because he had previously made a pact with him), obliged his former leader to consent to the alternating diarchy. The religious conflict took place against the background of these circumstances: Obregón feared it, Morones provoked it, and Calles made use of it. In August 1926 and again in March 1927, he defeated the attempts of Obregón; later, when the affair had become too hot to handle and agreement on the succession had been reached, he appeared to become more moderate. The violent death of Obregón, who had wanted to play the part of First Consul and pacifier, involves the problem of the double game being played by Calles, but the important thing is that anyway he got rid, at the same time, of the Obregón faction and of Morones's group, by means of the fierce struggles provoked by the National Revolutionary Party, the history of which has still to be written. After that, Calles could make peace with the Church.

The 1926–36 period raises the problem of the totalitarian nature of the Mexican system, which has often been confused with absolutism exercised by one man and is therefore called *callismo*. In the course of that decade, and only for a limited time, the Mexican state became God and hid behind its own myth, that of the Revolution, a myth which disguised the existence of the new ruling class. The bureaucracy, which expanded at this time, was the outward and visible sign of the requirements of the state, which, once a certain limit has been passed, can only grow and swallow everything. Then there is strong temptation to overcome the resistance of 'fanaticism and obscurantism', which are typical of the peasantry. However, the state had a more ambitious project in mind: it had both the temptation and the means to militarise people's minds by submitting them to its truth, to its orthodoxy. Knowing nothing of the legitimacy of tradition or of formal legality, this power fell back on its own absolutism, and gave itself an official ideology, a single mass political party, a monopoly of information and propaganda, and finally it declared war on society in order to assure its own dominance over the scene of dislocation. The police and the army were thrown against vast social groups, the peasants, the city dwellers, the middle classes, in order to break down the social structures and the basic rural social nucleus. The 'colonial' war waged against the Cristeros was similar, with its enforced resettlement of the population, to the totalitarian systems based on concentration camps. The attempt to destroy the Church and, in the shorter term, the family (especially in Tabasco and after the experiment with 'socialist education'), was accompanied by the systematic partitioning of the population by the Party and its satellite organisations (the *agrarista* militias, Garrido's Red Shirts, and so on).

In spite of the obsessive efforts to assert constitutional continuity, after 1911 the system of domination was to a greater or lesser degree based on charisma: Madero, Carranza (the 'First Chief'), Obregón (the 'Cripple from Celeya') and Calles (the 'Supreme Chief') all had, or attempted to acquire, the charisma of the apostle, the father, the warrior, the man of steel. Other types of legitimacy had been destroyed in order to ruin the system created by Porfirio Díaz. Around the great man there were the table companions, who were paid in presents, donations, and booty. The year 1929, a critical one, witnessed the transition to the institutionalisation of charisma: the emaciated revolutionaries, who had already become the pleasure-seeking table companions, found themselves transformed into officials of the state and the party, of which they were to create the dogma, doctrine, and theories. The period between 1926 and 1929 was that of the confluence of charisma and tradition; and the fundamental problem that had to be resolved was that of the succession, which at every attempt provoked a crisis. Caesar designated his successor, who was acclaimed rather than elected by the people.

Calles had been designated by Obregón, thanks to his obscurity and his unpopularity, which were guaranteed not to cast into shadow the glory of his master. Calles tried to compensate for this lack of charisma by building up the bureaucratic system and encouraging economic activity, and later by a remarkable display of aggressive behaviour. On the look-out for sensational exploits, he refused to acknowledge the value of Obregón's views and finally came into conflict with the United States, ignoring the golden rule, and with the Church, and he felt a tragic pleasure when there was war against the Yaquis. In 1929 one was even to see him on the battlefield, anxious to achieve military glory; but it was above all after July 1928 that he showed his greatness, in the storm which, between the death of Obregón and the battle of Jiménez, nearly destroyed everything. From then on he was to govern without interference from anybody, the dark, immense, black power of the *Máximo* who was to be visited in his cave. Legitimacy and charisma mattered little to him now that he had ensured his dominance and made and unmade Presidents. When he came to grief in 1935, everybody at once forsook him, as they had Carranza in 1920.

The conflict with the Church came to a head in the fullness of time; there was no element of chance involved. In the course of history this conflict had occurred on three occasions – under the Bourbons, under Lerdo de Tejada, and under Calles – and on all three occasions the masses had reacted violently, in 1810, 1874, and 1926. This happened because the problem of the Church was entirely central: Caesar, in expanding, was bound to supplant God, and from 1759 (the expulsion of the Jesuits) to 1934 the Regalist state revealed itself as essentially anticlerical. Díaz and Cárdenas were not successful as pacifiers because of their goodness or their understanding; they could afford to be peacemakers because they had inherited the victory of the state, which henceforth could be magnanimous. The two phases, attack and compromise, were inseparable, and the role of personalities is reduced to its proper place if one bears this in mind.

Calles's state suffered from a lack of legitimacy (Calles had Obregón behind him and needed to assert himself), and compensated for this by requiring absolute obedience. This obedience was considered as a patriotic duty, and, if it was refused, the people concerned were branded as traitors. Against the Church, a rival drawing its strength from many accumulated legitimacies, the state used as a weapon the Calles Law.

It lost the little legitimacy that it possessed, when it ceased to be obeyed in this particular sphere. This was felt as a challenge, as an insult which had to be expiated.

Calles had set the trap; he had provoked the disobedience, which was inadmissible, and brought the crisis to a head again, challenging the bishops to rise in arms. The state had been anticlerical for sufficient time to win victory, sufficient time to obtain by blackmail the benevolent neutrality of the Church. After this, Calles, who was now as anachronistic as the last guerrillas, was bound to disappear from the scene.

The Church

During these events, Rome demonstrated its authority over the Mexica:. clergy and laity; it also manifested its absolute indifference to the nature of political regimes, a policy which was in theory entirely orthodox but in practice cynically opportunistic; it consisted of simultaneously displaying human prudence and Divine wisdom, of satisfying interest and consciences: 'It was providential that there were Cristeros, and providential that they ceased to exist.' The Church (Rome and the Mexican bishops), as well as the state, were responsible for the outbreak of the war. It would be to under-estimate the convictions of the Christian people to suppose that they would suffer the suspension of public worship and the consequent suspension of the Sacraments, which did not affect the well-to-do classes. It was ill-treating the people to use their war as a trump card in negotiations, and to sign the peace without consulting them, abandoning them to the butcher's knife by obliging them to lay down their arms without guarantees. Rome made every effort to avoid the events of 1926, and it imposed peace in 1929; it never gave its approval to the insurrection, and it forbade priests to take part in it. That does not mean that the state bore the entire responsibility for the conflict.

It is a well-known fact that the Church, as an institution bearing and administering an official charisma, has often clashed with the state throughout history. Considering itself as the only perfect society and as God's instrument for the good of society, it has tended to put political power at its service. In Mexico, depending on the strength or weakness of the state, an upsurge of Caesaro-Papism (1759, 1874, 1926) or of clericalism has been evident. At times, when the two sides unfurled their banners simultaneously, there has been a spectacular collision. Between 1890 and 1925 there developed eschatological expectations based on

Christian Socialism, directed hierarchically (the trade unions were led by priests and approved by the bishops); during the democratic interlude under Madero, the Church created a party (the PCN), and indulged in the same demagogic behaviour as the other political forces, multiplying the number of mass organisations (Catholic Action on a sectoral basis, trade unions, schools, and leagues) and accentuating their bureaucratisation. The conflict with the state became aggravated at the very moment when the clergy, because of the political crisis, was least in control of its troops: in 1926 the League escaped from its tutelage, as the PCN had done in 1912–13 when it took a stand against Madero, whom the hierarchy supported.

Since Church and state both required, in totalitarian fashion, the acknowledgement of the monopoly of charisma, and since they both strove for universal domination, the war was bound to be total. 'The Episcopate has voluntarily embarked on an inexpiable struggle from which it can only emerge victorious or vanquished,' wrote Lagarde, the French observer. This was the feeling of certain bishops who, like Mgr Lara y Torres, preferred 'the iron gauntlet of Calles to the perfumed glove of Díaz'. This view was not shared by Rome, which broke the power of the combative bishop because it wanted to reach a compromise: in 1929 the Church renounced its right to exercise complete control over a field which was accessible to it, namely, legislation governing worship; this renunciation led, between 1930 and 1940, to an agreement between the two powers to form a condominium, by means of a reciprocal delimitation of spheres of influence. The state acknowledged the impossibility of extirpating the Church and religion, and the Church legitimised the state and lent it its authority to domesticate the subject people. The quarrel was not, therefore, the result of a misunderstanding, and the violence displayed by the state was not in any way blind, for it led to a kind of Napoleonic concordat, without this ever being embodied in written form.

This agreement corresponded, *mutatis mutandis*, to the crisis of the Action Française in France and the reconciliation in Italy embodied in the Lateran Treaty. The Catholics, as organised masses, ceased to ally themselves with contingent movements of opposition, the principal of these being that of Vasconcelos; they ceased to be the potential popular reserve for *coups d'état*, which the electoral struggles were tending to eliminate, and they tended to form a submissive majority, hoping one day to form a governing party. The Church abandoned its own, got rid of its servants who were a nuisance, and won victory in the game of loser takes all.

After the Peace

The Cristeros

Against this background of events, the Cristeros constituted a nuisance, because they displayed an ascetic indifference to the rightful place of the state, which they understood in eschatological terms in the light of the text, 'Render to Caesar . . .' Their attitude towards Caesar was not that of the Church, and this explains the hostility of the majority of the clergy towards the Cristeros, who were guilty of having lost patience. 'With what right are they raising taxes?' exclaimed Mgr Garribi, 'Do they think they're the Government?'

They did not think that they were the Government, or the Church, with the exception of the 'illumined' followers of the Wooden Cross, but they were utterly convinced that they were Mexico and Christianity. Having had only rudimentary instruction in the history of the nation and the Church, they were all the more free to have an invented interpretation of the present. They proved that they were capable of making for themselves an image of the state and of its legitimacy, of rendering to Caesar that which is Caesar's but of being prepared to be cut in small pieces rather than to give him those other things which did not belong to him and which he so ardently desired.

Some have interpreted this war as a movement similar to that of Salazar or Franco – a precursor of *Sinarquismo*, the Mexican variety of Fascism (1937–45); an attempt at counter-revolution, led by the Church, the big proprietors, and the reactionary petty bourgeoisie. This was not true, for the simple reason that Calles's Government was not, by any definition, revolutionary. (It is necessary to establish precisely in what sense one can speak of a 'Mexican revolution'.) Furthermore, the great agrarian reform movement did not take place until ten years later, and then the reaction occurred in the form of *Sinarquismo*.

One should ask a different question. Is it not the case that the Cristiada – the most important, if not the only, mass movement of the period – calls into question many myths? Of peasant radicalism, the Cristeros shared the traditional aspects (tradition being equivalent to transmission) and its looking backward to the past. One cannot have any doubts as to their independence, and even if they were later glorified (though only to a relative extent) by the reactionaries, they were never the creation of the latter. The distrust, hatred, and condescension displayed by the Marxist towards them might be based on ideological grounds for three reasons: because they belonged to the historical arsenal of the right, because they were Catholics, and because they were capable

212

of acting on their own initiative. Much has been said about the passivity of the rural masses, but the Cristeros were able, subject to all the limitations inevitable in such a process, to organise a movement without external leaders, to imagine a rational and positive political programme, and to encourage a fundamental solidarity within the people. These people wanted their conditions of life to change, but it was a change that had little resemblance to that which was imagined on their behalf by the *avant-garde*, which was imposing its revolution *manu militari*. After the event historians, theorists, and sociologists wrote the history of the 'Revolution', on the basis of this myth – namely, that the masses had desired and had carried out this revolution; they have therefore been obliged to transform, to cut out, to condemn, to expel the data at their disposal, because nothing fits the theory. Either Zapata was a revolutionary, or the workers of the Red battalions which fought him were revolutionaries (that is to say, supporters of Carranza's movement), but it is impossible for both to have been revolutionaries. By what feat of legerdemain can one reconcile the Zapatistas and the Red battalions? *A posteriori*, when one writes history. With the Cristeros the same problem arises, in a more serious form because of the national scope of the movement, which resembled Zapata's movement in its methods of mobilisation, recruitment, organisation, and ideology; faced with the impossibility of integrating the Cristeros into this historical vision, writers have denied their numbers, their strength, and their nature, in order to avoid having to say that the peasants were counter-revolutionary. Nevertheless, this was what was said in 1914, in 1928, and in 1936, at the moment of the confrontation.

One might simply say that the Cristiada was a movement of reaction against 'the Mexican Revolution', a revolution which was continuing the undertaking of modernisation commenced by Porfirio Díaz, by bringing up yet again the question of the relationship between Church and state; against a radical, summary, and brutal anticlericalism, there stood the Catholic people of the rural areas, who took up arms to defend their faith. In this connection, it should be noted that the Cristero movement, including the fringe movements common to all peasant rebellions, had a very special style. The supposed Mexican (or American) taste for pure violence ('Let's go to the riot! Let's go with Pancho Villa!'), and the idea of revolution considered as a way of life (more dangerous, it is true, but better, as portrayed in Júan Rulfo's *La Perra*) – these elements are absent. The clientele of this movement was different: they were people without experience of war, people who had not taken part in the Revolution;

and those who had taken part in it (and there were certainly a large number of them), now took up arms in a different spirit, often as though it were an act of expiation. The Cristiada was, therefore, doubly counter-revolutionary: it was against the Revolution, that movement which had triumphed with Carranza, Obregón, and Calles, against the revolution in the Mexican sense of the term; and also in the sense of the term as employed in classical political science (rather than the Marxist and progressive sense), in the technical and sociological sense of the term: 'squabble, quarrel, conflict, riot'.

A radical consciousness emerged in the course of the struggle, and important leaders called into question the established powers. At the end of 1927 the Cristero army took the name of the Army of National Liberation. As Gorostieta said, in Mexico the principal form of conflict was war, and civil organisation existed parallel to military organisation and subordinate to it. The primary objective was the war, since the Mexican Revolution was an extraordinary and diffuse military event extending over twenty-five years and progressing, not as a result of sudden political events, but of armed expansion. The putschist organisation which had served Huerta, Obregón, Calles, and Cárdenas, the instrument for territorial conquest used by Villa, became, in the hands of the Cristeros, an organisation for mass mobilisation. That was why the Cristero army was a popular army, and that was why Gorostieta was not obsessed by military victory as such. To withdraw when the Federals were advancing, to advance when they were withdrawing (1929), was not a way to win the war, but a way to make it last long enough to win it on the political plane, and meanwhile it encouraged the mobilisation of the people. The Cristero army was not an instrument of domination like the armies of the Mexican revolution, because its place was within the people, 'like a fish in water', and at the same time it was the incarnation of the people. The Cristero army even included women and children, and fought on every front: production, education, morals, health, and religion. This is why one can speak, objectively, of a revolutionary army.

If armed resistance was able to express certain objectives and a certain ideology, it did so in religious terms, and this is not surprising, for it was the revolt of a persecuted people who had exhausted legal methods of resistance, a people who had a peculiar vision of the world, a religious rhetorical arsenal. Those of whom it has been too often believed that they are empty of spirit, and whose taciturnity has been mistaken for idiocy, knew how to distinguish between Caesar and God. It was the Church that chose to suspend public worship (though not the Sacraments); it was Caesar who in reprisal prevented it from distributing the Sacraments; and the people, cut off from the roots of their spiritual life, administered to themselves the comprehensive sacrament, that of the bloody sacrifice. Laying down their arms when ordered to do so by the clergy, and having gained no temporal advantage, the people were perhaps the only party to the dispute which understood what it sang on the twenty-second Sunday after Pentecost: 'Serve God first, but render to Caesar that which is Caesar's'.' As participants in the work of redemption of the Church as the Body of Christ, martyrs, saints, loving friends and servants, the Cristeros lived for the Parousia, and believed that there was a number of saints, a number of martyrs needed before history reached its appointed term; they remembered the bargain made by Abraham. This was accompanied by a radical criticism of Caesar, whose goodness was called into question, and in the course of the war this moral consciousness took political shape.

The Mexican Revolution

It is a remarkable fact that for forty years Mexican Catholics, in common with the Latin American left, have been faced with the problem of choice between the violent and the peaceful roads to the conquest of power. The Cristeros demonstrated to the city dwellers, and to the forces of political opposition, that in Mexico it was necessary to abandon armed insurrection. Their failure gave birth to *Sinarquismo* and later to the PAN (National Action Party). Was their failure due to the lack of personal capability on the part of the leaders, or to the inability of the peasantry to raise itself above the context of local self-government? This was an old story, ever since the time of Morelos; the Cristeros, in the absence of an autonomous political movement of the popular classes, in order to win, depended on the urban 'political classes', the members of which were distributed between all the parties, both of government and of opposition. From the mediocre leaders of this petty bourgeoisie there was nothing to hope, until the moment when Vasconcelos arrived to upset the political equilibrium. Then, in 1929, there was a possibility of an alliance between the cities and the countryside, behind that remarkable man, who had a real sense of statesmanship. This threat, which was the greatest that ever faced the 'revolutionaries' between 1914 and the present day, was thrust aside at the right moment by the collaboration of the tutelary powers, Washington and Rome.

The second stage of the Cristiada, between 1934 and 1938, consisted of the reaction of the peasantry to the process of 'socialist education', to religious persecution (in Veracruz and Chiapas), and to certain aspects of the agrarian reform (the problems of the *ejido*, or communal lands, and of the militias). In Morelos, Puebla, and Veracruz, along the crescent line of the volcanoes, it was like the last flicker of Zapata's movement; the movement was stronger than it had been in 1926–9 in Sonora, Oaxaca, Puebla, and Morelos, regions which were less involved, and therefore less devastated, during the first war and its immediate aftermath. The Western Centre participated to a much lesser extent, and Jalisco, which was a bastion of the movement in 1926, hardly at all. This second stage was characterised by dispair, rebellion (particularly against the Church, which condemned and excommunicated the Cristeros), and violence. Terrorism, which had been unknown between 1926 and 1929, was unleashed against the leaders of the regime, the schoolteachers, and the agrarian authorities. Finally, at the moment when Cárdenas changed his policy, there developed great mass movements, of a non-violent character, in Veracruz, Chiapas, and Tabasco, where perhaps *Sinarquismo* learned its first lessons.

How should one situate the Cristiada within the context of the Mexican Revolution? After the explosion of 1913–14, the return to order was extremely difficult: between 1914 and 1920, there was repression, and between 1920 and 1925, reconstruction, a process deeply affected by the crisis within the ruling faction. Between 1926 and 1929, in response to the religious persecution, there was a ground-wave from the peasantry, the most important of the entire Revolution; so traumatic was the experience of those three years that fifteen years were to be needed for the extremely difficult return to peace.

What were the consequences of the Cristiada? The peasants were decisively crushed, and this was the last insurrection of the masses. Henceforth they were conscious of their weaknesses, of their isolation (the treachery of the well-to-do church-goers and the feebleness of the League were not forgotten), and the peasants resigned themselves to their violent and prejudicial integration into the regime, which was now firmly established.

The opposition (and later forces of opposition) learned from the affair. *Sinarquismo* was the result of the reflections of the politically minded young men of the middle classes. Another result was the PAN, which was based on the failure of the traditional forms of political struggle, and of rebellion, and on the need for a national organisation grouping all the forces under one banner. The Cristiada thus accelerated the modernisation of politics, and, respecting as it did a government which had learned never to drive it to take extreme measures, the opposition accelerated the integration for which it so diligently searched.

The Government accelerated its policy of geographical and moral integration: there was a road-building programme, and a policy for information and the mass media (Calles was the first President to speak over the radio); there was an unsuccessful attempt at 'socialist education' aimed at wiping out 'fanaticism', the strength of which was now acknowledged, agrarian reform, and, finally, the abandonment of anti-clericalism and its replacement by an entirely pragmatic system of collaboration which governed the relations between Church and state after 1938. The Government learned from the conflict that it must not drive the opposition to desperation, and that repression should be accompanied and reinforced by integration into the system; the democratic rules of the game were accompanied by the seduction and utilisation of all talents, in order to prevent the development of forces outside the system, while the army, subjected to close surveillance, guaranteed the impotence of the opposition. Finally, the history of the conflict confirms the fact that the support and friendship of the United States were an indispensable condition of success, whether of the opposition or of the Government. American hostility had overthrown Díaz and Huerta; it had prevented Villa, the Cristeros, and Vasconcelos from winning victory. The United States had maintained Carranza and Calles in the saddle, and obliged Cárdenas to give it the head of Múgica and to choose Ávila Camacho as his successor.

The years 1926–9 were crucial as regards the crystallisation of the present-day political, economic, and social system. Rome understood that it was the end of the uncertainty, of the void created by the crisis of 1923–4. Everything was staked in 1929, when the *modus vivendi* was achieved, and the electoral campaign of Vasconcelos was a mere duel fought after the event.

Envoi

It is only with difficulty that the men of the better classes come to have a clear discernment of what is going on in the souls of the people and in particular of the peasants.

> De Tocqueville, The Ancien Régime and the Revolution

To a Callista revolutionary and to a Cristero peasant, the Mexican Revolution was not the same process, and the 'meta-process', integrating the antagonistic experiences, if it is at all possible to achieve in retrospect, should begin by paying attention to the words of those who have never been understood. It is possible to level an accusation of *mujikism* against the author for having asserted the rustic sanctity of these men executed as disturbers of order, for having expressed an admiration for those who, like so many others – like the Spanish Republicans, for example – have affirmed that there are frontiers here on this earth on which one must not yield. At certain moments the free man has only one enemy, Leviathan, who says to him again in the lost language, 'Worship me or die.' Then the insurgents are the incarnation of the spirit of revolt, and refuse to yield an inch, defending the ethical and mythical kernel of humanity in order not to lose both heaven and earth at once.

Neutrality was impossible. The author has found this by experience, having begun with a personal point of view hostile to the Cristeros. This does not mean that social and historical analysis has been discarded, but it does mean that such an analysis will always conflict with the interests of a group. It means that it will call into question the declarations of the victors. The author has refused to be caught in the trap of the official mythology, and had no need to fabricate another mythology; there is, moreover, no desire to conceal feelings, which are the third dimension of history. Personally and totally concerned for history itself, and preserving a childlike faith in the power of the mind to order the information at his disposal, the author is obliged to acknowledge that, unless he engages in a process of reductionism, which would have truly traumatic effects, 'to write history is to surrender to chaos' – that is to say, one must respect the irreducible kernel of the historical event in itself, and be conscious of its survival within and of the modification of it inherent in any recalling of the event. An epoch and a war which are now almost forgotten, because history has failed the Cristeros, just as justice and glory have been denied them, have awakened a consciousness of all that has not occurred, of all that we aim at eternally.

Notes

CHAPTER 1: THE METAMORPHOSES OF THE CONFLICT

1 *Crown and Clergy in Colonial Mexico, 1579–1826: the crisis of ecclesiastical privilege* (London, 1968).
2 *Correo Americano del Sur*, no. 21.
3 Quoted in Francisco López Cámara, *La génesis de la conciencia liberal en México* (Mexico City, 1954), p. 325.
4 *Memoria de la Secretaría de Gobierno*, 1876.
5 Ciro Ceballos, *Aurora y Ocaso. Historia de la Revolución de Tuxtepec* (Mexico, 1912).
6 Paul Murray, *The Catholic Church in Mexico* (Mexico, 1965), vol. I, p. 301.
7 Quoted in Rafael Montejano y Aguiñaga, *El valle de maíz* (San Luis Potosí, 1967), pp. 320–1.
8 *Reminiscencias de Monseñor Gillow* (Mexico, 1922), p. 283.
9 Mgr J. de J. Oritz, Archbishop of Guadalajara, to Mora y del Río, Archbishop of Mexico City, 28 May 1911, *Archives of the Archbishopric of Guadalajara*, folder 253.
10 *Guia teórico-práctico del Partido Católico Nacional* (Guadalajara, 1911), p. 1.
11 *Archives of the Archbishopric of Guadalajara*, folder 253, 24 July 1911.
12 Mgr Ruiz y Flores, *Recuerdo de recuerdos* (Mexico, 1942), p. 65.
13 Bishop Francis G. Kelley, *El libro de rojo y amarillo, una historia de sangre y cobardía* (Chicago, 1915), p. 63.
14 Aquiles Moctezuma (pseud.), *El conflicto religioso de 1926* (Mexico, 1960), vol. I, p. 264.
15 Luis Cabrera, 'The religious question in Mexico', *Forum Magazine*, quoted in F. C. Kelley, *Replies to Luis Cabrera and J. Castellot* (Catholic Church Extension Society, 1916), p. 13.
16 Abbé Testory, *El Imperio y el clero mexicano* (Guadalajara, 1914).
17 *Diario de los debates del Congreso Constituyente* (Mexico, 1960), vol. I, pp. 643–4 (Deputy Rojas).
18 *Ibid.* p. 622–3 (Deputy Cravioto).
19 *Diario Oficial*, 21 November 1918.

CHAPTER 2: THE ROOTS OF THE PROBLEM

1 With regard to this point, and for this chapter as a whole, see Jean A. Meyer, *Histoire de la Révolution Méxicaine* (Paris, Payot, 1973).
2 Lorenzo de Zavala, *Ensayo histórico de las revoluciones de México* (Mexico, 1845), vol. I, p. 276.
3 Charles W. Hackett (ed.), *Progreso económico y social de México, una controversia* (Mexico, 1935).

4 Marjorie Clark, *Organised labour in Mexico* (Raleigh, NC, 1934), p. 92.

5 AAA.

6 Fall Committee, *Investigation of Mexican Affairs* (US Senate, 66th Congress, Washington, DC, 1919), vol. 9, p. 42. S. Inman, letter of 31 July 1919.

7 AGN. Presidentes. Obregón. Packet 35–2–4/438–I–4; packet 116, leg. 4/104–L–23.

8 *Crisol* (August 1929), p. 116.

9 A. Rius Facius, *Méjico Cristero* (Mexico, 1966), p. 13.

10 DSR 812.00, Coahuila 17.25, February 1929.

11 Zalce y Rodríguez, *Apuntes para la historia de la Masonería en México* (Mexico, 1950), vol. II, p. 295.

12 *Ibid.* vol. II, p. 92–3.

13 MID 2657 G 616/36, 'Extracts referring to the clergy and clericalism from the speech of General J. Amaro, Minister of War, on the occasion of the inauguration of the Historical Section of the General Staff, on October 22, 1929' (translation).

14 'Diversos aspectos de la propaganda del Clero'.

15 MID 2257 G 70/7 of 2 October 1930. 'Mexican War Department attitudes toward US', by Col. Gordon Johnston.

16 *Cauterios y látigos* (Jalapa, 1933); *Puyas y puyazos* (Mexico, 1944); ¡*Mujer, confiésate y verás!*; *Labor liberal*; *Sobre la brecha*; *Banderillas de fuego: libro de doctrina desfanatizante*; etc.

17 Printed and illustrated speech, AAA.

18 'arranged in accordance with the catechism of Christian doctrine according to the Jesuitical Roman ritual, this being required by the fanaticism of the present generation in Mexico'. (Official editions, 1914–26).

19 Narciso Bassols, *Obregón* (Mexico, 1968), pp. 165–7; *El Universal*, 14 January 1923.

20 Calles, at Guadalajara, 20 July 1934.

CHAPTER 3: THE CONFLICT BETWEEN THE TWO SWORDS, 1925–6

1 R. Salazar, *Líderes y sindicatos* (Mexico, 1925), p. 16.

2 See I. C. Enríquez, *La cuestión religiosa en México, por un católico mejicano* (Mexico, 1915); articles in *El Universal* by Fr Orihuela (16 October 1916), Fr R. Ramírez (19 January 1917), Fr José Cortina Márquez (27 January 1917).

3 Pedro Vera y Zuria, *Cartas a mis seminaristas* (Barcelona, 1926), p. 159.

4 AAA, 27 February 1925 (signed Nahum Toquiantzi).

5 Pedro Vera y Zuria, *op. cit.* pp. 318 and 605.

6 Senate Debates, 19 February 1926, pp. 3–10.

7 Ernest Lagarde, *Foreign Affairs* (Paris, 18 September 1926), p. 6.

8 *Ibid.* p. 35.

9 *Ibid.* p. 37.

10 *Ibid.* p. 14.

11 *Ibid.* pp. 15–16.

12 *Ibid.* p. 18.

13 DSR 812.6363, Sheffield to State Department, 24 December 1925.

14 Lagarde, pp. 19–20.

15 *Ibid.* p. 38.

16 *Ibid.* p. 34.

17 *Ibid.* p. 35.

18 Pius XI to the Mexican bishops, 2 February 1926, in W. F. Montavon, *The facts concerning the Mexican problem* (Washington, National Catholic Welfare Conference, 1926), pp. 48–51.
19 Lagarde, p. 64.
20 *Ibid.* pp. 65–6.
21 Telegram sent by Cardinal Gasparri to the Episcopal Committee, Jesuit Archives, Puente Grande, Jalisco.
22 DSR 812.404/578
23 *El Universal*, 30 July 1926.
24 David Kelley, *The ruling few* (London, Hollis & Carter, 1952), p. 163.
25 Lagarde, pp. 83–4.
26 *Ibid.* pp. 71–2.
27 Interviews by the author with Domingo Lavin, F. Torreblanca, and F. X. Gaxiola, 1967–8.
28 Liga Nacional Campesina, *Primer Congreso Nacional de Unifficación* (Puebla, 1927), p. 30.
29 Interview by the author with Cardinal Dávila Garibi, 1968.
30 P. Díaz, 'State vs. Church in Mexico', *North American Review*, CCXXV (April 1928), 408.
31 Anacleto González Flores, *El plebiscito de los mártires* (Mexico, 1930), p. 20.

CHAPTER 4: THE CONFLICT BETWEEN THE TWO SWORDS,
1926–1929

1 For the history of this war, see Jean Meyer, *La Cristiada* (Mexico, Siglo XXI, 1973, 410 pp.).
2 Juan Juárez MS (Tlaltenango, Jalisco).
3 Interview by the author with Acevedo.
4 Josefina Arellano, MS: 'Narración histórica de la Revolución Cristera en el pueblo de San Julián, Jalisco'.
5 J. J. F. Hernández, MS: 'Tierra de Cristeros'.
6 In the Revolutionary wars of the period 1940–65, it has been estimated that a regular army must have a numerical superiority of 15 to 1, or of 20 to 1 to achieve victory.
7 Letter from Gorostieta, 28 January 1929, to Colonel Manuel Ramírez de Olivas; private archive of Ramírez.
8 Gorostieta to Manuel Ramírez de Olivas, 28 December 1928.
9 DSR 812.00, Jalisco 36, 2 December 1928.
10 *Ibid* 40, 31 January 1929.
11 *Ibid* 44, 27 February 1929.
12 Debates of the Chamber of Deputies, Senator Caloca, 13 February 1929, pp. 11–12.
13 DSR 812.00, Jalisco 40, 17 January 1929.
14 *The New York Times*, 11 March; *Laredo Times*, 15 March.
15 Gorostieta to Viramontes and Acevedo, 31 March 1929, AAA.
16 Interview by the author with H. Navarrete, 1968.
17 Interview by the author with Santiago Dueñas, 1966.
18 Interview by the author with Manuel Ramírez de Olivas, 1967.

19 SJ; telegram from Consul Arturo Elías to Ministry of Foreign Relations, 23 August 1927 'Interview Mestre-Bertoni-Prelates: it appears that what they want is for the clerical party to give its support to General Obregón himself in exchange for these guarantees.'

20 10 February 1927.

21 SJ; 'Something very important that should be known', MS of 9 pp. countersigned by Fr Pío Ramírez, O.P., and 'Memorandum of Fr Macario Román', 2 pp. Government Archives, Jalisco, March 1927.

22 Harold Nicolson, *Dwight Morrow* (New York, 1935), p. 339.

23 For a full account, see DSR 812.00, P. H. McDevitt's papers, University of Notre Dame; D. W. Morrow papers, Amherst College (Mass.); and SJ.

24 DSR 812.404/931 6/12, extracts from the diary of Fr Burke in Morrow to Clark, 19 October 1928.

25 Portes Gil to Morrow in Rublee Memorandum, Morrow Papers.

26 DSR 812.00 Ags/7.3 May 1929; emphasis by the State Department or by Morrow.

27 DSR 812.00 Sonora 546, 23 March 1929.

28 Fernando Robles, *Un surco en el agua* (Mexico, 1970), Vol. I, p. 409.

29 SJ; Interview between General Degollado and Mgr Díaz, July 1929; memorandum of Fr José Romero Vargas.

CHAPTER 5: CHURCH FOLK AND TOWNSFOLK

1 SJ; declarations of the Episcopal Committee regarding an official bulletin, 1 November 1926.

2 Memorandum of the League to the CE, 23 November 1926; interviews between the author and Juan Lainé (21 May 1967), Fr Méndez Medina (23 May 1967), and Palomar y Vizcarra (27 May 1967).

3 Original sheet in the author's possession (double sheet written on recto and verso).

4 Bishops González, Valverde, Méndez del Río to Mgr de la Mora, Rome, 11 March 1927: 'The Holy See, for its part, maintains the most circumspect silence' (SJ).

5 SJ; memorandum from Mgr González to the Episcopal Committee, Cologne, June 1928; Mgr Manríquez to Palomar, 24 October 1928; the Nuncio, Fumasoni-Biondi, to Mgr Díaz, 12 December 1927; circular of Mgr Placencia, 1928.

6 DSR 812 404/949/6/8, 19 March 1929.

7 AAA; San José, Texas, 2 December 1928, to the priests of Huejuquilla el Alto, in reply to their letter of 6 November.

8 SJ; memorandum of Fr José Romero Vargas. Díaz to Degollado: 'Why did they get mixed up in politics?'

9 SJ; Ruiz to X, Washington, 19 February 1929.

10 An interview by the author with Cardinal Dávila Garibi, 14 January 1968.

11 AAA; notes on the religious persecution, armed defence, and agreements, by Fr Adolfo Arroyo, MS of 8 pp., 24 January 1934.

12 AAA; letter of 16 May 1929.

13 Interviews by the author with Castañeda (1966) and Fr J. J. Pérez.

14 Professor M. Cruz Solano; Fr Nicolás Valdés, archives of Fr Casas. Civil authorities West Guanajuato, R. L., to Civil Government, Jalisco, 17 January 1928.

15 Interview by the author with Aurelio Acevedo.

16 AAA; collective letter of the Quintanar Brigade to the parish priest of Mesquitic, Norberto Reyes.

17 Interviews by the author with Alberto Loyola, 1967, and Frs Federico González, José Santana García, Nicolás Valdés, E. Casas, and others.

18 *Las Noticias, Excelsior,* of 28 February, 1, 3, and 21 March 1929. Government Archives, Jalisco.

19 Interview by the author with Vicente Zepeda, Xochihuehuetlán, 1969.

20 UNAM, fo. 74, leg, I, Mérida, 6 February 1928: 'enjoying tranquillity in practice, because the local government is extremely tolerant, not only has an accurate idea of our conflict been lost, but the little that is known of it there is held to be excessive and exaggerated'. Also UNAM fo. 59, leg. 27, 4 May 1928, Guerrero Diario ... Senadores, 25 March 1928, p. 5 (Chiapas); UNAM fo. 59, leg. 27, 4 May 1928, Puebla, Oaxaca.

21 *Excelsior,* 7 January and 14 October 1928.

22 Juan Carlos, MS.

23 Archives of Fr Casas, December 1927.

24 Archives of Fr Casas, 29 March 1929.

25 Interview by the author with Acevedo.

26 Interview by the author with Acevedo. See *David,* III, 335, 342, 360, and 382; and IV 4, 29, 41, 130.

27 Interview by the author with Toribio Valadés.

28 The information and statistics reproduced here are based on the author's files and interviews.

29 *Ibid.*

30 After 1929, it broke up into several small groups. The most extreme elements did not give up the struggle until 1940.

31 The information given in this section is based on the archives of the League, of Miguel Palomar y Vizcarra, of VITA – Mexico City, and Antonio Ruis Facius, and on interviews with Capistrán Garza, Juan Lainé, Palomar y Vizcarra, Jorge Téllez, Carlos Díez de Sollano, Andrés Barquín y Ruiz, Jiménez Rueda, and Fr Méndez Medina, S.J.

32 Of the 24 national leaders there were 9 engineers, 6 lawyers, 4 doctors, 3 civil servants, and 2 ex-generals, Jesús Rebollo and José Ortiz Monasterio (who had belonged to the General Staff of Porfirio Díaz). Three Jesuits, 1 Dominican and 5 other priests, with or without formal appointments, were advisers and participants in the activities of the League.

33 Segura led the commando which attempted to kill Obregón on 13 November 1927; he gave himself up, to clear the Pro brothers of the accusation. The Pro brothers were shot on the 23rd.

34 Lagarde, pp. 77–8; MID 2025–383/12, 7 January 1927; DSR 812.404/668; DSR 812.404/560/599/658.

35 Reported by Palomar y Vizcarra.

36 Testimony of Díez de Sollano and Luis Beltrán y Mendoza; archives of the League, 10 November 1926, archives of Fr Casas, report of A. González Flores, 19 October 1926.

37 Archives of Palomar, Note to the letter of Fr Burke, General Convention, 3 May 1926.

38 Memoirs of Ceniceros; Mgr Díaz, *Report to the Episcopate, 23 November 1928* (New York, 42 pp., ed. of 100 copies); League, *Memorial ... a S.S. Pío XI,* 6 April 1927; correspondence of Fr Parsons, etc. Capistrán Garza continued to receive $250 per month.

39 League; Letter of the CD to the Pope, 5 August 1927. SJ; Mgr Lara y Torres to Palomar, 15 May 1928; Palomar to Mgr Orozco, 15 August 1928; Orozco to Palomar, 6 December 1928.

40 The Andrés Salazar incident.

41 To be more exact, peasants are not editors, even though the example of Aurelio Acevedo refutes this assertion. That they are historians, and conscious of being so, this book proves.

CHAPTER 6: THE RECRUITMENT OF THE CRISTEROS

1 Interview by the author with General C. Rodríguez, 1967.

2 'The revolutionary leaders know full well that to recruit men they have to go to the North, the South, or the coastal areas, but that it is useless trying to recruit in the central plateau (Hidalgo, Puebla, the Federal District and Mexico City) because the great majority of the men of that zone do not make good soldiers.' José Vasconcelos, *Obras completas* (Mexico City, 1958), vol. II, p. 891.

3 Interview by the author with Acevedo. The phrase was used by M. Viramontes in December 1926.

4 The lowest estimate was 45,000, plus the temporary bands in Coahuila, San Luis, Chihuahua, Tabasco, the Tuxtlas and Huatusco (Veracruz). In 1929, 14,000 had been issued with a safe conduct, and the Government estimated that these comprised one-third of the total. Personal calculations confirmed by DSR 812.00, Sonora/391, 21 March 1929; ditto, Sonora/715, 12 April 1929; Sonora/517 1/2, Clark memorandum on military situation, 4 April 1929; DSR 812.00/28456, Gordon Johnston (Military Attaché) to Stimson, 3 May 1929; DSR 812.404/974 12/17, Lane with Montavon, 23 May 1929.

5 Thanks to Aurelio Acevedo, the editor of *David*, the monthly periodical acting as a link between the old Cristeros, the author was able to organise an inquiry based on a questionnaire, supplemented by interviews and local monographs. A total of 378 questionnaire forms were filled in completely, covering 19 states and 112 villages, which gives a satisfactory geographical spread, despite the strong representation of Jalisco (110). Obviously, the questionnaire applies to only two-thirds of the population in terms of age, because the men who were over 50 years old in 1926 are absent. This sample lays itself open to criticism: is it really representative? Death has been responsible for a selection on two occasions – during and after the war. One can, however, dispose of one possible objection: those who answered the questionnaire were definitely not the leaders or the educated people (there are 64 officers, ranging in rank from second-lieutenant to general; 58 had never attended school). Finally, the results have been verified and completed by all possible methods.

6 Luis González, *Pueblo en vilo: microhistoria de San José García* (Mexico City, Colegio de México; 1st ed., 1968; 2nd ed., 1972); Paul S. Taylor, *A Spanish Mexican peasant community, Arandas in Jalisco* (Berkeley, Calif., 1933).

7 'It does appear that the Cristero Counter-Revolution recruited the majority of its partisans among those groups of Creole or *mestizo* small proprietors – from Zacatecas to the Altos de Jalisco – who had little to expect from distribution of the land and the establishment of *ejidos.*' François Chevalier, in *Revue Historique*, CXXII (July 1959), 17.

8 DAAC, Banco Nacional de Crédito Agrícola, municipal archives.

9 See DAAC file on Santiago Bayacora.

10 Figures based on answers to questionnaires, interviews, and other research.

11 See Chapter 7, the Women's Brigades (pp. 131 ff.).

12 Interview by the author with Acevedo, Partida, Campos.

13 Interview by the author with A. Campos.

14 Luis Luna, Acevedo, Ezequiel Mendoza; see plates.

15 *Previous military experience*

As a follower of Zapata	15
As a follower of Villa	27
As a follower Carranza	3
In self-defence movements	23
Total	68 (of the 378 who answered the questionnaire)

16 Interview by the author with Uriel Mendoza, 1969.

17 Some of them continue to exercise their functions, paying money to the Federal troops so that the village should not be burnt, or so that the parish priest and the hostages should not be hanged. However, most of rich inhabitants of the villages took refuge, financially ruined, in the towns, while the *caciques* fought the Cristeros.

18 AAA; Manuel Frías, commander of the Cross Brigade, report of 3 January and 31 February 1929; UNAM fo. 88, leg. 1, 4 June 1929. AAA; summary made on Minita Hill, 8 July 1928; etc.

19 Testimony of Buenaventura Iriarte.

20 This information was collected in interviews.

21 For a history and critical analysis of the agrarian reform, see Jean Meyer, *La Révolution Méxicaine* (Paris, Payot, 1973), pt. II, ch. 2.

22 DSR 812.00, Durango; AAA, March 1929; AAA, MS of J. Abacuc Román and archives of Fr Casas; correspondence of General Manuel Michel.

23 162 questionnaires completed by veterans of the war; 55 per cent were obliged to have a second occupation.

24 Interview by the author with Federico González, 1967, which revealed the treacherous behaviour of the men of El Valle. The *agrarista* leader of Chilapa stated quite honestly that he could not become involved in the movement but that his sentiments of friendship were unchanged.

25 The *agrarista* leaders of Valparaíso, captured by the Cristeros and then released, returned the favour by saving the hostages taken by the army.

26 Interview by the author with Luna and Acevedo, 1968.

27 SJ; 9 April 1929.

28 Interview by the author with José Gutiérrez.

29 Announcement by the Minister of Agriculture, 19 January 1927, published in *Excelsior*.
30 Banco Nacional de Crédito Agrícola Archives; Ramón Fernández y Fernández, 'Evolución económica del jornalero del Campo', *Crisol* (January 1931).

CHAPTER 7: THE CRISTERO ARMY

1 Archives of Manuel Michel, in the possession of Fr Casas.
2 Archives of the San Gaspar Regiment, in the possession of Luis Luna.
3 AAA, complete archives of the Quintanar Brigade, with promotion structure and strengths of the regiments and squadrons (name, occupation, age, marital status, home address, mount, make and calibre of weapon and date of enlistment).
4 See Chapter 9. For recruits, the Federal army relied chiefly on Indian infantry, and this tendency had been accentuated by General Amaro's desire to modernise the army. There was also a desire for, and later a positive need for, 'Americanisation', which impelled the army to buy horses from the United States; these were big, fine-looking horses which did not stand up to the fatigue of campaigning so well as the native Mexican horses.
5 Archives of the Civil Governor of South-Western Guanajuato, papers of Fr Casas.
6 Nominal rolls of the 3rd Regiment, 28 October 1928. Papers of Fr Casas, M. Michel I.
7 Reports of the 'Free Men of Huejuquilla' Regiment, 21 October 1928, Castañón Regiment, 13 November 1928, Guadalupe Regiment, 4 October 1928: a total of 649 men with 318 30–30 rifles and 223 Mausers.
8 AAA, archives of the Valparaíso Regiment.
9 Archives of Luis Luna.
10 Interview by the author with Pedro Martínez, 1968.
11 M. Michel, Degollado to Bouquet, 23 January 1929: 'I want them to send a team to teach them how to blow up trains without charging the batteries, which are very heavy, and the detonators.'
12 M. Michel I, Aniceto Arias to Michel, 26 November 1929: 'If you have clothing send it, also sandals, we are very short, and also the day-labourers are destitute.'
13 M. Michel, 26 February 1929, archives of Fr Casas.
14 AAA; Durango, F. Vázquez, 9 December 1929.
15 Interview by the author with Acevedo.
16 Interview by the author with Ezequiel Mendoza.
17 Interview by the author with Ezequiel Mendoza.
18 Interview by the author with Ezequiel Mendoza.
19 *Informador*, 26 February 1927.
20 Death of the American engineer Wilkins, April 1927. As a reprisal, the Government razed Santa Ana Tepetitlán to the ground. In June 1928 a rich *hacendado* was killed, and in October 1928 the American mining engineer Charles Smith (*Excelsior*, 13 October 1928); also, J. M. Underwood and C. C. Aisthorpe, employees of the Guanajuato Reduction Mines Company (*Informador*, 24 February 1929), Rosalio Rivera, the sixth hostage (26 May 1929).
21 *Excelsior*, 23 October 1928.
22 For their activities in Guadalajara, see *Informador* and *Noticias*, January to July 1929: kidnapping of A. Nuño. Dr R. Mendiola, Dr Altamirano, Manuel Ramírez, and others.

23 AAA, Valparaíso Regiment, 'Free Men of Huejuquilla' Regiment, both belonging to the Quintanar Brigade.

24 Marcos Valdivia, the mayor of Monte Escobedo, remitted 1,500 pesos (Colonel Viramontes to Gorostieta, 8 March 1928).

25 AAA, list of tax payers: taxes were levied only on grown and branded cattle and on horses. Donkeys were exempt. The lists of tax payers give an idea of the wealth of this society. At Peñablanca, 71 proprietors owned 515 head of cattle; of these, 4 persons owned 218.

26 AAA, 26 August 1929, kidnapping of Lino Etzel, of the Mexican Corporation SA, at Fresnillo; kidnapping of an old Englishman and a young American from the mine at Vacas, Durango.

27 Manuel Chaparro did the same at Angangueo, Michoacán.

28 Interview by the author with Acevedo.

29 Interview by the author with Acevedo.

30 Accounts of the headquarters of the 'Free Men of Huejuquilla' Regiment, 1929, for details of receipts and expenditure, of which every centavo is recorded: oil for weapons, an oil-can, etc.

31 The sums are justified under various headings and supported by receipts.

32 Miscellaneous items included 60 straw hats, at 50 centavos each, 63 pesos to pay for repairs to the rifles of the Indians ('*poblanos*'), and assistance to families, widows, and the wounded.

33 The following men reached the rank of general, which was undeserved in only about ten cases: Valente Acevedo (Dgo.), Aurelio Acevedo Robles (Zac.), Ramón Aguilar (Mich.), Salvador Aguirre (Jal.), Andrés Alberdi (Gto.), Luis Alcorta (Gto.), Miguel Anguiano (Col.), Lorenzo Arreola (Jal.), Justo Ávila (Zac.), Victorino Bárcenas (Gto.), Maximiliano Barragán (Mich.), Clemente Barrales (Pue.), Dámaso Barraza (Dgo.), Emilio Barrios (Zac.), Eleuterio Batista (Tlaxcala), Raimundo Beltrán (Gto.), Carlos Blanco (Jal.), Juan Manuel Bonilla (Mex.), Carlos Bouquet (Jal.), Esteban Caro (Jal.), Juan Carranza (Gto.), Ángel Castillo González (Mich.), Simón Cortés (Mich.), Lucas Cueva (Jal.), Vicente Cueva (Jal.), Epigmenio Cueva (Jal.), Jesús Degollado (Jal.), Nicolás Domínguez (Chihuahua), Isabel Fávila (Mex.), Manuel Fernández de Lara (Pue.), Donaciano Flores (Nay.), Manuel Frías (Qro.), Ignacio Galván (San Luis Potosí), Rodolfo Gallegos (Gto.), Luis García Granados (Mich.), Fernando González (Mich.), Enrique Gorostieta (Commander-in-Chief), Gregorio Guillén (Mich.), Librado Guillén (Mich.), Pancho Guillén (Mich.), Sebastián Guillén (Mich.), Luis Guízar Morfín (Mich.), Rubén Guízar O. (Mich.), Alberto ('Chema') Gutiérrez B. (Col.), José Gutiérrez Gutiérrez (Jal.), Aureliano Hernández (Dgo.), Miguel Hernández (Jal.), Luis Ibarra (Jal.), Primitivo Jiménez (Gto.), Lucas López (Ags.), Porfirio Mayorquín (Nay.), José María Méndez (Mich.), Benjamín Mendoza (Morelos), Prudencio Mendoza (Mich.), Manuel Michel (Col.), Ladislao Molina (Mich.), Trinidad Mora (Dgo.), Luis Navarro Origel (Mich.), Dionisio Ochoa (Col.), Manuel Orihuela (Mex.), Nabor Orozco (Mich.), Anatolio Partida (Mich.), Vicente Pérez (Gto.), J. Jesús Pinedo (Zac.), José Posada Ortiz (Gto.), Pedro Quintanar (Zac.), Jesús Rebollo (Federal District), Manuel Reyes (Mex.), Lauro Rocha (Jal.), Abacuc Román (Gto.), Andrés Salazar (Col.), Herminio Sánchez (Jal.), Felipe Sánchez Caballero (Jal.), Ignacio Sánchez Ramírez (Mich.), Juan Trujillo López (Pue.), José María Valenzuela (Dgo.),

Federico Vázquez (Dgo.), José Velasco (Ags.), Elías Vergara (Mich.), Maximiliano Vigueras (Gto.), and Candelario Villegas (Gto.).

Colonels: Fr Aristeo Pedroza, Fr Reyes Vega, Ramón Acosta (Mich.), Cayetano Álvarez (Jal.), Gabino Álvarez (Jal.), Joaquín Anguiano (Zac.), Catarino Ávila (Pue.), J. Refugio Avilés (Gto.), Agapito and Francisco Campos (Dgo.), Raimundo Cárdenas (Zac.), Perfecto Castañón (Zac.), Alfredo Cerda (Gto.), Serapio Cifuentes (Mich.), Candelario Cisneros (Cd.), V. Damián (Ags.), Santiago Dueñas (Ags.), Florencio Estrada (Dgo.), Frumencio Estrada (Dgo.), José María Fernández (Mich.), Antonio Flores (Pue.), Gabino Flores (Jal.), Ricardo García (Gto.), Víctor García (Col.), Honorato González (Mich.), Isidoro González (Gto.), Luciano González (Mich.), Sabino González (Mex.), Vicente Guízar Z. (Mich.), J. Jesús Hernándes (Gto.), Miguel Jaime (Jal.), Miguel López (Jal.), Víctor López (Gto.), Rodolfo Loza Márquez (Jal.), Pedro Martínez (Nay.), Ezequiel Mendoza Barragán (Mich.), Fidel Mora (Dgo.), J. Refugio Morales (Gto.), Ignacio Moreno (Mich.), Manuel Moreno Adrete (Jal.), Ignacio Navarro Origel (Mich.), Manuel Ocampo (Federal District), Filomeno Osorio (Gto.), Vicente Osorio (Gto.), José Padrón (Gto.), Porfirio Pedroza (Mich.), Narciso Pinedo (Jal.), Simón Quijada (Gto.), Germán Quirarte (Jal.), Victoriano Ramírez (Jal.), Manuel Ramírez de Olivas (Jal.), Felipe Sánchez (Zac.), Vicente Sánchez (Zac.), Pedro Sandoval (Zac.), Fernando Tamariz (Pue.), Alfonso de la Torre (Ags.), J. Jesús de la Torre (Jal.), Marcos Torres (Col.), Marcos Torres (Mex.), Teófilo Valdovinos (Zac.), Antonio Vargas (Col.), Antonio Vargas (Gto.), Francisco Vargas (Gto.), Wenceslao Vargas (Gto.), Sixto Vargas (Pue.), Eulogio Vázquez (Morelos), José Verduzco (Col.), Esteban Villanueva (Mich.), Candelario Villegas (Gto.), Román Villegas (Gto.), Porfirio Yáñez (Pue.), Gabino Zepeda (Pue.).

Lieutenant-colonels: Macedonio Alatorre (Jal.), Norberto Ávila (Zac.), Luis Barragán Orozco (Mich.), Trinidad Castañón (Zac.), Manuel Chaparro (Mich.), Julián Cháves (Mich.), David Galván (Mich.), J. Guadalupe Gómez (Jal.), Filemon Gaona (Pue.), José Huerta (Jal.), Francisco Loza (Jal.), Ángel Jaime (Morelos), J. Jesús Márquez (Jal.), Pablo López (Jal.), Francisco Loza (Jal.), Florencio Monasterio (Gto.), J. Reyes Montes (Jal.), Florencio Navarro Luna (Jal.), José María Ramírez Casillas (Jal.), Mateo Rangel (Mich.), Pablo Reyes (Dgo.), Enrique Rodríguez (Mich.), Miguel Rodríguez Rubalcaba (Jal.), José Sahagún (Jal.), José Santana (Jal.), and Francisco Zepeda (Mich.).

Majors: Antonio Acuña (Coah.), J. Trinidad Álvarez (Jal.), Luis Álvarez (Jal.), Esmael Chávez (Mich.), Vicente Contreras (Col.), Isidoro Flores (Dgo.), José María Gómez (Jal.), Epitacio Lamas (Zac.), Heliodoro López (Mich.), Norberto López (Ags.), Plácido Nieto (Ags.), Miguel Ortiz (Jal.), J. Félix Ramírez (Jal.), Plutarco Ramírez (Col.), and David Rodríguez (Oaxaca).

The list of field officers is considerably less complete than that of the generals. Colonels, lieutenant-colonels, and majors often had more men under their command than did some of the generals.

34 After the capture of Colonel Perfecto Castañón, his regiment elected Reinaldo Cárdenas as colonel and Aureliano Ramírez as lieutenant-colonel. After the death of General Luis Guízar Morfín, his soldiers elected Martínez as lieutenant-colonel. Trinidad Mora (Dgo.), Carlos Bouquet (Jal.), and Pedro Quintanar (Zac.) were elected by their soldiers. Subsequently, General Gorostieta confirmed the appointments of most of the senior officers, contenting himself with reducing their rank

when it did not correspond to the real military situation; he suppressed the generals without armies, and recognised as colonels only officers commanding complete regiments.

35 Interview by the author with Acevedo.

36 Interview by the author with Pedro Cordero.

37 Acevedo: 'The animal or bird that came into the sights of his carbine was sure to end up in the cooking-pot.'

38 Insurrection of the Chalchihuites, August 1926.

39 For a more detailed account, see Chapter 9.

40 Conspicuous by their absence were Esteban Caro, Vicente Cueva, and Fr Vega, who were excluded on account of their moral failings.

41 DSR 812.00, Aguascalientes, 8–15 May 1929.

42 Archives of Fr Casas, correspondence of the civil governors of the zone, interviews by the author with Yerena, Santiago Dueñas, Toribio Valadés, Aurelio Limón, and Acevedo. Interviews by Fr Valdés with Paz Camacho, Rosendo Flores, and Jesús Herrera.

43 Interview by the author with Acevedo.

44 *Excelsior*, 25 February 1928: two men arrested at Tacuba railway station with 16,000 rounds in their possession; *Excelsior*, 22 March 1928: a man arrested at the moment when he was consigning 35 boxes, and so on.

45 Interview by the author with Yerena. The transaction had been made by 'Don Wences'.

46 *Excelsior*, 9 May 1927, dissolution of muncipalities that had collaborated with the Cristeros; *Excelsior*, 4 April 1929, severe sanctions against 'employees of the Government who co-operate with the insurgents, this constituting not only rebellion, but treason'; *Excelsior*, 28 January 1929, dissolution of the militia of Tres Palos (Gro.), execution of Federal soldiers at Zapopán and Jamay, etc.

47 Lauro Rocha equipped his troops by purchasing ammunition from the commanding officer of the 74th Regiment, and the Cristeros were using recently manufactured cartridges, whereas the Federal troops were still using those of previous years. This situation provoked telegrams nos. 394 and 408 of 18 and 20 April 1929 to the zone commanders in Michoacán, Jalisco, Colima, Zacatecas, and Aguascalientes (Archives of the Government of Jalisco).

48 It has not been easy to write the history of the Women's Brigades, and it would have been quite impossible without the archives of Fr Casas and the friendly co-operation of Fr N. Valdés, who introduced the author to the heroines of this epic struggle. In fact, persecuted by the League, the brigades became the victims of the intervention of the Church, obtained through the intrigues of the Leaguers. Consequences of this were the destruction of the archives by Mgr Darío Miranda, when he became their superior on the conclusion of peace, and the refusal to speak on the part of the survivors, an attitude motivated by obedience, the desire to avoid scandal, and an understandable bitterness. As 'Celia Gómez', the Commander-in-Chief, expressed it, 'What was done was done for God.' I wish to express my thanks to her, and also to María Refugio Ramírez, Carmen Macías, Elodia Delgado, and Antonio Castillo, whom I met in 1968 and 1969. María Refugio Ramírez gave me valuable documents (here referred to as MRR) which were still in her possession.

49 He became a renowned man of letters, Governor of Jalisco, and Minister of Education (1964–70).

50 This military necessity made it possible for the League to obtain from Mgr Orozco and Rome the abolition of the oath of secrecy, by invoking the Church's condemnation of secret societies.

51 See *La Cristíada*, op. cit. vol. I, pp. 50–95.

52 He caused such annoyance and scandal, that Mgr Orozco requested his Provincial to expel him from the archdiocese, and this was duly done.

53 SJ. Gorostieta to the League, 28 December 1928: 'If it were not for the sources of supply which I have organised so that each regiment can obtain equipment, during the last conflict between you and the Women's Brigades, we should have all succumbed.'

54 C. Michel to his sister, 15 January 1929: 'I must repeat that the Devil has us well cornered here, this is the best way for them to defeat us . . . people are confused by politicking, and this certainly upsets things and the work gets behindhand.'

55 MRR, Mexico City, 12 January 1929:

The General Staff of the women's army [Saint Joan of Arc Women's Brigades] informs each and every one of the sisters who are members of the said Brigades, that it has agreed to abolish for the present the oath and promises which you previously gave, for the reasons given in the message which it duly sent to the Venerable Mexican Episcopate, the terms of which are as follows: To the Venerable Episcopal Subcommittee . . . as a proof of our submission and respect we take the liberty of informing Your Illustrious Worships that:

(1) whereas attempts have been made, we do not know whether in good faith or otherwise, to take the declaration made by His Grace the Archbishop of Guadalajara concerning the oath and promises, and assert without justification that these declarations apply to the Women's Brigades, with grave damage to the Catholic cause;

(2) whereas, if the Women's Brigades cease their activities, the Crusaders, their families and their wounded . . . would be left abandoned in the most extreme distress;

(3) whereas, finally, the most practical way of avoiding undue and compromising problems for Your Illustrious Worships . . . is to suspend the oath and promises for the present . . . the Women's Brigades will continue to work . . . abolishing from henceforth and until there is a just settlement of the dispute, the oath and promises . . . Prayer and action: therefore the General Staff of the Women's Brigades . . . calls on each and every member . . . actively to continue her work according to the system already established, but henceforth doing without the oath and promises. Therefore, the General Staff leaves each of the sisters on her own responsibility to observe the discretion required by the matters and tasks on which she is engaged . . .

56 Testimony of Cardinal Dávila Garibi: 'it is not fitting'.

57 DSR 812.00, Jalisco 51, 26 March 1929: 'As yet no definite organisation supplying arms to the rebels has been discovered.'

58 *Excelsior, Informador*, 13, 16, 17, 22, and 23 March, 2, 3, 4, 12, 13, 14, 17, 19, and 21 April, 9, 14, 18, 19, 23, and 30 May, 8, 9, 11, 12, 15, and 17 June, 1929; MID 2657 G 616/28 of 14 May 1929.

59 She was released in August.

60 As soon as peace was concluded, the Church wanted to bring the Women's Brigades under close control and integrate them into Catholic Action; placed under the authority of Fr Darío Miranda, the head of the Social Secretariat, they were obliged to suspend their activities (which had ceased to be military) and disappear, because their existence might have threatened the enforcement of the 'arrangements' by providing a focus for discontented Catholics. It was then that Fr Miranda destroyed the archive sent to him by Luis Flores.

61 The original is in the archives of Fr Casas.

62 Born at Ejutla, and a general at the age of 30, she was killed in November 1927, together with two assistants and Dionisio Ochoa, the Cristero commander in Colima, after the accidental explosion of bombs which she was making. 'She praised God for her sufferings.'

63 She was one of the few married women in this organisation made up of latter-day St Joans and St Judiths. She was a general for the last few months of the war; her husband, a commercial traveller, knew nothing of her activities.

64 María Ortega and Candelaria Borjas, arrested with the Cristeros with whom they were going to deliver ammunition (24 June 1928), were tortured and hanged; they had been forced to stand beside the Cristeros when they faced the firing-squad, and afterwards carry the bodies away. They did not talk, and apart from them nobody was arrested until June 1929, when 40 people were arrested in a raid at Comala.

65 Sara Ochoa at Cotija, María Arregui at Sahuayo, Herminia Vuveros at Morelia, and Carlotita and María de la Luz Castorena in Zacatecas.

66 These were not part of the brigades: each soldier could recruit auxiliaries, without initiating them.

67 MRR, testimony of the mother of Rigoberto and Octavio Becerra (2 and 7 years old), who said that they voluntarily transported ammunition to the 2nd ('Luis Padilla') Brigade.

68 The initial nucleus at Colima was provided by the College of the Sacred Heart.

69 Archives of Fr S. Casas (C/29): biographies edited by Luis Flores. SJ; autobiographies of Elodia Delgado (11 pp.) and Albina Michel (10 pp.). The only professional women were schoolteachers (the author has traced eight of these) and office-workers; the rest were peasant-girls or working-class women from the towns. If a member had children, she was usually a widow (e.g., María Luisa Ubiarco).

70 Testimony of Antonia Castillo.

71 Sara Flores Arias, María de los Ángeles Gutiérrez, and Faustina Almeida died as a result.

72 Testimony of María del Refugio ('Cuca') Ramírez.

73 Assassinated after the 'arrangements', as was Andrés Nuño, who disappeared.

74 A large reward was offered to informers (see *Excelsior*, 12 August 1928).

75 *El Minutillo*, later *La Honda*.

76 Testimony of Juan Bravo, who was a courier for the Women's Brigades and Gorostieta.

77 Archives of Fr S. Casas: report by Rafael Martínez Camarena, April 1928.

78 Carmen Macías.

CHAPTER 8: CRISTERO GOVERNMENT

1 AAA; archives of his regiment, the Quintanar Brigade, Fr A. Arroyo, of the mayors and judges, and of Aurelio Acevedo.

2 AAA; regional committee of administrative and judicial authorities appointed by the liberating army in Mezquitic, Jal., in May 1928, at the instance of the Valparaíso Regiment.

3 AAA; General Ordinance, prepared by the permanent committee on the functioning of judicial, administrative, and military authorities, which remained in force until things returned to normal, 5 June 1928.

4 AAA; criminal proceedings against Juan Díaz, for the crime of theft.

5 Criminal proceedings for aggravated rape against the soldier Norberto Victoria, 2 November 1928; against the soldier Miguel Domínguez, 2 January 1929; the sentence reads: 'Having investigated the matter, we found that this man had been deceived and he allowed himself to be led astray by human nature; we therefore inform you, Colonel, that the above-mentioned Domínguez has been released.'

6 *María del Socorro Navarro* vs. *Claudio Robles* for murder (2 May 1929); *the Authority* vs. *Isabel Magallanes*, the murderer of Serafín Ramos, etc.

7 20 June 1929, Isabel Magallanes.

8 Manuel Muñiz, the officer, for desertion and service in the Federal army; Isidoro Ruiz, for treason, March 1929. For rape, G. V. Candelaria and T. Escobedo, 5 February 1929.

9 7 January 1929, Manuel de la Paz was condemned for having said, 'I hope the Federals come soon and screw these fucking bandits who have stolen much from me.'

10 AAA; 20 September 1928, to Manuel Soto (Zacatecas) against Arellano.

11 AAA; accounts submitted every fortnight to the *ad hoc* committee.

12 AAA; Sebastián Arroyo, circular of 19 March 1929.

13 Acevedo, circular of 24 March 1928.

14 Interview by the author with Acevedo.

15 Interview by the author with Acevedo.

16 On 6 February 1929, Trinidad Castañón found a dance going on at La Labor; he imposed a fine of 59 pesos and broke the violin. On 7 February, he collected 200 pesos in fines for drunkenness from two *agraristas*. On 13 February 1929 Pilar Herrera accused the commissioner of Tenzompa of organising a dance. On 15 March 1929 the report of the commissioner of San Antonio stated that S. Mascorro had been fined 15 pesos for selling wine, F. Prieto 5 pesos 'for being under the influence of drink', J. Salas 2 pesos for the same reason, Preciliano Escobar 'for having a woman in the house as his wife', and Martín Pacheco 10 pesos 'for making passes at a married woman'.

17 The figure of the *agrarista* bore witness to this disintegration.

18 Accounts of the municipal council of Huejuquilla, the 'Free Men of Huejuquilla' Regiment, the Valparaíso Regiment, and the Quintanar Brigade. The accounts were very carefully kept, and submitted every fortnight to the supervisory committee.

19 AAA; A. Arroyo to Acevedo, 29 January 1929.

20 AAA; 19 June 1929: 'They bring from the Canyon cattle belonging to the enemy, and bring it at any time to sell.'

21 AAA; Acevedo to Quintanar, 24 October 1928.

22 AAA; Valparaíso Regiment, Orders 172, 182, 218, and 255 of 1929.

23 AAA; Acevedo to Captain F. de la Torre, letter 172, 16 February 1929; decree of 25 February 1928; F. de la Torre to Acevedo, 2 December 1928, concerning the harvest of Luz Robles, Casa López, and Vino Severo.

24 AAA; 29 April 1928, Valparaíso; Valparaíso Regiment, letter 88, Acevedo to Pinedo, 8 October 1928, concerning the harvest.

25 AAA; Acevedo to the municipal inspector of the hacienda of Ameca, 10 May 1928.

26 AAA; Manifesto, Huejuquilla, 2 June 1928.

27 AAA; P. B. Montoya to Acevedo, 15 June 1928.

28 The author has been unable to find the archives of Manuel Frías, except for his reports to the League, in which he mentions municipal councils installed and schools

opened in 1929; from Colima and Coalcomán there are few documents but numerous eyewitness reports; for Jalisco, there are the archives of Miguel Gómez Loza, General Degollado, General José Gutiérrez y Gutiérrez and General Manuel Michel; for western Guanajuato, there are the archives of the civil governor of the region.

29 The year 1929 did not provide a solution of continuity: the governor and General Lázaro Cárdenas appointed Mendoza commander of the rural defences of the zone; he remained in this appointment until 1942, when he migrated to Guerrero.

30 They were shot on 31 May 1929, after a swoop by the Federal Army.

31 Each regiment had a sector, from which it recruited its men and found its supplies.

32 Official correspondence of Manuel Michel, 3rd sector of South Jalisco, 3rd Regiment, and Generals Degollado, Salazar, Anguiano, Bouquet and F. Ortiz, December 1928 to July 1929 (1,000 pp.). First section, military matters, 500 pp.; second section, civil matters connected with military matters, 250 pp.; third section, requisitions, taxes, civil government, and miscellaneous, 100 pp.

33 Michel, 1–21 January 1929, received the submission of Telcruz and Ayotitlán, and answered, 'Ask the communities of Zapotitlán, Tetapán, Mazatán, Santa Elena and Sacoapán whether or not our movement gives them guarantees and protects them.'

34 Michel I, 19 January 1929.

35 Michel I, 9 January 1929, execution of the Cristero Captain Alfonso Rodríguez Tapia ('he committed serious abuses against certain civilians, and he also had innocent people shot'); 23 February 1929, warrant to arrest Rincón and Carrión, who were extorting money from the people of El Chante; letters to Generals Anguiano and Salazar (17 April and 18 May 1929) denouncing unjustified requisitions by their soldiers 'who really are exacting an impossible amount of assistance from them, without bothering to take things from the haciendas or the enemy'.

36 18 January 1929: 'various people of San José earnestly requested me to close down the houses of ill fame which abound in the principal streets'; 25 February 1929: 'from henceforth I will impose severe punishments [for the consumption of alcohol], since reasonable exhortations have not succeeded in establishing order and morality'.

37 Sebastiana Acuña, widow of Vázquez, recorded by Fr N. Valdés.

38 Michel III, letters to rich sympathisers (or people reputed to be so) and enemies, with demands for money, announcement of requisitions, and sequestrations; III, 8 December 1928, claim for a ransom of 3,000 pesos for the son of Don Francisco; 30 March 1929, letter to Alejandro Alfaro in Sayula: 'I have taken the liberty of assigning to you a good sum, 1,000 pesos . . . I am requesting your assistance in this friendly way, and I can assure you that your refusal will be taken as an authorisation for me to act differently.'

39 13 January 1928, receipt given to Domingo Encarnación; 22 February 1928, 'we earnestly request you to supply us with 2 or 3 hectolitres of maize, or what you can, we need maize, whether it is lent, sold or given to us; we'll pay you for it if you can't supply it free. And I am telling you that if you do not supply maize to the soldiers, they will take it where they can. God and my right.' Michel I, 8 March 1929; a convoy of 30 animals went to look for maize in Totolimispa and Telcampana.

40 Michel I, 15 January 1929, to Captain Aniceto Arias.

41 Michel III, February 1929, to Francisco Santana.

42 Michel III, 22 March 1929.

43 Michel II, 5 May 1929; 1929 Michel III, correspondence with the authorities

of San José del Carmen, Toxin, La Salada, El Mamey, Tetapán, Tolimán, Tajipo, Tuxcacuesco, Alista, Mazatán and Hitzome (all Cristero authorities), and San Gabriel, Ciudad Guzmán, Zapotilitic, Tuxpán, Sayula, and Atoyac (where the authorities collaborated with the Cristeros).

44 Archives of the Southern Division (Degollado, J. Gutiérrez); archives of the Altos (Gómez Loza, R. Martínez Camarena, A. Sánchez, Aristeo Pedroza, Gorostieta); archives of Guanajuato (Civil Governor of Manuel Doblado, Pénjamo, Cueramaro, Irapuato, La Piedad, Jesús María, Ayo, Degollado; General Vicente Pérez). Informants: David Dávila (Santa Fe, San Juan Cutzala), Juan Ramírez (Teocaltiche), Aurelio Limón, María Torres (Arandas), José Jiménez (Aranda and Capilla de Guadalupe), Felipe Figueroa (commander of Ayo), Guadalupe Tejeda (commander of Arandas), Daniel Alcalá (commander of Lagos), Mónica Martínez (Lagos), Ausencio Gómez (commander of Moya).

45 Their organisation is better known, thanks to the archives of Miguel Gómez Loza (MGL), in the possession of Fr Casas (C): correspondence, rough jottings, notes, and letters from 8 August 1927 to March 1928, account book; archives of Rafael Martínez Camarena (RMC).

46 Ramón López to MGL, 31 January 1928: 'We only had contact with the UP, there is a great bond of sympathy between the Catholics of this region and those of the Altos, and a certain community of feelings, aspirations and interests, because a great number of families affected by the resettlement took up residence in this city [Manuel Doblado].'

47 Report of MGL, 26 December 1927.

48 Ramón López to MGL, 24 November 1927, Elicerio J. Travelea (Cecilio E. Valtierra) to MGL, 27 November 1927, concerning the hacienda of Jalpa.

49 Issued at Guadalajara, 3 September 1927, MGL, National Government of Liberation of the State of Jalisco.

50 Decree No. 2, 20 May 1928, RMC. See receipts and forms in the annex to this decree.

51 MGL, December 1927.

52 Accounts submitted to the civil administration by those appointed by MGL (daily accounts to the nearest cent). Between 24 January 1928 and 6 February 1928 he sent, in four shipments, $7,655 (16,553 pesos).

53 MGL, 25,000 pesos in December–January 1927–8, plus 16,000 pesos in January–February, letters of MGL to Fr González Pérez in San Antonio asking him to see what the League has done with the money, 30 December 1927, January 1928, March 1928.

54 AAA; Gorostieta, 30 May 1929.

55 'Automobile traffic is only authorised with a permit, but seeds or livestock may be taken,' circular of General Degollado. SJ.

56 R. Martínez C. to J. G. Pérez Flores, Lagos, April 1928: 'For all items of clothing, food, etc., money is to be obtained by special collections and contributions, thus avoiding spending revenue from taxes and leaving it intact to purchase the military equipment we so urgently need.'

57 Circulars of Degollado (SJ): 'In view of the fact that some bad elements have outraged certain families, this headquarters orders that all abuses of this nature be punished with death'; 'This headquarters, taking into account the fact that most of the abuses committed by the troops are committed when they are drunk, forbids the sale of intoxicating liquors throughout the territory of the Division.'

58 MGL, 23 January 1928, J. G. Rodríguez.

59 UNAM, fos. 75 to 81, archives of Fr Pedroza, fo. 151, leg. 9, 28 February 1929.

60 Fo. 151, leg. 9, 18 April 1929; leg. 14, 8 March 1929 and leg. 40, 8 April 1929; 20 May 1929. MGL, black notebook 12 × 7 cm, 58 pp., miscellaneous matters.

61 MGL. Gómez Loza, even before the affair of the finances, had informed the League that its *War Bulletin* was a tissue of errors and lies.

62 Zapata was, much against his will, surrounded by intellectuals. Anacleto González Flores and Miguel Gómez Loza were born in villages and preserved the mentality and the ideology of the villages. Gorostieta was the only exception; he was the only one to speak of a political party and elections. Pedro Quintanar and Aurelio Acevedo were really typical figures.

CHAPTER 9: THE WAR

1 MID 2347–G–44/3, 7 February 1928; 44/7, 8, 9, March to September 1928; 48/1, 28 May 1929; MID 2657–G–670, 22 May 1929.

2 MID 2655–G–161/1 to 20, 14 February 1928.

3 *Ibid*, 2 January 1930.

4 DSR 812.00/29132, 13 February 1928, and MID 2347–G–48/1, 28 May 1929: 'When the internal and external debts are taken into consideration the Mexican Government is insolvent.'

5 MID 2025.386/3, 2657–G–605/62; MID 2025–259/175, /62; MID 2025.259/178 and 187.

6 MID 2025.386/3; 2025.259/150 and 208.

7 MID 2025.403, March 1927, *The Mexican Army, study made in the Latin American section, General Staff* (37 pp.); and MID 2025.259/208, 16 May 1930.

8 MID 2025.475/4, 29 April 1935.

9 DSR 812.00, Colima, 19 March 1929, 125 men of the 90th Regiment went over to the Cristeros; MID 2657–G–605/122, 16 February 1928, forcibly enlisted miners deserted in Sinaloa.

10 MID 2025.293/106, 7 September 1928.

11 MID 2025.403, *The Mexican Army*.

12 Purchase of rifles, machine-guns, ammunition, horses, and aircraft, MID 2724–G–38 and 45, report of Lt.-Col. Gordon Johnston, 19 June 1929.

13 MID 2657–G–666, Col. McNab.

14 Interview by the author with E. Mendoza.

15 See Chapter 6.

16 H. Navarrete, *Por Dios y por la Patria*, pp. 142–3.

17 AAA; archives of the Valparaíso Regiment; SJ, correspondence of Colonel González Romo (Coalcomán).

18 MID 2025–403, March 27. M32–7. Interview by the author with Acevedo.

19 Interview by the author with Acevedo.

20 SJ, letter to Colonel González Romo, Coalcomán, n.d.

21 AAA; Acevedo to Quintanar, 16 April 1929.

22 Fr J. Jesús Pérez, recorded by Fr Rafael Ramírez, S. J.

23 Fr J. Jesús Pérez, quoted by Fr Rafael Ramírez, S. J.

24 AAA; Aureliano Ramírez, captain in the 'Free Men of Huejuquilla' Regiment, bought himself horses and soap with regimental funds; Florencio Estrada, accused of violence towards the families of the enemy; Francisco Sánchez, colonel of the 'Free Men of

Chalchihuites' Regiment, suspended after an inquiry; Colonel Ignacío Serrano, suspended for collecting taxes illegally.

25 Interview by the author with Aurelio Acevedo.

26 UNAM, fo. 46, leg. 2; and AAA.

27 Interview by the author with Genaro Gómez López, 1967.

28 Archives of the Government of Jalisco, 1927–9: nine safe-conducts delivered in three years, of which one was given to Rito López, who later returned to the fight. The archives of the MID do not mention any Cristero soldiers as having gone over to the Government, but they insist that there were tens of thousands of Federal deserters.

29 Interview by the author with Fr N. Valdéz, 1968.

30 Interview by the author with Luis Luna, 1967.

31 Testimony of the sister of Reynaldo Cárdenas (sister-in-law of Castañón).

32 Interview by the author with Acevedo.

33 Interview by the author with Luis Luna, 1968.

34 Lagarde, p. 98.

35 See the accounts in 1926–7 of the war in Durango; in the battle fought halfway between Zitzio and Pamatacuaro 'comrade Cenobio struggled fiercely with a *guacho* [Federal], and when the latter felt himself to be badly wounded he said to him: brother, do not kill me, I am Ignacio Zepeda, Lieutenant Colonel. When he heard these words, comrade Cenobio let him go like a chicken, and took away his rifle, and left him there.' *David*, III, 170.

36 *Excelsior*, 23 October 1928. He was released on payment of a ransom of 20,000 pesos, with which Pedro Martínez bought 600 uniforms, flour, and cartridges. (Interview by the author with Pedro Martínez, 1967.)

37 Anonymous (Fr Valdés's collection).

38 Interview by the author with Ezequiel Mendoza.

39 See the account of the war; the Federal General Ayala was killed there; cf. report of the battle of the hill of Encinal (Mich.)

40 Interview by the author with Acevedo.

41 'They just fired shots at us wildly, without any order; we were like dear hunters, and with few weapons we were good marksmen.' (Interview by the author with Ezequiel Mendoza).

42 ' ... because you yourselves take them arms and equipment, you take them horses and money and everything, and not in a basket but in big shipments', said Joaquina Sierra to General Enrique León, who accused her of taking ammunition to the Cristeros in a basket (letter of Francisco Campos to Meyer, 1970). The Government forces besieged in Colotlán fired 42,300 rounds, and the Cristeros who were attacking them, 4,000. The former lost 50 killed and the Cristeros, 9. Report of the ex-Governor Luis Reyes to Calles, 22 April 1929, MID and AAA.

43 Luis Luna, interviewed by the author.

44 'Que muera Cristo y su Madre la gran chingada, viva el demonio, viva el diablo mayor!'

45 Gonzalo Arellano interviewed by Fr N. Valdés.

46 AAA, report of Acevedo to Quintanar, 12 June 1928.

47 7 April 1929, Manuel Ramírez to Gorostieta, report of the battle of Encarnación (Jal.).

48 Interview by the author with Cristóbal Rodríguez, 1968.

49 AAA, archives captured from the federals, telegram from Major A. Méndez to General Ortiz, 8 December 1926.

50 'I was with Lt.-Col. Azcárraga in Yurécuaro, he is with the 42nd Regiment, where the Cristeros do not let him rest for a moment'; AAA, letter of Lt.-Col. Luis Muñoz Cienfuegos, 23 January 1929.

51 Silvano Barba González, *La rebelión de los Cristeros*, pp. 174–5; 'in practice, nothing could be done against them with the infantry we had with us'.

52 P. J. Jesús Pérez to P. Rafael Ramírez.

53 MID 2657-G-605/125, report of Lt.-Col. Gordon Johnston, 20 May 1928.

54 MID 2657-G-651/12, 30 September 1930, 'Memorandum on the Mexican agricultural situation.'

CHAPTER 10: CULTURE AND RELIGION, FAITH AND IDEOLOGY

1 AAA, Report No. 14: 'I address myself to that delegation from this headquarters under my command. I say the following: I did receive your sincere messages into my hands and was informed of their contents. With the same affection as always I say to you that I am on the alert in every way; I am only awaiting the right hour, and immediately the messenger by word of mouth will tell you the following. What I want, and hoping that the last sacrifice will be made to achieve this opportunity. I remain in hopes of my (?)' [Abbreviated formula of greeting] [Initials of F. V.].

2 As late as 1972, one could hear and see a troop of actors from Tenango del Valle act in the sanctuary of Chalma 'Charlemagne and the Twelve Peers of France'.

3 Doña Tere de García, 1969, Xalpatlahuac, Guerrero.

4
    A turkey found a mirror
    and to see its own handsome features
    got too close to a candle
    and its tail caught fire.
    A certain monkey heard
    his bitter laments,
    and seeing his sad countenance
    said to him with great pleasure
    the madness of vanity
    always receives its just reward.

And:
    A certain greedy thief
    had to suffer the penalty
    of the poisoned good,
    and how he says: honey is very good,
    it has a delicious taste,
    but because of the cursed good,
    I shall not return to the beehive
    because that is certainly to find
    the penalty after the crime.

The poetry magazine *La Délirante* (Paris) published in its number 4/5 (December 1972) 'Un Combat de Pacotille' by Ezequiel Mendoza, illustrated by Pelayo.

5 *Excelsior*, 21 October 1927, 13 December 1927, and 29 October 1928.

6 Numerous documents in AGN, national press etc.

7 C. E. Valtierra, 'Memorias de mi actuación en el movimiento Cristero en Jalpa', MS.

8 Interview by the author with Ezequiel Mendoza.

9 Interview by the author with Acevedo.

10 Interview by the author with Ezequiel Mendoza.

11 M. Azuela, *Obras completas* (Mexico, 1960), vol. III, p. 592.

12 See section on the clergy and the war; the vast majority neither provoked nor supported the Cristero movement, even though later they supported, or were extremely sympathetic towards, the *Sinarquista* movement.

13 See Luis González, *Pueblo en vilo: microhistoria de San José de Gracia* (Mexico, 1968), 365 pp.

14 It is worth noting that the police reports never mention the arrest of priests in the course of demonstrations.

15 Drought, Spanish flu, famine, banditry in 1917; testimony of Aurelio Acevedo and Beatriz Espínola, 1968–9.

16 Police reports, Archives of the Government of Jalisco.

17 José Gutiérrez, quoting his uncle Luis (Jalostotitlán).

18 '... because I felt remorse at not having religious liberty'.

19 It is worth remembering the scepticism of Mgr Díaz, that of Rome, or that of the priest of Colima who wrote, 'Our people is a tortoise' (Fr Emeterio Covarrubias to the Liga Nacional de Defensa Religiosa (LNDR), 25 August 1926).

20 For the most concise account, see J. Lloyd Mecham, *Church and State in Latin America* (Chapel Hill, N.C., 1934), p. 507.

21 Gabriel le Bras, *Études de sociologie religieuse* (Paris, 1958), vol. II, p. 567.

22 Fr Hernández Cueva, quoted by Fr N. Valdés.

23 Interview by the author with María Refugio Ramírez, 1968; interview by the author with María del Rosario Ochoa, quoting her brother, 1966.

24 *David*, II, 220.

25 Interview by the author with Ignacio Villanueva, 1966.

26 Interview by the author with Ezequiel Mendoza.

27 *David*, I, 67.

28 Josefina Arellano MS, booklet no. 3, p. 3.

29 Jesús Herrera, quoted by Fr N. Valdés.

30 Carlos Vargas to Manuel Michel, 31 March 1929.

31 Interview by the author with Petra Cabral, 1967. One thinks of St Pol Roux 'astonishing the beggars with the hope of a palace'.

32 *David*, VI, 10.

33 Interview by the author with Petra Cabral, 1967.

34 This was Fr José María Espinosa, the parish priest of Tacáscuaro, 'the son of a small *ranchero*, a man of very little intelligence ... giving safe-conducts to Heaven, where he said that if they died in the revolution, whatever sins they had, they would be completely forgiven'. Interview by the author with Fr José Romero Flores, 1965.

35 The most important of these were: the Sacred Heart of Jesus, the Rosary, the Perpetual Adoration, the Daughters of Mary, Saint Francis, Saint Luis Gonzaga, the Holy Deposit, the Sacred Viaticum, and the Perpetual Veil. We have only mentioned here the ones which were active throughout the country.

36 Fr C. Brambila, *El Obispado de Colima* (Colima, 1964), and the parochial archives of Cuauhtémoc, Ahuijullo, Tuxcacuesco (complete from 1668), Comala, La Merced, and the archives of the diocese of Colima.

37 Archives of the diocese of Zamora, of the archdiocese of Guadalajara, and the

parochial archives of Chavinda, Sahuayo, Tangamandapio, San José de Gracia, Ciudad Guzmán, Jaripo, Jacona, Villamar, Emiliano Zapata, Tingambato, and, in the Altos region, San Francisco de Asís, San José de Gracia, Atotonilco, Ayo, Arandas, Jesús María, Lagos, San Juan de los Lagos, and San Miguel el Alto.

38 Parochial archives of Tlaxiaco, Miahuatlán and Huajuapám in Oaxaca; of Huejutla in Hidalgo, of Tlapa, Chilapa, Buenavista de Cuéllar, and Chilpancingo in Guerrero.

39 It was because the Government had him executed that the Huicholes of San Sebastián, whose priest he had been since 1920, became Cristeros.

40 This accounts for that abstract and rich vocabulary which surprises the inquirer and provokes incredulity in the reader.

41 At the end of the nineteenth century, there were in the canton of Coalcomán 105,000 souls and 28 priests. The majority of the population lived in remote places, several days' march from the 19 parish priests. This was still the case in 1925 and, in Colima, in the region of Minatitlán and Juluapán.

42 In Huazamota, a village without priests, men said the Rosary every day and celebrated all the liturgical festivals, the dying were attended by 'holy women', and for christenings and marriages people made the journey to Huejuquilla.

43 This was done, for example, by Pedro Sandoval, the Cristero leader in Florencia (Zac.), after which this man of forty was soundly beaten by his father.

44 Parish archives of San Francisco de Asís, Fr Angulo to Mgr Orozco, 8 August 1929: 'the most admirable thing about them is their heroic sacrifice, to which they submit themselves completely, immediately and with that heroic sincerity which characterises them, at the first indication which they received to cease from the war, by order of the Apostolic Delegate, whose order they obeyed, with the promptitude of an Angel and the simplicity of a child, even though they have gone on killing them'.

45 Francisco Campos to the author.

CHAPTER II: TEN YEARS LATER

1 DSR 812.00, Durango 29, 1 October 1929; MID 2657–G–605/196–8.

2 DSR 812.00, Jalisco 69, 15 October 1929.

3 Interview by the author with E. Mendoza.

4 Interview by the author with Ezequiel Mendoza.

5 20 July to 1 August 1934, in A. Bremauntz, *La educación socialista en México* (Mexico City, 1943), pp. 212–13.

6 Or 'the *albérchiga* war' (*albérchiga* – fruit picked late in the season).

7 22 episcopal condemnations between 1930 and 1932, repeated every year until 1938; encyclical *Acerba animi*.

8 *The New York Times*, 8 July 1935.

9 4 March 1936, to the schoolteachers of Guadalajara.

Bibliography

I. PRIMARY MANUSCRIPT SOURCES
A. Public Archives

Mexico

Archivo General de la Nación, division concerning Presidents Obregón, 1921–4, and Calles, 1924–8.

State archives: Coahuila, Jalisco, Oaxaca, Querétaro.

Municipal archives: Guanajuato; San Francisco del Rincón, Jalisco, Arandas, Atotonilco, Ayo el Chico, San José de Gracia, Tapalpa, Tepatitlán.

National Autonomous University of Mexico, Vasconcelos collection; Palomar y Vizcarra collection (archives of the League).

Departamento de Asuntos Agrarios y Colonización.

USA

Department of State Records relating to the internal affairs of Mexico 1910–29, 812.00, 812.404; 711.12.

Military Intelligence Division, War Department General Staff 1925–40.

Josephus Daniel's private papers, Library of Congress; National Archives and State Department.

Dwight Morrow papers, Amherst College, Amherst, Mass.

Sheffield papers, Yale University Library.

Bishop MacDevitt's papers, Notre Dame University.

Catholic archives of Texas (Austin).

Archives of the archdiocese of San Antonio (1913–17).

William Borah manuscripts: DSR rolls 384–385 (1934–6).

France

Diplomatic and consular correspondence: 'M. Ernest Lagarde, chargé d'affaires de la République française au Mexique à son Excellence, M. Aristide Briand, ministre des Affaires étrangères', 18 Sept. 1926, 100 pp., typed, large format, Box 105.

B. Private Archives

Church Collections
Archbishopric of Guadalajara.
Parish archives – Jalisco: San Francisco de Asís, San José de Gracia, San Miguel el Alto, Totatiche.
    Michoacán: Ciudad Hidalgo, Tacámbaro, Zacapu, Zitácuaro.

Bibliography

México: Tenancingo.
Morelos: Santa María Ahuacatitlán.
Guerrero: Buenavista de Cuellar, Huitzuco, Chiepancingo, Tlapa, Chilapa.
Jesuit archives: Puente Grande (Jalisco) and San Ángel (DF).

Private collections
Miguel Palomar y Vizcarra (bequeathed to UNAM).
Antonio Rius Facius (Mexico, DF).
Aurelio Acevedo.
Fr S. Casas (Guadalajara).
Fr Nicolas Valdés (Guadalajara).
Jesús Sanz Cerrada (Durango).
José Gutiérrez by Gutiérrez (Mexico, DF).
Felipe Brondo (Saltillo).
J. J. F. Hernández (Capilla de Guadalupe, Jalisco).
Emiliano Guardián (Tenancingo)

II. PHOTOGRAPHIC DOCUMENTATION

350 photos given by individuals cited and by about a hundred other donors.

III. ORAL SOURCES

The refusal of Church and state to open certain collections of archives – those of Mgr Díaz, of the Episcopal Committee, the Ministry of War, the Ministry of the Interior – and especially the systematic destruction of documents force the researcher to rely on eye-witnesses, and to fall back on oral sources. For obtaining facts written material is deficient, and will always be so, for the historian; pursuit of oral material, on the other hand, leads to a wealth of information on attitudes of mind, social structures, and ideology. The records containing the material gathered by Fr N. Valdés were completed after slightly fewer than 500 interviews with 420 Cristeros from every region, with government personnel, with representatives from the army, the clergy, and the League; about a hundred hours of recorded material are the result.

IV. QUESTIONNAIRES

400 questionnaires filled in by Cristeros, and 160 by *agraristas*.

V. PRIMARY PRINTED SOURCES

A. Government

Boletín Judicial.
Diario de los Debates del Congreso Constituyente, 1916–17.
Diario de los Debates de la Cámara de Diputados, 1926–9.
Ibid. Senadores.
Diario Official, 1917–38.

Bibliography

Gruening, Ernest. *Mexico and its heritage.* 747 pp. New York, 1929, pp. 398–504. Contain documents of the Ministry of the Interior (government).

Investigation of Mexican affairs. Hearings before a subcommittee of the Committee on Foreign Relations, United States Denate, 66th Congress, first session, pursuant to S. res. 106 directing the Committee on Foreign Relations to investigate the matter of outrages on citizens of the United States in Mexico. 3 vols. Washington, DC, 1919.

Jurado de Toral y la Madre Conchita, el. What was and was not said at this sensational trial. Shorthand version. 2 vols. 350 pp. Mexico, 1928.

Ley reformando el Código Penal para el Distrito y Territorios Federales, sobre delitos de Fuero Común y delitos contra la Federación en materia de culto religioso y disciplina externa. Pamphlet. Mexico, Telleres Gráficos de la Nación, 1926.

Memorias de la secretaria de Gobernación. 1926–32. 7 vols.

Memorias de la secretaria de la Defensa Nacional. 1926–41. 16 vols.

Navarrete, Félix. *De Cabarrus a Carranza: la legislación anticatólica en México.* 150 pp. Mexico, Jus, 1957.

Navarrete, Félix, and Pallares, Eduardo. *La persecución en México desde el punto de visto jurídico.*

   Colección de leyes y decretos relativos a la reducción de sacerdotes. 361 pp. No indication of date nor editor. Mexico, 1936?

País, el. Official government periodical; in Jalisco *La Sombra de Arteaga* . . . Querétaro.

Pérez Lugo, J. *La Cuestión religiosa en México: recopilación de leyes, disposiciones legales y documentos para el estudio de este problema político.* 428 pp. Mexico, 1926.

Periódico Oficial del Gobierno Constitucional del estado de Aguascalientes, 1913–33.

Ibid. Colima (state of Colima), 1913–38.

Ibid. Chihuahua, 1913–38.

Ibid. Durango, 1913–38.

Ibid. Guanajuato, 1913–38.

Ibid. Guerrero, 1913–38.

Ibid. Hidalgo, 1913–38.

Ibid. Michoacán, 1913–38.

Ibid. Nuevo León, 1913–38.

Ibid. Oaxaca, 1913–38.

Ibid. Sinaloa, 1913–38.

Ibid. Tamaulipas, 1913–38.

Ibid. Tepic, 1913–38.

Ibid. Tlaxcala, 1913–38.

Ibid. Yucatán, 1913–38.

Ramos V., Roberto. *Revolución y régimen constitucionalista.* Vol. 3, part 1, collected *Documentos Históricos de la Revolución Mexicana,* XV. 270 pp. Mexico, Jus, 1969.

B. On the Mexican Catholic Church

Carreño, Alberto María. *Pastorales, edictos y otros documentos del Excmo y Revmo Sr Don Pascual Díaz, Arzobispo de México.* Mexico, 1938.

   El Arzobispo de México Exmo Sr Don Pascual Diaz y el conflicto religioso. 2nd ed., annotated and enlarged. 628 pp. Mexico, 1943.

Correa, Eduardo J. *Pascual Díaz S.J. el Arzobispo Martir.* 262 pp. Mexico, 1945.

Bibliography

Díaz Barreto, Pascual. *Informe que rinde al V. Episcopado mexicano el obispo de Tabasco en relación con las actividades de la L.N.D.L.R. en los E.U.A.* 54 pp. New York, 1928.

Lara y Torres, Leopoldo. *Documentos para la historia de la persecución religiosa en México.* 1,104 pp. Mexico, Jus, 1954.

C. On the Holy See

Acta apostolicae sedis: monthly official publication of the Holy See. See especially the Encyclicals:

    Benedict XV: *Exploratum Vobis Est* (1917).

    Pius XI: *Paterna Solicitudo sane* (12 February 1926).

    Pius XI: *Iniquis afflictisque* (18 November 1926).

    Pius XI: *Acerba Animi* (29 September 1932).

    Pius XI: *Firmissimam constantiam* (28 March 1937).

D. Journals and periodicals

The Ministry of the Interior has imposed a severe censorship on all inquiries concerning military operations and has seen to it that only official communiqués shall be published.

Daily journals of the Centre
El Demócrata;
Excelsior.
El Hombre Libre.
El Machete (daily from 1926).
El Nacional.
Omega;
La Patria.
La Prensa.
Reconquista.
Restauración (journal of the schismatic church, 1925–28).
El Universal.

Regional dailies
Guanajuato: *El Diario de León, El Heraldo del Centro.*
Jalisco: *El Informador, El Sol, El Tiempo, El Heraldo, Las Noticias.*
Oaxaca: *El Mercurio.*
Tabasco: *Redención.*
Veracruz: *El Dictámen.*
Zacatecas: *El Amigo del pueblo, El Iris, El Preludio.*
Cayetano Reyes undertook the prevention of the distribution of *Excelsior* and *El Informador.*

Dailies published in the United States
El Diario de el Paso (published by Mexicans).
The New York Times.
The New York Evening Post.

Bibliography

The Wall Street Journal.
Oklahoma News.

L'Osservatore Romano

Foreign periodicals
United States: Baltimore Catholic Review, The Catholic World, Columbia, Current History,
 Extension, Foreign Affairs;
Belgium: Les études religieuses, Revue catholique des idées et des faits;
France: Les Etudes;
Italy: Civiltà Cattolica.
Ross, Stanley R. Fuentes de la historia contemporánea de México; periódicos y revistas.
 Vol. I, 1910–17. Vol. II, 1917–42. 1,006 pp. Mexico, 1965. This is essential
 reading.

VI. SECONDARY PRINTED SOURCES

A. State versus Church

The Porfiriato and the Conciliation
García, Ignacio. Exposición al sumo pontifice sobre el estado que guarda el clero y la
 religión bajo la dominación secular en esta arquidiócesis. 2 vols. Mexico, 1890.
Garza, Jr, Emeterio de la. La política de conciliación. 35 pp. Mexico, 1903.
Gillow, T. Mgr. Apuntes históricos 166 pp. Mexico, 1889.
 Reminiscencias. 300 pp. Los Angeles, 1920.
Hernández, Ciro. Some aspects of the Mexican Catholic social congresses 1903–1909.
 Master's thesis, Mexico City College, 1959. Unpublished.
Juárez, Joseph Robert. Conflict and cooperation between church and state: the archbishopric
 of Guadalajara during the Porfiriato 1876–1911. Ph.D. thesis, University of Texas,
 Austin, 310 pp., typed. Exciting work on the archives of the archbishopric;
 unique of its type.
Pardo, Agustin. El clericalismo en acción. 184 pp. Mexico, 1908.
Schmitt, Karl M. 'Catholic adjustment to the secular state: the case of Mexico 1867–
 1911.' The Catholic Historical Review, XLVIII, 2 July 1962.
 Evolution of Mexican thought on Church-State relations, 1876–1911. Ann Arbor,
 Michigan, 1954 (microfilm).
Tarrant, Daniel J. The Catholic church in Mexico: a survey, 1877–1910. Catholic
 University of America, 1954. MS.
Terrazas, J. Joaquín. La lucha patriótica entre México, España y los Estados Unidos en
 sus relaciones con la cuestión religiosa. Voz de alarma para que la Iglesia condene
 la Doctrina Monroe. 220 pp. Mexico, 1897.

The conflict with the Carrancistas
Branch, H. N. 'The Mexican Constitution of 1917 compared with the Constitution of
 1857.' Annals of the American Academy of Political and Social Sciences. 1917,
 Supplement.

Bibliography

Cabrera, Luis. *The religious question in Mexico.* 9 pp. New York, 1915.

González Flores, Anacleto. *La cuestión religiosa en Jalisco.* Ed. with Régis Planchet, *La cuestión religiosa en México.* 310 pp. El Paso, 1927.

Kelley, Francis C., Mgr. *El libro de rojo y amarillo, una historia de sangre y cobardía.* 131 pp. Chicago, 1915.

Memorial del cabildo metropolitano y clero de la Arquidiócesis de Guadalajara al C. Presidente de la Republica Mexicana Don V. Carranza y voto de adhesión y obediencia al Ilmo y Rdmo Sr Arz. Dr. y Mtro Dn Fr. Orozco y Jiménez. 46 pp. n.p. 1918.

Menendez Mena, Rodolfo. *La obra del clero y la llamada persecución religiosa.* 23 pp. Mexico, 1916.

Orozco y Jiménez, Francisco, Mgr. *Acerquémonos a Dios! Memorándum.* 99 pp. Guadalajara, 1918.

Memorandum. 32 pp. n.p., 1917.

Paredes, Antonio J. and Herrera, Gerardo M. *Carta a los fieles cristianos de la ciudad de México.* Mexico, 1915.

Rivera, Luis M. *El clericalismo y el militarismo en la evolución política de México.* 76 pp. Guadalajara, 1914.

Voice of the Government

Báez Camargo, Gonzalo (Pedro Gringoire), and Grubb, Kenneth G. *Religion in the republic of Mexico.* 166 pp. London, 1935.

Balderrama, Luis. *El clero y el gobierno de Mexico, apuntes para la historia de la crisis en 1926.* 2 vols, 302 and 234 pp. Mexico, 1927.

Beltrán, Enrique. *La lucha revolucionaria del proletariado contra la Iglesia.* 47 pp. Mexico, 1931.

Díaz Soto y Gama, Antonio. *Discurso pronunciado al Congreso de la Unión.* 22 pp. Mexico, 1926.

El Gobierno de México ante los problemas sociales y económicos. 2 instalments. Mexico, 1936.

Elías, Arturo. *The Mexican people and the church.* New York, 1926.

Elías Calles, Plutarco. 'The policies of Mexico to-day'. *Foreign Affairs,* V–I, October 1926, 1–6.

Federación Anticlerical. *Estatutos.* 33 pp. Mexico, 1923.

Fray Polilla. *Desde mi púlpito.* 151 pp. Mexico.

Galarza, Ernest. *The Roman Catholic Church as a factor in the political and social history of Mexico.* 188 pp. Sacramento, 1928.

Gobierno de Vera-Cruz. *La cuestión religiosa en Veracruz.* 47 pp. Jalapa, 1926.

Islas, Felipe and Muzquiz Blanco, Manuel. *De la pasión sectaria a la noción de las instituciones.* 284 pp. Mexico, 1932.

L.G.M. *¡A las armas ciudadanos!* 109 pp. Mexico, 1926.

Liga Central de Resistencia. *ABC socialista para uso de los niños campesinos.* 45 pp. Mexico, 1929.

List Arzubide, Germán. *Práctica de educación irreligiosa.* Mexico 1934.

Obregón, A. 'Declaraciones de prensa.' *El Universal,* 14 January 1923.

El problema religioso en México. 14 pp. Mexico, 1926.

Portes Gil, Emilio. *La lucha entre el poder civil y el clero: estudio histórico y jurídico.* 133 pp. Mexico, 1934. A thematic indictment published at the time of the 1934 crisis, by the ex-president, *procurador general.* Also in English and French.

Riveros, Francisco. *El decreto del 2 de julio y la pastoral colectiva.* 211 pp. Mexico, 1927.

Bibliography

Rodríguez, Cristobal General. *Sobre la brecha.* 228 pp. Mexico, 1930.

Ruiz, Jaoquín. *La revolución en Tabasco.* 123 pp. Mexico, 1934.

Sender, Ramon. *El problema religioso en México, católicos y cristianos.* 236 pp. Madrid, 1928. The great Spanish novelist, though an Iberian liberal, takes on logically the positions adopted by the Mexican government.

Tellez, Manuel C. 'The church and the state in conflict in Mexico. The Mexican official view.' *Current History,* XXIV, 1926, 496–8.

Toro, Alfonso. *La Iglesia y el estado en México.* 288 pp. Mexico, 1932.

Uroz, Antonio. *La cuestión religiosa en México.* 282 pp. Mexico, 1926.

Valdez, S. and Lazcano, F. *Abajo las religiones, la apostasía clerical.* 19 pp. Mexico, 1929.

Vargas Vila, José Maria. *La cuestión religiosa en México.* 35 pp. Mexico, 1926.

Voice of the Church

Arquímedes (Benjamin Flores Cárdenas). *Los 'arreglos' religiosos y la pastoral del Ilmo Delegado Apostólico examinados a la luz de la doctrina católica.* 44 pp. Mexico, 1929. An aggressive rebuttal.

Barraquer. *La lucha de los católicos mexicanos.* 583 pp. Tarragona, 1926.

Blanco Gil, Joaquin (Andrés Barquin). *El clamor de la Sangre.* Mexico, 1947.

Curley, Michael J. (Archbishop of Baltimore). *Mexican tyranny and the Catholic Church.* 64 pp. Brooklyn, NY, 1926.

Deister, John L. *Mártires mexicanos, soldados de Cristo Rey. Ofrenda que México glorioso deposita ante tu trono. La Iglesia en una noche de persecución.* 165 pp. n.p., 1928.

Díaz, Pascual (Archbishop). 'State vs. Church in Mexico.' *The North American Review,* CCXXV, April 1928.

Echeverría, José. *Der Kampf gegen die katholische Kirche in Mexiko in den letzten 13 Jahren.* München Gladbach, 1926.

El Modus Vivendi, la verdad sobre los arreglos de la cuestión religiosa celebrados entre el Lic. E. Portes Gil y los Ilmos Srs L. Ruiz y Flores y P. Díaz. 23 pp. Mexico, 1929. Official Church viewpoint.

Galvez, J. Leopoldo (priest). *Grande ofertorio de opiniones y esperanzas para un sacrificio.* 60 pp. Chicago, 1929. Against the 'arreglos'.

Gutiérrez, Agustin. *Elucidario, conferencia leida en la Sociedad de Geografía, Historia y Estadística de Guadalajara.* 3 pp. Guadalajara, 1936. The 'arreglos' and their results.

(priest). *Que somos?* 99 pp. Guadalajara, 1933. Against the 'arreglos'. Condemned by Mgr Orozco for its insults to the Pope, the Cardinal Biondi, and to the Episcopate. Banned for three months.

Kelley, Francis C. (Bishop) *Blood-drenched altars, Mexican study and comment.* 522 pp. Milwaukee, 2nd ed., 1935.

López Ortega, J. Antonio. *Las naciones extranjeras y la persecución religiosa.* 374 pp. Mexico, 1944.

McCullagh, Francis. *Red Mexico, a reign of terror in America.* 415 pp. New York, Montreal, London, 1928.

McFarland, Charles S. *Chaos in Mexico: the conflict of Church and State.* 284 pp. New York, London, 1935. The first important work written by an American Protestant condemning the Mexican Government's policy. It had great influence in changing the attitude of Cárdenas.

Bibliography

Manríquez y Zarate (Bishop). *A mis compatriotas.* 25 pp. San Antonio, 1928.

Marin Negueruela, Nicolas. *La verdad sobre México.* 368 pp. Barcelona, 1928.

Miles, César. *Víctimas y verdugos, estudio sobre la persecución antireligiosa en México.* 124 pp. Belfast, 1927.

Navarrete, Félix. *¡Si, hay persecución religiosa en México!¡ aquí estan las pruebas!* 50 pp. San Francisco, 1935.

Obispo mexicano, Un. *Breve estudio para contribuir a la mejor comprensión del actual conflicto religioso en México.* n.p., 1928. 2 parts: the 1st is lost; the 2nd, *La revolución y nuestras libertades*; the 3rd, *Memorial del Episcopado y la ley reglamentaria de cultos promulgada para el distrito y los territorios.*

Ruiz y Flores, Leopoldo (Archbishop). *Recuerdo de recuerdos.* 181 pp. Mexico, 1942. Succinct and evocative; interesting; dispassionate.

B. General Studies

Books

Bailey, David C. *The Cristero rebellion and the religious conflict in Mexico 1926–9.* 449 pp. Doctoral thesis, Michigan State University, 1969; published, 1974, by Texas University Press, Austin. Excellent study of the political conflict and the converging pressures brought to bear by Rome and Washington to lead the adversaries to a compromise.

Callcott, Wilfrid Hardy. *Liberalism in Mexico 1857–1929.* 410 pp. Stanford, Calif., 1931; new edition, Hamden, Conn., 1965. Indispensable reference work.

Campbell, Hugh G. *The radical right in Mexico 1929–49.* Unpublished thesis, University of California, Los Angeles, 1968.

González, Franklin S. *Church-State controversy in Mexico since 1929.* MS master's thesis, University of California, Los Angeles, 1948.

Larin, Nicolas. *La rebelión de los Cristeros.* 260 pp. Mexico, 1968. Original Russian ed., 1965. Deals more with the church and state than with the Cristeros, employing a conceptual framework of 'demo-bourgeoisie' and 'national bourgeoisie'.

Olivera Sedano, Alicia. *Aspectos del conflicto religioso de 1926 à 1929, sus antecedentes y consecuencias.* 227 pp. Mexico, 1966. First Mexican work of historiography to break with the Manichaeist tradition. This doctoral thesis is a pioneer work on the archives of the League which Alicia Olivera had been appointed to put on microfilm at the residence of Mgr Palomar y Vizcarra; it is the first objective study. In this respect it marks an epoch in Mexican historiography, which had not until then had the courage to tackle a subject that was taboo. The author highlights the steps in the confrontation between Church and state, one that was inherited and reinforced by the social tendencies of the two powers, as well as by the action of the League. From the reports of the League, she outlines a history of the conflict and underlines both the importance and complexity of the rebellion.

Quirk, Robert Emmett. *The Mexican Revolution and the Catholic Church, 1910–1929, an ideological study.* Doctoral thesis, Harvard, 1950; 1st ed., Indiana University Press, 1960; 2nd ed., New York, 1963, paperback.

Quirarte, Martín. *El problema religioso en México.* 408 pp. Mexico, 1967. Ideological synthesis from the Conquest until the twentieth century.

Bibliography

Rubino, Elena. *Aportación al estudio histórico de las relaciones entre la Iglesia Católica y el Estado Mexicano durante los gobiernos de Obregón y Calles.* Unpublished thesis. Mexico, UNAM, 1963. A curious Marxist–Toynbean endeavour.

Articles

Broderick, Francis L. 'Liberalism and the Mexican crisis of 1927: a debate between Norman Thomas and John A. Ryan.' *Catholic Historical Reivew,* XLI, 2 May 1960, 191–211.

Brown, Lyle C. 'Mexican Church–State relations 1933–1940.' *A Journal of Church and State,* VI-2, Spring 1964, 202–22.

Dewey, C. 'Church vs. State in Mexico.' *New Republic,* 25 August 1926.

James, Earl K. 'Church and State in Mexico.' *Foreign policy reports,* XI–9, 3 July 1935, 105–16.

Jones, Chester L. 'Roots of the Mexican conflict.' *Foreign Affairs,* XIX, 1 October 1935, 135–45.

Kenney, Michael R. P. 'La crise méxicaine.' *Etudes Religieuses,* Liège, 25 February 1928.

Lloyd Mecham, J. 'State vs. Church: Mexican religious problem.' *Southwest Review,* XXIII, April 1938, 295–6.

Lugan, Alphonse (Abbé). 'Religious fight in Mexico and the peace.' *Current History,* 25 September 1929.

'The Mexican Church conflict.' *Current History,* February 1931, 672–7. 'Mexico's religious conflict.' *Current History,* XXIV, 4 July 1926.

Wilkie, James W. 'The meaning of the Cristero religious war against the Mexican revolution.' *A Journal of Church and State,* VIII–2, Spring 1966, 214–33.

C. The Role of the United States

Bailey, David C. *Op. cit.*

Berbusse, Edward J., SJ. 'The unofficial intervention of the United States in Mexico's religious crisis, 1926–1930.' *The Americas,* XXIII, 1 July 1966, 28–63.

Bucher, Betty R. *Catholics and W. Wilson's Mexican policy, 1914–1916.* Unpublished master's thesis. The Catholic University of America, 1954.

Cirieco, Joseph. *The United States and the Mexican Church-State conflict 1926–9.* Unpublished master's thesis. Georgetown University, 1961.

Committee on Religious Rights and Minorities. *Religious liberty in Mexico.* New York, 1935. W. Borah arouses American public opinion.

Cronon, Edward David. 'American Catholics and Mexican anticlericalism, 1933–1936.' *Mississippi Historical Review,* XLV, 2 September 1958, 201–30.

Ellis, Ethan. 'D. Morrow and the Church–State controversy in Mexico.' *Hispanic American Historical Review,* XXXVIII, 4 November 1958, 482–505.

Lippmann, Walter. 'Church and State in Mexico: the American mediation.' *Foreign Affairs,* VIII, January 1930, 186–207. Lippmann's sources are valuable: Morrow, the State Department, the editor of the *New York World,* informants from Rome and Mexico.

Nicolson, Harold. *Dwight Morrow.* 409 pp. New York, 1935. Essential.

Rice, Elizabeth Ann, O.P. *The diplomatic relations between the United States and Mexico, as affected by the struggle for religious liberty in Mexico, 1925–9.* 224 pp. Washington,

DC, 1959. The first work of research into the American diplomatic archives. A reference book that will be a classic.

Ross, Stanley R. 'Dwight Morrow, ambassador to Mexico.' *Americas*, XIV, 13 January 1958, 272–90.

'Dwight Morrow and the Mexican revolution.' *Hispanic American Historical Review*, XXXVIII, 4, 1959, 506–28.

D. The Cristeros

Few works have been devoted to the Cristeros, whether of a polemical or academic nature or by witnesses. Only very few publications have concentrated solely on this subject:

Texts

Bailey, David C. *Op. cit.*

Barba González, Silvano. *La rebelión de los Cristeros.* 212 pp. Mexico, 1967. Recollections that are a little confused: serious errors in dates of the interim governor of Jalisco in 1926–7. Account of the first uprisings in Jalisco and of an interview with Calles.

Bonfil, Alicia O. S. de. *La literatura Cristera.* Mexico, 1970.

Camberos Vizcaino, Vicente, *Miguel Gómez Loza.* 2 vols, 309 and 325 pp. Mexico, 1953. A biography of the successor to A. Gonzáles Flores. Not much information on the Cristeros.

Cardoso, Joaquín. *El martirologio católico de nuestros días: los martirios mexicanos.* 481 pp. 2nd ed. Mexico, 1958. An ecclesiastical work, from which some information may be gleaned.

Casasola, Augustín V. *Historia gráfica de la Revolución 1900–1940.* 5 vols. Mexico, 1940. An interesting and useful collection of photographs, documents, and press extracts.

Chowell, Martin (pseudonym of Alfonso Trueba). *Luis Navarro Origel, el primer Cristero.* 159 pp. Mexico, 1959. Panegyric, edited from original documents, on the leader of the uprising at Penjame, Gto., in September 1926. The author is guilty of hagiography, notably when he deals with the brush between Navarro and the Cristeros of Michoacán. There is good evidence of what might be called 'League spirit' among urban Catholics.

Degollado, Jesús. *Memorias.* 307 pp. Mexico, 1957. The recollections of the leader of the South Jalisco Division, who was in command of 8,000 soldiers, before he took over command from Gorostieta as commander-in-chief of the National Guard. Highly coloured though accurate accounts are not overshadowed by errors in matters of detail, dates especially, revealed in the publication of documents from his archives and by photographs.

Gallegos, C. J. I. *Apuntes para la historia de la persecución religiosa en Durango de 1926 a 1929.* 95 pp. Mexico, 1965. Some information on the Cristeros of Santiago Bayacora.

Gelsky, Frank León. *Historia e ideología de la filosofía Cristera,* 262 pp. Manuscript doctoral thesis for the University of Salamanca, April 1961. A good analysis of Catholic literature favourable to the Cristeros, though little on the Cristeros themselves.

Bibliography

Gómez Robledo, Antonio (pseudonym). *Anacleto González Flores, el maestro.* 193 pp. 2nd ed. Mexico, 1947. The setting of the Altos is remarkably well evoked, as well as the tragedy of civilians compelled to fight.

Larin, Nicolas. *Op. cit.*

Meyer, Jean A. *La Cristiada.* Mexico, Madrid, Siglo XXI, 1973. In Spanish. 3 vols: I, *La guerra de los Cristeros*; II, *El conflicto entre la Iglesia y el Estado en México*; III, *Los Cristeros: sociedad e ideología.*

Apocalypse et Révolution au Méxique. Paris, Gallimard, 1974.

Morones, Felipe. *Capítulos sueltos o apuntes sobre la persecución religiosa en Aguascalientes.* 230 pp. Aguascalientes, 1955. A local martyrology written by a priest.

Navarrete, Heriberto, S.J.

Los Cristeros eran así. 105 pp. Mexico, 1968. Intimate account of Cristero daily life.

Por Dios y por la Patria. Memorias de mi participación en la defensa de la libertad de conciencia y culto durante la persecución religiosa en México de 1926 a 1929. 276 pp. Mexico, 1961. Account of an unusual witness, a young science student who, having been involved in urban political conflict and after deportation to the Islas Marias, joined the Cristero fighters. A clinical portrait of the Cristeros of the Altos de Jalisco, whom he knew as secretary and staff officer to Gorostieta. Endowed with an excellent memory and a lively style, though near-blindness forced him to record his experiences orally, he later entered the Society of Jesus. Inaccuracy is to be found in only one matter, the death of Victoriano Ramírez. Good photographs from the author's collection.

Olivera Sedano, Alicia. *Op. cit.*

Pérez, José Dolores. *La persecución religiosa de Calles en León.* 99 pp. León, 1942. The author, a priest, is concerned mainly with martyrs of the Church.

Ramírez, Rafael. *Breves respuestas al programma de Historia Patria.* Manuscript. El Paso, 1942. First attempt at a complete and detailed history of the war.

Rius Facius, Antonio. *Méjico Cristero, historia de la ACJM 1929–1931.* 1st ed., Mexico, 1960; 2nd rev. ed., Mexico, 1966, 446 pp. Accent placed on participation of ACJM members, outside this institution, in national events between 1925 and 1931. More about the ACJM than the Cristeros, but much of the information has been taken from the author's archives.

Rodríguez, Cristobal. *La Iglesia Católica y la rebelión cristera en México.* 2 parts, 250 and 251 pp.; the 2nd part is subtitled *Cristeros contra Cristianos.* Mexico, 1966–7. General Rodríguez, companion and friend of Amaro, Minister of War, sets out to prove that the Cristeros were the foolish victims of the clergy, who were neither Catholic nor patriotic and wanted to recover power and wealth. Invaluable testimony of a participant in the conflict, whose sincerity is evident.

Sodi de Pallares, Maria E. *Los Cristeros y José León Toral.* 157 pp. Mexico, 1936. Chiefly about Obregón's murderer.

Spectator (pseudonym of P. E. de J. Ochoa). *Les Cristeros del Volcán de Colima.* 1st ed. in Italian, Turin, 1933 (*Fe di popolo, Fiore di Eroi*); 1st ed. in Spanish, Mexico, 1942; ed. cited here, revised and completed, Mexico, Jus, 1961, Vol. I, 390 pp., Vol. II, 329 pp. The author was an eye-witness and a companion of Cristeros (brother of Dionisio Ochoa, leader of the Cristeros of Colima). A source of the first rank.

Valdes, Nicolas. *México sangre por Cristo Rey.* 104 pp. Lagos, 1964. Alphabetical list, with geographical location and date of death, of some 6,000 Cristeros fallen in combat, chiefly in the Altos de Jalisco and the Cañones area (Jalisco and Zacatecas). The author, a priest, spent nearly 80 hours recording oral material and has a remarkable collection of documents.

Fiction

Anda, Guadalupe de. *Los Cristeros, la guerra santa de los Altos.* Mexico, 1937.
  Los Bragados. Mexico, 1942.
Estrada, Antonio. *Rescoldo.* Mexico, 1961. A distinguished novel, noticed by Juan Rulfo. The author is the son of the Cristero leader Florencio Estrada, who died in combat in 1936.
Gallegos, Romulo. 'La Brasa en el pico del cuervo.' Chapter printed in *Cuadernos Americanos*, 1969, 164–200.
Garro, Elena. *Los Recuerdos del porvenir.* Mexico, 1963.
Gram, Jorge (P. David Ramírez). *La Guerra Sintética.* El Paso, 1956.
  Hector. 6th ed., Mexico, 1953.
  Jahel. El Paso, 1956.
Guzman, Vereo. *Viva Cristo Rey!* Mexico, n.d.
Menéndez, Miguel Angel. *Nayar.* Mexico, 1941.
Navarrete, Heriberto. *El Voto de Chema Rodríguez.* Mexico, 1964.
Paso, Fernando del. *José Trigo.* Mexico, 1966.
Rivero del Val, Luis. *Entre las patas de los caballos.* 2nd ed. Mexico, 1954.
Robles, Fernando. *La Virgen de los Cristeros.* Buenos Aires, 1934; Mexico, 1959.
Robles Castillo, Aurelio. *¡Ay Jalisco no te rajes! la guerra santa.* Mexico, 1937.

Index

Only the most important names have been indexed; but, wherever possible, people and places are covered by key-words such as Women's Brigades, battles

253

boycotts, 14, 43, 50, 64, 80, 131
brigades, *see* Women's Brigades; Cristero
 army; Federal army
Burke, Fr J., S. J., 60–2

CGT, *see* Great Workers' Union
CNCC, *see* National Catholic Peasant
 League
CNCT, *see* National Catholic Labour
 Confederation
CROM (trade union), 18, 22–4, 30, 34–
 5, 40
caciques, 84, 100–5
Calles, Gen. Plutarco Elias
 and the Cristeros, 31, 56–7, 185
 anticlerical policy, 30–1, 33–5, 41–4,
  210–11
 regime, 17–21, 25, 27, 40–1, 60–4
'Calles Law', 42–7, 63, 187, 209
Camacho, Joaquín, 131–2
Capistrán Garza, René, 77, 81
Cárdenas, Gen. Lázaro
 and the Cristeros, 162, 177
 conciliatory policy, 8, 31, 46, 187
 regime, 20, 27, 180, 205
Caro, Esteban, 127, 135, 168–9
Carranza, Juan, 112, 125, 127
Carranza, Venustiano, 11–15, 208–9,
 214
Caruana, Mgr, 42, 62
Castañón, Trinidad, 73, 107, 116
Catholic Action of Mexican Youth
 (ACJM), 50, 76–9, 211
Catholic Apostolic Church, *see* Mexican
 Catholic Apostolic Church
Catholic Church in Mexico, 2–16, 19–
 47, 57–75, 201–6, 209–17
 see also, Catholics; churches; priests
Catholic Church in Rome, 4–5, 16,
 37–40, 42–3, 46, 57–66, 68–9,
 132, 203, 210–11, 217
Catholic Church in United States of
 America, 15, 60, 80–1
Catholic Congresses, 9–10
Catholic Employees' Union (UCE), 131–
 2, 136
Catholic Extension Society, 15
Catholic Labour Confederation, *see*

National Catholic Labour
 Confederation
Catholic Party, *see* National Catholic
 Party
Catholic Peasant League, *see* National
 Catholic Peasant League
'Catholic Workers' Circles', 10
catholicism, *see* religion
Catholics
 and the Church/State conflict, 5–16,
  22–4, 33–6, 41–2, 47–56, 60–3,
  67–8, 75–82, 190, 202–6, 211, 215
 and LNDR, 41, 43–4, 50–1, 76
 trade unions, 10, 16, 22–3, 35–6, 76,
  131, 193–4, 211
 see also Catholic Action of Mexican
  Youth; Catholic Congresses;
  Catholic Employees' Union;
  Catholic Extension Society; National
  Catholic Party; National Catholic
  Peasant League
Cedillo, Gen. S., 56–7, 160, 177, 202,
 205
Ceniceros y Villareal, Rafael, 61, 77
chaplains, *see* priests
Chávez García, Ines, 112, 124
Christ-the-Kings, *see* Cristeros
Church, the, *see* Catholic Church in
 Mexico
churches
 desecrated, 28, 36–7, 41–2, 131, 165,
  188
 as fortifications, 119, 168, 175
 public worship suspended, 14, 43–4,
  48–9, 210
civilian losses, *see* losses
civilian support, for Cristero army, 93–8,
 119–20, 128–37, 144–53
clergy, *see* priests
'colonial war' *see* Cristero war
Columbus, Knights of, *see* Order of
 Knights of Columbus
combatant losses, *see* losses
combatant priests, *see* priests
Committee of the League of Free Nations,
 26
conciliation policy, 6–12, 15–16, 30, 37,
 46, 203